Reminiscences

of

Vice Admiral William Paden Mack
U. S. Navy (Retired)

Volume II

U. S. Naval Institute
Annapolis, Maryland

Preface

Volume II contains a transcript of six taped interviews (number 7 - 12) with Vice Admiral William Paden Mack at his home in Annapolis, Maryland during the months of March, April, and May of 1979. They complete his narrative of a most fascinating naval career. Highlights in this period were his duties as Chief of Legislative Affairs (1967-69); Deputy Assistant Secretary of Defense for Manpower and Reserve Affairs (1969-71); Commander of the Seventh Fleet (1971-2); and Superintendent of the U. S. Naval Academy (1972-75). The reader will note the strong impact of Admiral Mack's ideas in all the billets where he has served.

The Admiral has reviewed the transcript. Corrections have been made and the manuscript retyped. A subject index has been added for convenience.

An appendix to the volume contains some pertinent excerpts from speeches and articles of interest to the researcher.

                                                                 John T. Mason, Jr.
                                                                 Director of Oral History

                                                                 June 1980

VICE ADMIRAL WILLIAM P. MACK, UNITED STATES NAVY

William Paden Mack was born in Hillsboro, Illinois, on August 6, 1915, son of the late Commander A. R. Mack, USN, Retired, and the late Mrs. Josephine Paden Mack. He entered the U. S. Naval Academy on June 8, 1933, on Presidential appointment (at large). He was graduated with the degree of Bachelor of Science and commissioned Ensign in the U. S. Navy on June 3, 1937, and through subsequent advancement attained the rank of Vice Admiral, to date from January 28, 1969.

On graduation from the Naval Academy, he was assigned to the USS IDAHO (BB-42), and served as a junior officer in all departments of that battleship until December 1939. In December 1939 he joined the USS JOHN D. FORD (DD-228), on the Asiatic Station and was serving as Gunnery Officer of that destroyer at the outbreak of World War II in December 1941 The JOHN D. FORD was awarded the Presidential Unit Citation and the Army Distinguished Unit Citation for service during the Java Campaign.

From October 1942 until November 1943 he served as Aide and Flag Lieutenant to the Commander Amphibious Force, Pacific, attached to the USS PENNSYLVANIA, which won the Navy Unit Commendation for service in the Pacific Area from May 4, 1943 until February 10, 1945.

He assisted in fitting out the USS PRESTON (DD-795), and served as her Executive Officer from her commissioning in March 1944 until October of that year, the latter months of that period participating in Pacific operations.

In October 1944 he assumed command of the USS WOODWORTH (DD-460), and remained in command of that destroyer throughout the last months of hostilities and until April 1946.

From May 1946 until June 1949 he served as Officer in Charge of the U. S. Naval School (Academy and College Preparatory) at Bainbridge, Maryland. He next commanded the USS ANDERSON (DD-786) for eleven months, then had Staff duty, successively, as Assistant Chief of Staff for Operations to Commander Destroyer Flotilla ONE, and as Assistant Readiness Officer on the Staff of Commander Cruisers-Destroyers, Pacific. Detached from the latter assignment in May 1953, after participating in operations in Korean waters under the United Nations Command, he reported in June 1953 to the Navy Department, Washington, D. C. where he served for two years as Commander Detail Officer in the Bureau of Naval Personnel.

He was a student at the National War College from July 1955 until June 1956, and in July became Commander Destroyer Division TWENTY-TWO. A year later he returned to the Bureau of Naval Personnel for duty, and on October 8, 1958, was transferred to the office of the Chief of Naval Operations, to serve as Assistant Director, Special Projects, General Planning Group. On April 2, 1959 he was named Naval Aide to the Secretary of the Navy and served in that capacity until April 1961, when he became Commander Destroyer Squadron TWNETY-EIGHT.

In June 1962 he was assigned to the office of the Special Assistant for Counterinsurgency, Joint Chiefs of Staff, Washington, D. C. On August 19, 1963 he reported to the Secretary of the Navy as Chief of Information. On May 15, 1966 he became Commander Amphibious Group TWO and in February he returned to Washington as Chief of Legislative Affairs.

On January 19, 1969 the President nominated him for appointment to the grade of Vice Admiral and assignment as Deputy Assistant Secretary of Defense (Manpower and Reserve Affairs).

In June 1971 he assumed command of the Seventh Fleet and conducted the mining of Haiphong Harbor and operations against the North Vietnamese subsequent to their invasion of South Vietnam.

In June 1972 he became the 47th Superintendent of the Naval Academy.

He retired 1 August 1975 with the Rank of Vice Admiral.

Vice Admiral Mack was married to Ruth McMillin on November 11, 1939. They have two children, William Paden Mack, Jr. and Margaret Ellen Mack. Their home is 1109 Gaillard St., Alexandria, Virginia.

Vice Admiral Mack is President, Navy Marine Coast Guard Residence Foundation and Vinson Hall Corporation; Vice-Chairman and member of the Board, Northlake Community Hospital, Chicago, Ill.; member of the Board, Human Resources Research Organization; Director, Services National Bank, Alexandria, Va.; member of the Board, Premier Industries; member U.S. Naval Institute, New York Yacht Club, Navy League of the United States, U.S. Naval Academy Foundation, U.S. Naval Academy Alumni Association and the Army Navy Country Club.

THIS IS AN IMPORTANT RECORD — SAFEGUARD IT.

1. LAST NAME-FIRST NAME-MIDDLE NAME	2. SEX	3. SOCIAL SECURITY NUMBER	4. DATE OF BIRTH		
MACK, William Paden	M	224 52 3664	YEAR 15	MONTH 08	DAY 06

5. DEPARTMENT, COMPONENT AND BRANCH OR CLASS	6a. GRADE, RATE OR RANK	6b. PAY GRADE	7. DATE OF RANK		
NAVY-USN	VADM	09	YEAR 69	MONTH 01	DAY 28

8a. SELECTIVE SERVICE NUMBER	8b. SELECTIVE SERVICE LOCAL BOARD NUMBER, CITY, STATE AND ZIP CODE	8c. HOME OF RECORD AT TIME OF ENTRY INTO ACTIVE SERVICE (Street, RFD, City, State and ZIP Code)
NA	NA	5045 63rd Street, San Diego, California 95820

9a. TYPE OF SEPARATION	9b. STATION OR INSTALLATION AT WHICH EFFECTED
RETIREMENT	U.S. Naval Academy, Annapolis, Maryland 21402

9c. AUTHORITY AND REASON	9d. EFFECTIVE DATE		
	YEAR 75	MONTH 07	DAY 31

9e. CHARACTER OF SERVICE	9f. TYPE OF CERTIFICATE ISSUED	10. REENLISTMENT CODE
HONORABLE	NA	NA

11. LAST DUTY ASSIGNMENT AND MAJOR COMMAND	12. COMMAND TO WHICH TRANSFERRED
U.S. Naval Academy, Annapolis, Maryland 21402	Naval Reserve Manpower Center, Bainbridge, Maryland 21905

13. TERMINAL DATE OF RESERVE/MSS OBLIGATION	14. PLACE OF ENTRY INTO CURRENT ACTIVE SERVICE (City, State and ZIP Code)	15. DATE ENTERED ACTIVE DUTY THIS PERIOD		
YEAR NA MONTH -- DAY --	1617 Plymouth Avenue, San Francisco, California 94127	YEAR 37	MONTH 06	DAY 03

16a. PRIMARY SPECIALTY NUMBER AND TITLE	16b. RELATED CIVILIAN OCCUPATION AND D.O.T. NUMBER	18. RECORD OF SERVICE	YEARS	MONTHS	DAYS
3283-SCHOOL ADMIN	091-Superintendent, Schools	(a) NET ACTIVE SERVICE THIS PERIOD	38	01	29
		(b) PRIOR ACTIVE SERVICE	00	00	00
17a. SECONDARY SPECIALTY NUMBER AND TITLE	17b. RELATED CIVILIAN OCCUPATION AND D.O.T. NUMBER	(c) TOTAL ACTIVE SERVICE (a + b)	38	01	29
NA	NA	(d) PRIOR INACTIVE SERVICE	00	00	00
		(e) TOTAL SERVICE FOR PAY (c + d)	38	01	29
		(f) FOREIGN AND/OR SEA SERVICE THIS PERIOD	11	08	00

19. INDOCHINA OR KOREA SERVICE SINCE AUGUST 5, 1964	20. HIGHEST EDUCATION LEVEL SUCCESSFULLY COMPLETED (In Years)		
☒ YES ☐ NO	SECONDARY/HIGH SCHOOL ___ YRS (1-12 grades)	COLLEGE 06 YRS	

21. TIME LOST (Preceding Two Yrs.)	22. DAYS ACCRUED LEAVE PAID	23. SERVICEMEN'S GROUP LIFE INSURANCE COVERAGE	24. DISABILITY SEVERANCE PAY	25. PERSONNEL SECURITY INVESTIGATION	
TL-NONE	60	☐ $15,000 ☐ $5,000 ☒ $20,000 ☐ $10,000 ☐ NONE	☒ NO ☐ YES AMOUNT ___	a. TYPE BI	b. DATE COMPLETED 23 MAY 67

26. DECORATIONS, MEDALS, BADGES, COMMENDATIONS, CITATIONS AND CAMPAIGN RIBBONS AWARDED OR AUTHORIZED DISTINGUISH SERVICE MEDAL (3); SILVER STAR; LEGION OF MERIT; BRONZE STAR MEDAL; JOINT SERVICE COMMENDATION MEDAL; NAVY COMMENDATION MEDAL; PRESIDENTIAL UNIT CITATION; ARMY/AIR FORCE PRESIDENTIAL UNIT CITATION; NAVY UNIT CITATION; MERITORIOUS UNIT COMMENDATION; NAVY EXPEDITIONARY

27. REMARKS BLOCK 26 (CONT): MEDAL; CHINA SERVICE MEDAL; AMERICAN DEFENSE SERVICE MEDAL; AMERICAN CAMPAIGN MEDAL; ASIATIC-PACIFIC CAMPAIGN MEDAL; VICTORY MEDAL WORLD WAR II; NAVY OCCUPATION SERVICE MEDAL; NATIONAL DEFENSE SERVICE MEDAL; KOREAN SERVICE MEDAL; ARMED FORCES EXPEDITIONARY MEDAL; VIETNAM SERVICE MEDAL; NATIONAL ORDER OF VIETNAM, COMMANDER; VIETNAMESE CROSS GALLANTRY WITH PALM; VIETNAM PRESIDENTIAL UNIT WITH PALM; PHILIPPINE REPUBLIC PRESIDENTIAL UNIT CITATION; REPUBLIC OF KOREA PRESIDENTIAL UNIT CITATION; PHILIPPINE DEFENSE RIBBON; PHILIPPINE LIBERATION RIBBON; PHILIPPINE INDEPENDENCE RIBBON; UNITED NATIONS SERVICE MEDAL; REPUBLIC OF VIETNAM RIBBON;

Effective date of retirement: 1 August 1975, with the grade of Vice Admiral and with retired pay of that grade, pursuant to provisions of 10 USC 6322 and 6233. XXXXXXXXXXXXXXXXXXXXXXXXXXXXXXXXXXXXXXXXXXXXXXXXXXXXXXXXXXXXXXXXXXXXXXXXXXXXXXXX
XXXXXXXXXXXXXXXXXXXXXXXXXXXXXXXXXXXXXXXXXXXXXXXXXXXXXXXXXXXXXXXXXXXXXXXXXXXXXXXX
XXXXXXXXXXXXXXXXXXXXXXXXXXXXXXXXXXXXXXXXXXXXXXXXXXXXXXXXXXXXXXXXXXXXXXXXXXXXXXXX

28. MAILING ADDRESS AFTER SEPARATION (Street, RFD, City, County, State and ZIP Code)	29. SIGNATURE OF PERSON BEING SEPARATED
1109 Gaillard Street, Alexandria, Virginia 22304	X /signature/

30. TYPED NAME, GRADE AND TITLE OF AUTHORIZING OFFICER	31. SIGNATURE OF OFFICER AUTHORIZED TO SIGN
J. J. ANDRILLA, LCDR, USN, PERSONNEL AND ADMINISTRATIVE OFFICER	/signature/

DD FORM 214N, 1 NOV 72 — PREVIOUS EDITIONS OF THIS FORM ARE OBSOLETE. S/N 0102-LF-002-0202

THIS IS AN IMPORTANT RECORD — SAFEGUARD IT.

REPORT OF SEPARATION FROM ACTIVE

DECLARATION OF TRUST

The undersigned does hereby appoint and designate as his (her) Trustee herein, the Secretary-Treasurer and Publisher of the United States Naval Institute to perform and discharge the following duties, powers, and privileges in connection with the possession and use of a certain taped interview between the undersigned and the Oral History Department of the United States Naval Institute.

1. Classification of Transcript.

    (X)a. If classified OPEN, the transcript(s) may be read or the recording(s) audited by the qualified personnel upon presentation of proper credentials, as determined by the Secretary-Treasurer of the U.S. Naval Institute. *except that portion marked "closed"*

    ( )b. If classified PERMISSION REQUIRED TO CITE OR QUOTE, the user will be required to obtain permission in writing from the interviewee prior to quoting or citing from either the transcript(s) or the recording(s).

    ( )c. If classified PERMISSION REQUIRED, permission must be obtained in writing from the interviewee before the transcribed interview(s) can be examined or the tape recording(s) audited.

    ( )d. If classified CLOSED, the transcribed interview(s) and the tape recording(s) will be sealed until a time specified by the interviewee. This may be until the death of the interviewee or for any specified number of years.

2. It is expressly understood that in giving this authorization, I am in no way precluded from placing such restrictions as I may desire upon use of the interview at any time during my lifetime, nor does this authorization in any way affect my rights to the copyright of my literary expressions that may be contained in the interview.

Witness my hand and seal this ____ day of FEB 1980.

[signature]

I hereby accept and consent to the foregoing Declaration of Trust and the powers therein conferred upon me as Trustee:

[signatures]

Interview #7 with Vice Admiral William P. Mack, U.S. Navy
(Retired)

Place: His residence in Annapolis, Maryland

Date: Friday morning, 30 March 1979

Subject: Biography

By: John T. Mason, Jr.

Q: All right, Sir. This is a continuation of your story about the chief of information during the years 1963 to 1966.

Adm. M.: Perhaps I should precede this second part by saying again that the chief of information works directly for the secretary of the navy and the chief of naval operations, and the secretary, in turn, is beholden to the secretary of defense for all matters, including public affairs. The secretary of defense always has an assistant secretary who carries out these responsibilities for him. During most of my tenure there, he was Arthur Sylvester, who was, by his own rights, quite a famous person in terms of his dealings with the press during the first part of the Vietnamese War, and Phil Goulding was there as his replacement as assistant secretary with General Chappy

James as his assistant. During this part of my career there, this was a much happier period.

Arthur Sylvester was controlled very carefully by Mr. McNamara, and his relationships with the press, with the movie-making groups, and with the television groups were very poor. It was because he felt he had to support whatever Mr. McNamara wanted without question, and sometimes he would not give reasons for arbitrary decisions regarding the press and movies. In turn, he would give arbitrary decisions to the services, and that made it very difficult for us.

Q: He's a very positive man, isn't he?

Adm. M.: Very positive, and just as positive when he was right as when he was wrong, and he was wrong a good many times. Sometimes on his own, sometimes because Mr. McNamara was a poor public relations person and didn't realize what harm he was doing to the Defense Department and the president and the services when he made certain decisions.

I guess I could characterize the time there - we've already covered the main thing, which was the navy's responsibilities toward getting its problems known and its image out regarding the Vietnamese War.

Q: Yes, and how difficult that was to achieve!

Adm. M.: Yes, it was because Mr. Sylvester's ideas were that the services were just out there doing what the Defense Department wanted, and the Defense Department and the White House should take all credit for everything right and the services for everything wrong. That was the way he played the game, so it was difficult to get the navy's story told. I think as I said before, I had to get round that a little bit by putting a detachment of the Seventh Fleet ashore in Saigon and surreptitiously building it up man by man, officer by officer, over a long period of time until we had twenty or thirty people there from the initial two. But we still were not allowed, even though we had large forces of Marines and others in-country, to have our own public relations group in Saigon.

Q: Was it ultimately discovered by Sylvester that you had built that up?

Adm. M.: Oh, no, they knew it. It was just that they would not let us do anything. It seemed to satisfy Mr. McNamara that this was a Seventh Fleet detachment there because we had no permanent group, and General Westmoreland would run the total press affairs out there, his group would, and General Westmoreland's group was run, in a sense, by Barry Zorthian most of the time, who was Defense-oriented.

It was very difficult. The navy did all sorts of

good things out there and the public would never hear about it, and, of course the chief of naval operations and the secretary of the navy would be all over me, wanting to know why the navy's story hadn't been told. I would just have to say, "I can't tell it except by leaking it to the press or doing something else, because General Westmoreland doesn't want it out at the present time, and I have no way of getting it out, even through my Seventh Fleet sources because they are restricted and if they do something that's obviously wrong they'll be thrown out of the country."

It was a very difficult period.

Q: Leaking to the press is a very dangerous thing, too, isn't it?

Adm. M.: It depends upon what you call "leaking to the press." You can always answer a question. You're allowed to answer what's called a query. If the press asks the right questions, you can give the answers. So the trick was to leak the questions, have them ask the questions, and you could give them the answers, but you were not allowed to initiate anything. This seems a little silly, illogical, but that's the way the game's played.

Q: That's the way it's played on the Hill, too, isn't it?

Adm. M.: Exactly, and so I had to be very careful and it was a very difficult three-year period of our relations there with the Defense Department.

I'm going to discuss this in groups because these were the sorts of ways things happened.

One of the jobs of the chief of information was to handle press conferences on roll-outs for major aircraft. The first one in my career when I was early there was the F-111B, and this was an extremely controversial airplane, which the navy did not want and which Mr. McNamara forced upon the navy with the idea that it would be a one-time procurement thing, that is, you'd buy all the spares and all the airplanes at one time and that would make it cheaper.

Q: Sort of a simplistic idea?

Adm. M.: Yes. Also, it was an aircraft that was made for the air force primarily and, therefore, it had strength on its main longitudinals and things like that which would give it the ability to fly at low altitudes where it would be buffeted and would have to be very strong. But it had very skinny landing gear, not suitable for carrier landing, so the navy version had to be beefed up in terms of the landing gear and some other points. By the time this was done, the navy version was so heavy that the catapults wouldn't hold it. They couldn't launch it, and they had difficulty with the land system, the wires to catch it, and so forth. It was always a battle, week by week, how many pounds can you bring the F-111B down to. Mr. McNamara insisted it was coming down and the navy kept saying no, it still isn't suitable for carrier use.

When the time came in Dallas to roll it out, I was put in charge of relations with the press, which meant I had to dream up the secretary of the navy's and the chief of naval operations' statements which said this was a fine airplane but didn't commit them in case it didn't turn out to be as it was tested and flown. I had to skirt the hard places there, trying to have them satisfy the secretary of defense, still have their consciences clear, and have the assurance that when the change was made, which we knew was coming, it was junked and the navy, at least, would still be pure in the sense that if the press looked back at what they had said they could see they hadn't really said it was a fine airplane at all, they'd just made general statements.

This was an extremely controversial event, so there were thousands of people there, including almost two hundred, I guess, members of the press, which I had to arrange, get the cameras set up, and the people involved all in proper places, and get the company to give us an after-roll-out lunch and proper planes so that I could whisk the secretary of the navy out and he wouldn't have to speak too long or talk to the press too long. It was a difficult press conference but it was the first and biggest I conducted and it came off all right.

Subsequently, in this same vein, the A-7 was brought out and I also had some press conferences for minor aircraft that the navy brought out, one being the version of an ASW aircraft which the navy used for COD, that is "carry on board delivery," which was brought out in Connecticut by Grumman. I handled this one also.

Q: Were there any repercussions from the Department of Defense on any of these?

Adm. M.: No, never, except snide remarks by Mr. Sylvester, saying, "Well, you've done it again," which I took as a compliment, but nothing was ever -

Q: But you were under the gun all the time?

Adm. M.: Yes. Oh, yes, we never were home free. It was never cut and dried, really, as to whether things were good or bad.

Another grouping of events like this were the submarines, the Scorpion and the Thresher, where I had to handle most of the press queries, when they were discovered, when photographs were made of them, and the first press conference I held regarding the findings of the court that was held afterwards. This was very difficult in the sense that obviously the press wanted to know everything and the secretary of the navy was in favor of having them know a lot, but Admiral Rickover was very cautious and did not want much known because he didn't think there was enough evidence there to show what happened and people would make wrong conclusions that the nuclear system had failed rather than something else.

So this, again, was very difficult, having to sneak a look at the report, which even, as you say, the senior member couldn't see, after it was finished and none of the press could see it, and then trying to fashion answers that could be given by the secretary in his press conference which would protect Admiral Rickover and still give them such information as could be made available and give to the press a plausible cause for the loss of the submarines.

Q: Was the press aware of your position?

Adm. M.: Oh, yes. Their idea always is to press for more than you can give them and to ask questions they know you can't answer, but they have to do this and you know they have to do it. So they ask questions, you give them answers, and that's all right. If they didn't ask the questions, their editors would be all over them. It's a very friendly give-and-take thing. I was always very close to members of the press personally, in the sense that I liked them and they apparently tolerated me all right.

Q: That's terribly important, isn't it?

Adm. M.: Oh, yes, of course it is.

Q: Once they get down on a man -

Adm. M.: Yes - you can never tell a lie, not even a white one. If you don't want to say something, you just say so, but don't ever tell them something that's wrong because you're going to be in the soup then. Some people in these kinds of jobs did and they didn't last long. I just resolved that I would never tell even a white lie and I didn't. If I couldn't say something, I just said, "I'm sorry I can't answer that." As long as you tell them the truth, you're never in trouble, and it's not a difficult thing to do.

Q: Would you go off, for a moment, on a tangent and talk about the accountability of the press?

Adm. M.: The press is not accountable to anybody. If they print something that's secret information, or top secret, unless they stole it. They just do what they feel like.

Q: Yes, but I mean in terms of publishing truthful statements rather than untruthful ones, their sense of accountability.

Adm. M.: Their sense of accountability is protected by what is called speculation. If you look very carefully at press pieces, you'll find the things they do not know exactly or have not been told them exactly are couched in language that shows that they're speculating. In other words, they're guessing. If you look at it very carefully, you'll see that they don't say exactly. They'll attribute their remarks to some unknown spokesman or "it is said in Washington that," and that sort of thing. It gets them off the hook. They say, "Well, somebody told me," or "I heard it," or "Somebody in the Defense Department told me that and I can't reveal his name." They don't have to reveal their source.

So, if you look at what they say, every time they breach security or do something that's close to it, they will very carefully hedge it, and that's called speculation.

Of course, one of the problems is to get your bosses to realize that's what they're doing. They're guessing. I think we talked about the second Tonkin Gulf incident where on pure detective work and speculation a story was written that was about 90 percent true, which caused a terrible upheaval in the Defense Department. But, unless they deal with this thing every day, it's very difficult to get your seniors to recognize speculation or to recognize a true leak or violations of security. They just don't understand these things. They have difficulty in separating them. So you're always trying to explain to your seniors how this information came out, who gave it out, if it was leaked, how the press could have arrived at a certain conclusion even though they didn't know any facts. It's a very difficult thing.

The press does what it wants. It will ignore truth - I have in mind a case in point, where I went to an Overseas Press dinner in New York for overseas press conferees and correspondents. General Leslie Groves spoke there. He was talking about developing the A-bomb and, in the course of his remarks, he said that the United States developed the A-bomb to drop on Germany. It was configured to knock down buildings, the six- or seven-story type that Germany had, and when the war ended it was necessary that the bomb be reconfigured to be used against Japan, where you had lesser buildings but more space, so it was a different kind of explosive.

To me, that was interesting and it should have been interesting to the press, because all the time the United States had been accused of having dropped the A-bomb upon an Asiatic country and it was said that it would never have thought of dropping it on Germany or one of the countries in Europe, and that was used to degrade national policy and to degrade the feeling for President Truman, if he had done this sort of thing. I thought this was a time when the press could see that they were wrong in what they'd been writing but they wouldn't write it wrong again. So I wrote a little note to the AP and UPI desk men in Washington and said I'd been there for this speech and I'd heard this and they might like to have it for their files and perhaps put it out as a story. Neither one did, and they just kept right on writing the same old thing, that the United States dropped the A-bomb on Japan but never would have dropped it on Germany.

Here, they had the facts in a public speech by the expert who should know in New York and they ignored it. Sometimes they like to be misinformed.

Q: There are certain gradations, though, among reporters, are there not, in terms on honesty?

Adm. M.: Oh, yes.

Q: Some of them are scrupulous about that.

Adm. M.: That's exactly right, and I would say that the

Press Corps in Washington, particularly the Defense Department Press Corps, was absolutely outstanding. There wasn't a man there that I would not have been personally friendly with, even if he hadn't been a colleague. They were the tops. The press correspondents and their assistants who are sent to Washington are the best. The best go to the State Department, White House, and the Defense Department, not in any particular order. Sometimes the White House is best. Any of the correspondents in those three areas was outstanding. They were the cream of the crop. I never encountered a single correspondent I thought was dishonest or would have done something that, if he was going to do it, he wouldn't have told me first.

Q: What characteristics do these outstandings ones have that are different from the others?

Adm. M.: They're simply honest professional persons who have a sense of integrity, and they have good character like you'd expect of anybody in any profession, a minister, a lawyer.

Q: Therein comes the accountability for what they write, then?

Adm. M.: Exactly right.

The parent organizations, UPI, United Press International, AP, Associated Press, New York Times, Wall Street Journal, and so forth will not tolerate anyone who does not have that kind of character because they themselves are organizations of real integrity. They will not tolerate a direct lie.

I don't know what you think about the New York Times and some of its recent machinations about handling their correspondents and so forth, generally they are good organizations and their correspondents must match them. A correspondent will not last in that organization if he's not that way. You can generally tell from the character of the organization what the man representing it would be like. A Time correspondent would be tops.

There are other exceptions. For instance, I have in mind Mark Watson, one of the premier correspondents of all time for the Baltimore Sun. The Batlimore Sun is not necessarily a prestigious paper as compared to, say, the New York Times, the Wall Street Journal, but it's about second level. Some of the middle western papers, Chicago and other papers which sent correspondents to town, sometimes you would doubt them a little bit and be careful with them because their papers were not really of that kind of character. The New York papers are looking for sensational stuff, a one-day sensation, and they're not worried about what happens the second day, but the New York Times is.

They want to know what happens the second day. If they violated the confidence of someone and they go back for a story the second day, what happens. They're shut out.

You can generally tell. The big papers, big magazines, big organizations had good people working for them. The people represented the character of the organization. So you would never worry about the good ones.

Q: Baldwin told me about his feud with Secretary McNamara about the time that you were there, being faced with a lie detector and that kind of thing. Were there other reporters who were involved in that kind of thing?

Adm. M.: No, only because most reporters would have none of it. Sometimes, reporters were, in a sense, harassed or denied information by Sylvester if he didn't like something they had done, and soon they would sort of waft away and be replaced by somebody else because the organization wanted somebody who had a little more rapport with Mr. Sylvester. But very seldom did that sort of thing happen.

I started to speak about the two press conferences of the _Thresher_ and _Scorpion_. The third one was the dropping of an H-bomb by an air force airplane off of Spain.

Q: Accidentally.

Adm. M.: Yes, of course. It was just lying on the side of the underwater bank. The navy was heavily involved because we were charged with going over and recovering the bomb, which we did eventually. Although the navy did not directly run the show - it was an air force and Defense job to run the daily press conference which detailed the progress of this sort of rescue operation, I was involved because the navy wanted to take great credit for what it was doing and it was getting very little because the Defense Department did this and did so and so and such and such. Nobody knew that the navy was doing the rescue operation.

I guess what happened was really backhanded in the sense that the rescue submarine at one time picked up the H-bomb and then dropped it, and so, by using this as a gimmick, I was able to talk to the press and say that we now have the only submarine in the world that's dropped an H-bomb. They thought this was quite funny so this was written and then suddenly, since it came out that way, the Defense Department relaxed its control and we got this out backdoorwise and the navy was able to talk about what it was doing in Spain, and we eventually got credit for what we'd done, which was to recover the bomb.

Q: And was this your intention?

Adm. M.: Yes. Sometimes you had to work in devious ways, but honest ways. That was an interesting exercise in how to get around the Defense Department again. They were very difficult.

In another general area, the chief of information is charged with the navy's relationships with movie companies and also television movie series.

Q: Building up the image and recruiting and - ?

Adm. M.: Yes, all that. What happens is that when a movie company wants to make a movie and it involves the navy, sometimes it involves our ships and aircraft, they want to use our ships and aircraft as background or perhaps the main part of the plot and so forth, and they will submit their script to the Defense Department and ask for what's called "cooperation." The Defense Department will pass the script to Mr. Sylvester or one of his minions. Then, if he approves, the service, in this case the navy, is allowed to cooperate with that movie company, and generally this is good because the navy gets a lot of good publicity out of it. Sometimes the publicity is adverse, such as "McHale's Navy," a television series that portrayed the navy in what I thought was a rather sympathetic way but to Mr.

Sylvester's way of thinking it was not, and he would never let us cooperate with "McHale's Navy."

On one trip I made out there I did land right on the set of "McHale's Navy" by helo and went around and met all the people and watched them make a couple of series, and I did all I could to change Mr. Sylvester's ideas, saying that, well, this was a little funny and sometimes the characters were a little hard to imagine in real life but, totally, the effect for the navy was good and, anyway, it was going to be produced, so why didn't we improve it a little bit. He never would buy that.

I made several trips to Hollywood, looking at whatever we had, a movie in production, going out to see what was going on and try to help. Particularly when scripts were in the hands of the Defense Department, I would confer with the producers and so forth, and studio heads, trying to make a few changes, "The Bedford Incident" being a case in point. That was a movie story of a submarine, Soviet submarine, off our coast, starring Charles Heston and others. We made some changes in the script that would allow that to be passed and it came off as a pretty good movie.

Q: Charlie Lockwood was involved in that, too, wasn't he?

Adm. M.: Yes. One case in point being that the Soviet

submarine - this was fiction, of course - was said to be in U.S. waters and it was attacked with depth charges. Mr. Sylvester said you couldn't say that, and I said:

"Well, it's in accordance with international law, it's perfectly all right. You cannot submerge in anybody else's national waters. If you do, you're subject to anything that that country wants to do."

He wouldn't believe it, so finally I had to get the international law books out to show him that this was a fact. Eventually, he acceded to the fact that this was true, but he still wouldn't pass the movie for some time, until we got Mr. McNamara personally to get involved with the secretary of the navy and got it passed.

Q: He doesn't sound to be very well versed in military matters?

Adm. M.: No, he wasn't. He had very little concept of the military business. He was an ex-reporter and he took a reporter's view that the military wasn't much, anyway. He was very anti-military, which is not a way to be if you're going to be in that position.

Another big movie was made by Otto Preminger. It was going to involve half the navy. He wanted the navy to do a lot of things. Mr. Sylvester just balked at this. He would not let him do this sort of thing. This was a movie called "In Harm's Way," which turned out to be quite a good movie, but there were some sequences that he didn't like. This was a movie of the South Pacific with a great many ships being blown up and so forth. For some reason or other, he wouldn't pass it. I think mostly because Otto Preminger was very autocratic and wouldn't accede to small changes and he was very pressing and Mr. Sylvester just didn't like it.

So, in the end, what happened was, instead of having the actual ships, Mr. Preminger was forced to build exact-scale models, some 15 to 20 feet long, which had a man in them, who would be down below running these things. They took them down to a lake in Mexico and made his movie, and when it was all over he thought so highly of the navy we tried to do the best we could to help him. He gave us all the models and we sent Marine C-130s down, picked up all his models and flew them down to various parts of the country where they are now, even today, in some recruiting districts and used as recruiting props.

This was a typical example of where legally and officially you couldn't cooperate but on the other hand we made sure we appeared at the studio when they were doing certain things, and we helped when we could and we did everything we could that was legal to help these companies out when they were producing material that was, at least in our eyes, good for the navy.

This was quite a field, the movie and television series business. In those days military series were very popular because people still remembered the war and these sorts of things were quite popular, "Sergeant Bilko," on the army side, which used to make us pretty happy in the navy. We'd laugh at the army's problems with Sergeant Bilko.

Another thing, for instance, there was Buzz Sawyer, a comic strip of the day. We were allowed to cooperate with that since it was a pretty good vehicle for good navy propaganda. That was always a good comic strip.

We ran the combat art system. We had about 3,000 paintings of World War II and subsequent times, actually painted by artists of the Salmagundi Club in New York, who dedicated their services to doing this sort of thing, painted all these pictures free and gave them to the navy. The navy would run them around in exhibitions around the country in some large vans.

Q: People like Montgomery Flag?

Adm. M.: Yes. This was another enlarged Chinfo program. The Chinfo organization was involved in all sorts of things that people knew very little about, as well as running the day-to-day relations with the press which, of course, was the main thing.

Q: Did you actually make any movies, short ones, for recruiting purposes?

Adm. M.: Oh, many. Actually, we would contract out. All we'd produce was the script and, sometimes, provide some of the actors and acting services and so forth, and then cut and paste the final edition of it, and then have somebody make the prints. We were limited in doing that because the Defense Department thought that that was not a proper thing for a service to make. So many times we would arrange with a contractor, a submarine contractor, aircraft contractor, if that sort of thing impinged on his area, suggest he might like to do this, and he would do it with our script, direction, and so forth, and produce a fine movie, which we'd then take and distribute.

Q: If it was for recruiting purposes, why would it be beneath the dignity of the navy to do it?

Adm. M.: For recruiting purposes, these were the sorts of things you could do legally. You recruit all kinds of people, pilots, submariners, and so forth, and the Defense Department didn't think we needed to recruit those types of persons. All we had to recruit was the recruit, the seaman and the Marine private. As long as we were recruiting the recruit, that was all right, as long as we didn't do this esoteric bit about trying to persuade young men to be pilots and that sort of thing.

Q: You were operating, in a sense, within an iron maid, weren't you?

Adm. M.: Yes, we were. We had not very much money and a lot of things to do, so the problem was to stretch the money and get contractors to help us out, provided they joined in the cost of the film and we just provided the core of it.

But this, again, was a very exacting period because you were always between a rock and a hard place. If you were dishonest at all or stretched your mandate too much, somebody was on top of you, quite properly, I guess. It was a very difficult thing because the secretary, the CNO, and others wanted you to do certain things and you could only use certain tools and get certain cooperation out of the Defense Department to do what you had to do, which was to tell the navy's story. Also, of course, the difficulty of the period was measured by Mr. McNamara and his organization, through which you had to work, and the fact that the Vietnamese War was escalating and getting very difficult. The handling of the war was difficult because the Defense Department wanted to handle all the public relations in-country and yet correspondents and others wanted to know what was going on. They wanted to get a story out. All these factors made this a very difficult period in the life of the chief of information.

I was really surprised that I survived three years with nothing more than one lie-detector test.

Q: What about the other services? Did they fare any better under the aegis of the secretary of defense?

Adm. M.: I would say they had the same problems that we had. I like to think that we were a little cleverer than they, but I'm not sure. The other chiefs of information and I used to confer a lot. We were all very friendly toward each other and liked each other, helped each other whenever we could. Really, what you were doing was fighting Mr. Sylvester all the time. The four of us against Mr. Sylvester is what it amounted to. I think they had about the same problems we did.

Q: In the area of propaganda, I suppose propaganda coming out of Vietnam reached a peak a little bit later, after your term there, but did this involve the information office? I mean the sort of stories that came out of Haiphong, Hanoi, and the correspondents in Vietnam who were sending all these bloody pictures back, on television and that kind of thing.

Adm. M.: No. I was involved in that because the third year I was there the war was quite warm and all these things were happening. Correspondents were, in a sense, against the military out there. General Westmoreland was having his problems with body counts and that sort of thing, and I kept protesting that the body-count system was terrible and was going to get us in trouble, but since I was not an army type nobody listened to me.

We were able to get our stories out, because the navy was quite heavily involved with many sorties a day from its carriers and its river forces being expanded at a great rate. So they were heavily involved in-country. And, of course, the Marines were to the extent of more than a division out there, sometimes two divisions. So that in the last year of my tenure all the problems that eventually, in a sense, weighed so heavily on the country were beginning then. I guess there were some 200 or 300 correspodnents out there, heckling the Defense Department and General Westmoreland with a press briefing every day. The daily press conference was becoming a circus, really. It wasn't good, but there wasn't much that could be done about it.

Q: You could see it being turned against us?

Adm. M.: Yes, it was. Public opinion, through the press, was turning against the military at this time, so I was rather glad to leave.

Q: What about the speeches of the CNO and others of that level? Did Chinfo have anything to do with them?

Adm. M.: Yes. As a matter of fact, speeches made by anybody, if they involved foreign policy or defense policy, had to be cleared and, for that purpose, there was in the secretary of defense's office a four-officer clearance board, one of whom was a naval officer. We had our own clearance section, which would go over these speeches first and sometimes remove obvious errors. Then it had to go down below and there would be a constant fight between our man in our office and the man down in the Defense Department, who might even be a naval officer, over what could be said. Every speech had to be cleared that way. They were supposed to be delivered to us a certain number of days before they were to be given, but somehow the deadlines always got fudged a little - the secretary of the navy wasn't quite ready and wanted to change his speech, so there'd be one of these all-night affairs where I and my clearance guy would argue with the Defense type. Then, we'd have to come back and tell the secretary he couldn't say this or he'd have to change that a little bit.

The clearance business was quite heavy, in the sense that it seemed to precede weekends because a lot of the secretary's speeches were made on Saturday on trips he went on, and Friday night was a terrible time trying to get things cleared. This was a very heavy chore and, since we had to clear speeches for a lot of people, there were a lot of times when there would be problems to be resolved as to what they could say and couldn't say.

Q: Then did you also have the responsibility of seeing that there was proper coverage for a speech when it was being delivered?

Adm. M.: Oh, yes. The navy's information staff was at that time and still is rather small. We had a public affairs officer, for instance, on each commandant's staff and major staffs, CinCPac, CinCLant, and so forth, and a few at various places around the country. But normally when something like that was done — for instance, the secretary would make a speech in we'll say Cleveland, where there was no public affairs officer, his advance man would go out and make all the necessary preparations, but we had reserve companies in all major cities, reserve public affairs officers, who were very active and liked this sort of thing.

Q: They were professionals, were they?

Adm. M.: Yes, they would be perhaps reporters or public

affairs specialists in some business concern, and they would be commandeered to help out with whatever was going on in that particular city. They were very helpful, so our information staff at headquarters was augmented tenfold by the reserve companies around the country. Wherever we went they would materialize out of the woodwork and help out, not only for that event but at all times. They had monthly meetings and so forth so they would be given jobs to do. We gave them party lines, so to speak, and information to spread and they helped. Without them, we couldn't have done much, really.

Q: Did you - were you beginning to take into consideration - they did obviously later on - the headlines when it was best to have a public event so that it would appear in the headline the next day or the Sunday paper or something of that sort?

Adm. M.: Yes. The problem there was that you couldn't always do that, because if a speech was to be given somewhere it was keyed to the event. In other words, the secretary would go to a convention somewhere, say the American Legion convention, and he couldn't control the date of that convention. He had to give a speech and our problem was to figure out what he was going to say that would be timely and know it a week or ten days in advance.

We had a speech-writing bureau that generally was available to write speeches for any person who wanted it, and frequently would write for the secretary or the CNO. The problem was to try to keep our speech-writing bureau up to date on what we were pushing at that moment, what was going to happen ten days from now or two weeks from now, and try to anticipate what would be newsworthy on this particular date the speech was to be given, which was very difficult. You might have what you thought was a good timely speech and then something would happen on that same day, there'd be an earthquake or something you couldn't control, a natural event, that would preempt the headlines, even the front page. So it was always a little difficult to anticipate what you were going to get in the way of reaction and to get into newsworthy time slots, times of the days or times of the week when you would know there wouldn't be regulat news.

Another problem was that the White House always wanted to preempt good news, and if the navy had something to announce or to say, it was not uncommon for the White House to call Mr. Sylvester or somebody else and then have him call us and say, "The White House will announce so and so." So, there was the secretary's speech shot down in flames because this was going to be announced by the president, and all the good news the secretary had to say about we were going to build umpteen ships of something else suddenly was no good and you had to get another speech put together. The White House was very careful about wanting to announce good events but not bad ones. That was up to the secretary. He got to talk about the bad events.

Q: That happens especially when you have a real politician in the White House!

Adm. M.: Yes, one who cares about such things. I don't think Mr. Carter cares very much about that sort of thing, but in those days that was the way it was. They'd announce anything good.

Q: Was there any attempt at overall coordination, perhaps out of the Department of Defense or even out of the White House, of speeches that were being made in various parts of the country so that there wouldn't be any contradictions?

Adm. M.: No, none at all, at least not as is done today. What happened was that the president did what he wanted where he wanted and everybody else conformed. There was no overall planning system that said, in a sense, we're going to cover those events now. In other words, there was no public affairs plan anywhere in the navy.

Mr. Nitze insisted, when he became secretary, that the navy have one, and I put one together. So ours was coordinated in the sense that we put down in our plan what we wanted to do, the way in which we wanted to project the navy and what we wanted to tell the public about it, and then we said these are our policies. The secretary's direction that went out said this is what the secretary wants to do. He wants to project the navy's image as so and so and such and such, and it's suggested you do so by speeches, by using your public affairs reserve companies to do thus and so, to put out these little brochures and do these sorts of things that could be done.

Our plan said what was to be done, the tools to be used to do it with, and gave the coordinated annual schedule of what we'd be pushing in the various months and at various times. Everyone's speech was supposed to be coordinated around these general directions, and it worked very well. The only problem was that nobody above us had any plan and we would always find the White House or the Defense Department going off in some direction very suddenly, without any warning, and that would upset our plans. We kept telling Mr. Sylvester, "Why don't you have a plan?"

"Oh," he said, "I can't operate that way because Mr. McNamara has to react to the White House and he doesn't know from one month to the next what his plan will be."

So we never could get anything done in that direction.

We had our own plan but nobody else had any plans. The White House and Defense business was catch as catch can. They were always reacting to emergencies and never had any positive plan to try to tell the country what the Defense Department was doing.

Q: All vastly interesting.

In May of 1966, on 15 May, you took over an entirely different command, getting away from Washington for a change. You became commander of Amphibious Group No. 2. Was this in the Atlantic?

Adm. M.: Yes, this was a Norfolk-based amphibious group and, in my conversations with Mr. Nitze before I went to take it, he thought I should go to a cruiser division, since that was the popular thing of the day. I'd been a destroyer and battleship officer most of my life, except for a tour on an amphibious staff.

Q: He had your advancement in mind, didn't he?

Adm. M.: He didn't really know. That was his idea and I think he was perhaps egged on by destroyer-cruiser types. My idea was that when I went to sea as a flag officer I wanted to command something. I didn't want to command two cruisers. You hardly ever see two cruisers in the same place and I found the cruiser division lads were not very much, in my estimation. They had very little opportunity to exercise command, whereas I knew that an amphibious group, in my experience, was a very large affair. It had a PhibRon, which was three squadrons, each squadron having four or five amphibious ships in it, all big, APAs and that sort of thing. When it went off on a planned exercise, generally attached to it were two or more carriers, two or three cruisers, twenty or so destroyers, half a dozen submarines, and the resulting naval group was quite large for a rear admiral.

Q: I suppose there was also the possibility you might get involved in Vietnam?

Adm. M.: Yes, except that I went to an Atlantic-based group. There was no group that big in the Pacific, going to Vietnam at that time.

Q: Wasn't there a constant shift of ships from the Atlantic to the - ?

Adm. M.: Oh, yes. There was a possibility of it, which I liked, also the possibility that we'd go and do certain things in the Mediterranean, in case something happened. We were always ready for that. As a matter of fact, the

Dominican Republic affair was still a little warm down there and there were times when we'd go in to take people out of the Dominican Republic.

Q: That happened while you were Chinfo, didn't it?

Adm. M.: Oh, yes.

Q: Was there anything of particular interest about that?

Adm. M.: No, that was just a sort of routine operation. It was mostly done by the army.

Q: The president himself had a —

Adm. M.: Yes, but we just hauled things back and forth. The navy side of it was rather low key. I wasn't very heavily involved in it.

There was a possibility this would flare up again. Anything can happen in the Caribbean, so I foresaw that there might be some interesting things happening. I did plan and conduct several large-scale amphibious operations in the Caribbean area, at Vieques. The biggest one was done in conjunction with General Wheeler, who was then a brigadier general and had been a Marine aide to the secretary of the navy, to Mr. Connally, when I was a naval aide. This was very peculiar. Here I was the amphibious group commander and he was the landing force commander. At some later date we both made flag and general rank and here we were commanding the same group.

This was the biggest exercise we had down there. It was quite large.

Q: What was its purpose?

Adm. M.: It was simply to train the Marines in amphibious techniques. There was the equivalent of about two-thirds of a division of Marine troops, a company of artillery, and so forth, going ashore at Vieques in a landing against opposition which was mostly a counterinsurgency affair. However, we took about a thousand Marines, dressed them up in civilian clothes, and gave them Chinese weapons and stuck them back in the hills as guerrillas. Some of them were dressed as pregnant women, children, and so forth. The idea was that the Marines would go ashore and overcome the opposition, then do what they could with the guerrillas and the civilian population, again Marines dressed up. We built POW compounds and that sort of thing. The sort of thing you'd have if you were going to Vietnam. What we were doing was training for that sort of thing, or for anywhere else, as a matter of fact.

Q: What was this operation called?

Adm. M.: Beach Time was the name.

Subsequent to this time there were two amphibious group commanders in the Atlantic. One of them was Admiral Anderson. Admiral Anderson was suddenly detached to go to some particular chore in Washington and that left only one amphibious commander. So in the last three months of my time there I would plan one exercise with PhibGroup 2's staff and then go down and conduct it, while PhibGroup 4, the other group, was planning an exercise. Then I would fly back and take them down and so the next one. So I ended up spending several months in almost constant command, which was great for me, so that I proved to myself that if you wanted command at sea as a rear admiral the way to do it is in an amphibious group.

Q: You were almost overall commander?

Adm. M.: I was.

The other phase of the job here was that the amphibious commander was generally the recovery commander for the various space-recovery shots. I commanded three of these. The first one was so far back that monkeys were being used and my biggest problem in that particular one was to find bananas in the force for the monkeys, because NASA had failed to tell us that monkeys could only eat bananas, so we had to find some on one of the destroyers.

Q: Who was the famous monkey, Enos, or something like that?

Adm. M.: That was the one. I'd forgotten his name for the moment, but he wanted bananas.

Other recovery shots were Gemini X, which was the biggest one. That was the one in which Michael Collins and John Young were recovered. That was done without event and was a very accurate recovery, which was a fascinating thing to conduct in the sense that we had as flagship the Guam, which was an LPH, a small helicopter carrier. We were contemplating how we were going to get our communications going because communications in the navy are not always good, when NASA came aboard with their communications gear, set it up in flag plot, and told us they had three separate receivers on three separate particular frequencies, so that if one went down they could use another and they could have three different frequencies. We found out how you communicate. You have lots of expensive equipment, which they had. They were able to communicate around the world all the time in flag plot in our ship, whereas we could hardly find the ship next to us with our inexpensive and not very efficient equipment.

Mack #7 - 451

Q: Well, they had much more money than you did?

Adm. M.: Oh, yes, their money was absolutely unlimited.

Q: Would you tell me about your marching orders, to to speak, as arranged with NASA for these rescues?

Adm. M.: What happened generally on a rescue mission such as that was that the commander of the Atlantic Fleet, of course, would be in general overall charge because the recovery group was only one such group. Contingency groups were put 1,000 miles south of that in case of accident and it came down early. They were along the flight path of the space craft. They were 1,000 miles southwest, I think, and 1,000 miles to the north, slightly east, so that if there were some error there would be two other rescue groups that could be used.

Q: A considerable number of ships, then, involved?

Adm. M.: Oh, yes. These were small groups, only two destroyers, all they would be able to do was get the people out. They couldn't get the space craft up, but the main recovery force, of course, had an LPH in it with a good crane, helos, and frogmen, the usual things that you had to have to effect a recovery.

You were told the recovery area, then, as the mission ended, the NASA group would compute when to have the reentry vehicle come down and where it was going. They would try to give you as they could, as this progressed, last-minute corrections on where the landing would be, and it was up to the recovery commander to know where he was, first, with his ship and tell the ship where to go, tell the skipper of the ship here's the position we think it's coming down now and here's where we think you are. You go there at 25 knots or whatever.

Eventually, of course, you would see it coming down and you had to compute its fall with a parachute and make last-minute corrections. Then, at the last minute, you turned the recovery over to the recovery commander. We backed this up of course, with destroyers, that were spread out around us in case there was a helo casualty or something of that sort. There was a regular rehearsal done of this several times, to have the helos take off on time to the various rescue groups, and the frogmen, and so forth. They had to be spaced in various areas around the carrier so that you'd have helos in all directions. We had about six of them out there.

Then you had to know just how to maneuver the carrier to get the space craft onto the elevator just right under the crane. It was lifted up by the crane, placed on the elevator, and brought in. Then there was, of course, the business of several hundred members of the press aboard, and there were transmitters put aboard for major television companies to operate with, and there was a large radar dish put aboard, which was used to communicate with the shore so that the landing aboard could be shown on television to the country. One of the problems was keeping this dish clear of the island of the carrier and still try to maneuver to get to the people in the water because we didn't want to black out the picture at a critical time.

This was all very hard to coordinate. Then we had to arrange a ceremony on deck for the returning astronauts and so forth. There were certain things that could and coult not be done. They couldn't be touched by anybody until the doctors had seen them. The doctor called a lot of the shots, really, in terms of what the astronauts did. He would take them down to sick bay and examine them for several hours. Then they were allowed to come up and see the crew, have dinner, and do a lot of things that they had to do afterwards.

And then you were supposed to head for Jacksonville Beach at high speed to unload not only the astronauts but the capsule, on the beach there.

It was a very structured business. You had to do it exactly the same way every time, except that during the critical period you were put on your own and told, okay, now you can recover the capsule.

Mack #7 - 454

Q: That's where the matter of your judgment entered into it?

Adm. M.: Yes. NASA did all the little things and the navy had to do all the big things, which was to get the capsule up.

Q: And I understand that the air force got into the picture, too, did they not?

Adm. M.: Yes, they had what are called airborne recovery teams, which they could have used in an emergency actually to land. They'd drop by parachute somebody, frogmen, in case the capsule were way off course. This had to be coordinated. They were in Bermuda, and we had to tell them what we were doing. They were up in the air, of course, we'd tell them in the air. They were there under our command, in case we needed them.

Q: But they wanted it the other way around, did they not?

Adm. M.: Oh, yes, always! NASA didn't buy that.

There was a second recovery. I'll look it up and describe it later. I don't remember which one it was. We did so much.

Q: That must have made some diversity in your doings!

Adm. M.: It did. As I said before, during the last two or three months of my tour, I was commanding both amphibious groups, and just at the end of one of the landing exercises in Vieques I got a telephone call from the chief of naval personnel, Admiral Semmes, who said that I was being ordered to the secretary of the navy's staff as chief of legislative affairs and that as soon as I returned from port I would be detached without relief and I was to expedite getting to Washington. I protested and said, first, that that would leave the Atlantic Fleet with no amphibious commanders, and he said:

"That's the secretary's problem. Don't you worry about that."

And I said: "My second point of protest is that I will be going right back to Washington, to the same kind of job I had before."

I thought that would kill me careerwise because I needed to do something else. He said:

"You'll have to argue that one out with the secretary of the navy. You're being brought back because he needs you desperately because he wants to sell the FDL program to Congress."

Q: The secretary of the navy at that point being?

Adm. M.: Nitze. He was still the secretary. He was there

when I left and he was there when I got back.

So I did exactly that. I left the ship as soon as we got in port, in about one day's time.

Q: Would you go back for a minute to the amphibious group and talk about any new techniques that may have been developed by that point, that you employed?

Adm. M.: There were no new techniques that I developed at this time. I'd been in on the development of these same techniques back in the first days of the amphibious force, when I was on Admiral Rockwell's staff. For instance, I found that the fire-support doctrine, in other words communications procedures, how you plot, how you conduct gunfire support, was roughly that that I'd developed and had my name on parts of way back in the days when the amphibious force was put together.

Q: And they were still doing this?

Adm. M.: Yes. The Marine techniques, of course, were changed somewhat in that helos were mostly used now to supplement landing craft, and the landing technique had changed in the fact that in the old days we had preplanned loads that were loaded into the transports in a certain order and came off in the reverse order, with very little flexibility. Now, you had what was called on-call loading. After the first few loads of real combat material, ammunition and so forth, went ashore, after that, using computer techniques, the landing force commander called for what loads he wanted. In other words, as he saw what was happening ashore, if he wanted more wirecutters, more mines, or more troops of a certain kind, or he wanted medics and so forth, he would send back and say, "I want load No. 17-22." A group commander, in that case, would tell the APA to get that particular load in amphibious craft or in a helo and take it to so and so ashore. This was all done on call, highly automated and computerized, which was quite a departure from the early days of the amphibious business.

Q: Yes.

Adm. M.: But I had nothing to do with that. That's just the way it was being done.

Q: Were there new types of craft, also?

Adm. M.: Oh, yes. The basic LCVPs and LCMs were still in use, although much larger versions, but there were new craft in the sense that the armored personnel carriers, amphibious armored personnel carriers, were really rudimentary in the early amphibious days. They were made by

Food and Machinery Corp. They were slow and tended to sink. The new armored amphibious tractors were quite good, much improved over the old days.

That was the biggest change, the amphibious tractors that were used. They were used in the assault wave, no more landing craft trying to go ashore under fire. The assault wave was amphibious armored tractors or helos. Of course, the helo business is a big change since the early days.

I had very little to do with advancing techniques. There wasn't that much time for it. We would try some new wrinkles in terms of getting into the area and protecting the amphibious area from submarines, mines, and so forth, but they were just the results of ASW techniques I knew about that were new and different.

So I had little impact on the amphibious business. There wasn't much impact that was possible in those days, not much change to be made.

Q: You intimated that you made full use of the facilities on Vieques. Culebra?

Adm. M.: Oh, yes, Culebra was for the full fire-support practices you did. What you'd do would be fire on Culebra and then do very little on Vieques.

Q: What about the navy's loss of those facilities?

Adm. M.: I think it's a blow in the sense that you're talking about places that are left to have amphibious exercises. We looked for spots on the southern coast of Puerto Rico and other places we were going to use just for a little variation in landing techniques, beaches, and so forth. As a matter of fact, I was planning such an operation when I left and that was subsequently canceled. There aren't many places you can go and have a full-scale landing without either tearing up the roads or the beaches or terrain, farms and so forth, and that's difficult to do.

Q: Yes, it's pretty heavily populated, isn't it, the southern coast of Puerto Rico?

Adm. M.: Yes. And that leaves you no places but the beaches along Camp Le Jeune, which are old and known to everybody and not much use, but you can do it.

Q: I suppose in Puerto Rico, also you get involved with the nationalist sentiment?

Adm. M.: Yes. If you go ashore and get much away from the beach, you run into the politics of the place. They don't like it. They think they're being used for warmongering.

Q: So what, if there's a future for the navy, does the navy do?

Adm. M.: I think maybe more and more they have to rely on perfecting techniques, which can be done at Camp Le Jeune even. You can use helos there to load and unload. In any event, it's very difficult to project amphibious warfare in the future in terms of predicting what kinds of beaches you'll go across, what kinds of areas you'll come to. The beach doesn't make much difference any more because you're going to do the main assault and all the rest of it by helo. So all you're looking for is a flat place to land the helos. Fire support doesn't mean an awful lot because you're not going to be landing against entrenched opposition any more, at least we don't think so. If you are, it's going to be after a period of time, not in the initial parts of a war, and so you really don't need fire support techniques that we had so well down in the Vietnamese War and before. As a matter of fact, we don't have many ships any more that have fire support potential, anyway. There are very few guns on our destroyers and other ships. We don't have any capability for it and we don't think we need it, so I think what is happening is that we're evolving new techniques that really call for using helos.

Q: What kind of a command ship did you have?

Adm. M.: Did I have at the time?

Q: Yes.

Adm. M.: I had a fast transport, the Marion.

Q: Was she fully equipped for communications?

Adm. M.: No, she was very poor in that. She was the best APA in the force, and the reason I had her was because we had two regular flagships, one of which was occupied by the force commander, the Amphibious Force, Atlantic Fleet, the other was given to PhibGroup 4 to experiment with.

Generally what happened was when we went on a landing, the active phibgroup commander took the second AGC and used it as a flagship. So we would plan on our APA and then when the time came to go on an operation we would shift flagships to either one that was normally occupied by PhibGroup 4 or, on some occasions, the force commander would let us have his flagship and he would go ashore, and we would use that flagship.

So whenever we went on an operation we had a full-scale AGC. That was interesting in the sense that I had helped plan these AGCs back when I was in the amphibious force before. I planned the first two variations of the flag plot in the old Pennsylvania to make it useable as an amphibious force flagship.

Q: Yes, I remember.

Adm. M.: Then, at that time, the Bureau of Ships' representative came out to question us very carefully on what we had in the way of what we wanted and what we should have in an amphibious force flagship. We gave him our back-of-the-envelope designs, told him what we did have and didn't have, and what we should have. That was my job because nobody else had the time to do it. Then BuShips' representative went back with this information and planned the AGCs, the kind we have now, the Rocky Mount and the others that are still in commission. Then, during the latter part of my tour, the Bureau of Ships again were designing what was the ultimate AGC, a new one, completely automated, computerized, with three-story level display in the interior of a large well in the ship, where the amphibious force commander would have one deck, the landing force commander one deck, and the supporting intelligence and air defense groups would have the other deck, all using the same large plot. Obviously, this cost too much money and was never built, but at least we had a hand in designing it.

Q: The ideal ship!

Adm. M.: Yes, the ideal AGC.

Q: Did you employ UDTs with the amphibious groups?

Adm. M.: Oh, yes. There were two UDTs at the amphibious base in Norfolk, which were always in training, and we took detachments from these groups. They were part of every amphibious exercise. Not only were they there to destroy token mine defenses which we would put in and tell them to find and destroy, but they usually had guerrilla or offensive-type missions given to them, where they were landed twenty-four hours or so in advance and would go inland and seek out the disposition of the enemy and so forth.

Q: Did you use them for breaking up coral formations and that kind of thing?

Adm. M.: Well, Vieques is so worked over that there wasn't much you could do there. You generally had to put in artificial barriers and say find and destroy this.

Q: You were going back to Washington to be chief of legislative affairs. Tell me about your job sheet. Was this an office that existed or were you simply going to set up one?

Adm. M.: It was an office that had existed for some time and the responsibilities of it were that the occupant worked again both for the secretary of the navy and the chief of naval operations. It was a two-hatted job just like the chief of information job. My job was, first, to train, in a sense, inform and train congressional witnesses. For instance, each year when the budget was to be presented I would assemble the secretary of the navy, the chief of naval operations, and all their underlings, the deputies of the chief of naval operations, and go over the budget with them, and we would assign duties for who was to stress this and what congressmen were in this particular committee and subcommittee —

Q: You mean matched the personalities?

Adm. M.: Yes. The idea was, of course, to sell our budget. First the authorization groups. In other words, each budget year the main weapons that the navy produces, and all services produce, had to be authorized by the Armed Services Committee of the House and then by the Senate. Once they

are authorized, then they're appropriated for by the
Appropriations Committees of both houses.

Q: There's a time lag there, isn't there?

Adm. M.: Yes, there is. The authorization meetings are
quite early in the year. First, you establish navy
policy, what you can do and what you can't do and what the
navy's going to be designed for. You talk in rather large,
grand terms, that you need so many ships, so many aircraft,
and so forth, and the money aspect is not much talked about.
It's the size and shape of the navy you're getting authorized.

Then, later on, the comptroller of the navy goes to
the Appropriations Committee and without much help he dickers
with the appropriations committees of both houses for the
money to carry out the authorized navy. When the comptroller
goes to the appropriations committees, the appropriations
committee is very jealous of its prerogatives and will not
permit legislative affairs personnel even to be in the
hearings. So it's a divided affair and you have to work
through the comptroller and try to get him prepared before
he goes over there as to what he has to get for the navy.

But with the authorization hearings the chief of
legislative affairs accompanies the secretary and the chief
of naval operations and is the principal backup person there.
In other words, if the secretary wants to know facts, the

chief of legislative affairs has to know them, how many of this we want, how many of that, what the history of procurement is for these kinds of weapons and ships and so forth.

Q: I would think he'd be an awfully good resource person for the appropriations committees, too?

Adm. M.: He would be. The only reason he's not there personally is because the appropriations committee doesn't want him there and will not allow anybody there except the comptroller types. They don't want to be, as they say, propagandized. They only want to talk numbers with their opposite numbers in the comptrolling business.

Q: Well, when the authorization hearings are under way, even though they don't mention money in the large sense they must have it in the back of their minds?

Adm. M.: Oh, yes, but they talk about gross figures. They're talking only about gross numbers of people, for instance, and numbers of ships, so much money for logistics and so forth. The appropriations group talks about the nitty gritty details, exactly how many men of each kind are you going to have, how many lieutenants, commanders, and so forth. Even this is preceded by hearings in the

House Armed Services Committee and the Senate Armed Services Committee, say, with the chief of naval personnel, going over his grand figure, so to speak, of how many people he wants and what he has to do.

After all these hearings are done, then the appropriations committee gets together with the comptroller and figures out how much money is going to be put aside for all these things that the chief of naval personnel wants, and the secretary and the CNO want in the way of weapons, ships, and aircraft.

Q: You say that your basic job, at the beginning, was to train all the people who were going to present these things.

Adm. M.: So they all present the same figures and, in a sense, talk with one voice.

Q: This involves a dry run, then?

Adm. M.: This involves, I would say, something like ten days of four-hour sessions where the chief of legislative affairs, in those days, went over the budget piece by piece, with the chief of naval operations and the secretary pointing out the highlights of the points they had to make, and there'd be discussion back and forth about who would say what. These were quite lengthy briefing periods.

Q: You certainly had to digest the budget, then, in all of its details?

Adm. M.: Yes.

Q: This involved real study, didn't it?

Adm. M.: Yes, it did.

Q: And with the assistance of the comptroller?

Adm. M.: Well, the comptroller was there because he would be asked occasionally how much money this would cost and if we substituted three F-4s for two F-8s, what would be the price differential, and that sort of thing, so he had to know the numbers.

It was quite a lengthy period each year -

Q: How long did it take you in advance of these rehearsals and so forth to really master the budget yourself? It's very complicated.

Adm. M.: Yes, it is and, actually, this all starts I guess maybe three months before the January hearings, the posture hearing, so called authorization hearings - the slang name for these is posture hearings - usually take place in late January, and, in those days, the budget was put together and finished up about October. So October, November, December were budget-study periods for the chief of legislative affairs.

Q: You also said that when they went before the committee certain points of emphasis were directed toward individual members of the committee. How did you achieve this knowledge of the individual members and their interests?

Adm. M.: A lot of this is known to everyone. All you have to do is read the papers and that sort of thing. The chief of Legislative affairs has a rather large organization. He has an office in the House and an office in the Senate, each one headed by a captain. These two individuals, together with a staff in each place of about ten or fifteen, some officers and some yeomen, were supposed to feel the pulse of the people in that particular house, who felt which way and so forth, so they were in constant communication with the members of the Senate and House of the armed services committees, the appropriations committees, the committees dealing with nuclear power and any other senators and representatives who might have navy feelings or who could control what happened to the navy.

But, of course, the biggest group that you dealt with was the House Armed Services Committee and the Senate Armed Services Committee. If you knew the idiocyncrasies of each one of those two committees you could do your job. The chief of legislative affairs had to rely upon his staff to keep him informed on the various areas that these people were interested in, and he had to spend a lot of time on The Hill. I used to spend half my time over there, calling on these people, having lunch with them and breakfast, talking to members of the staffs. The members of the staffs are extremely important. You had to know those people like you know your own brother. I'd just see them all the time and they many times could give you more information than the principal could.

Russ Blandford, who was the chief counsel for the House Armed Services Committee during my time there - he was a Marine colonel promoted during my tenure to brigadier general - and I were in constant communication because he wanted what was best for the navy and Marine Corps as well as what was best for the country. He was always slipping us information as to what we should be doing and how we should take care of Mr. Rivers, who was the chairman. Senator Stennis was the chairman of the Senate Armed Services Committee, a very fine old gentleman who would not deal with his staff quite as completely as did Mr. Rivers.

Mr. Rivers.

In other words, you started out the congressional year with the authorization hearings, but frequently there were other hearings after that all year long, on personnel, on drugs, anything that happened to come along, if they were interested in it, and you had to round up appropriate witnesses in the navy hierarchy and get them over there and tell them what they were supposed to talk about, get them over to testify before the appropriate either committee or subcommittee, or you had them go over and call on congressmen in particular.

Q: What power did you have to snatch these people?

Adm. M.: Absolute, in the sense that if I said it I did it with the secretary of the navy's backing and nobody ever refused. That was their first priority, to see what they had to do in terms of Congress.

Q: And you could call them from the field or anywhere?

Adm. M.: Oh, yes, call anybody you wanted.

Then I had to arrange lunches and dinner for various members of Congress who'd come over and be briefed and propagandized in the Pentagon by, again, the CNO or Sec-Nav or whatever person wanted to do it. Whenever congressional delegations traveled, the navy had a certain proportion of these delegations to send escorts with, so we had certain trained escorts who knew the idiocyncracies of certain congressional groups and would go round the world with them, providing all their funds and entertainment and arrangements.

So you saw quite a bit of the Congress.

Whenever there was a joint session I had to accompany the chief of naval oprations over there, get him into his seat at the joint session, and get him back. If a congressman wanted anything, he'd call me and I'd have to get somebody to do it or go over and see him.

The two offices handled something like 1,000 phone calls and perhaps 3,000 queries a day, letters and so forth from congressmen. They'd get these letters from Congressman A, for instance, who wanted to know why his constituent didn't have thirty days' leave this year, and get it to the proper place in the chief of naval personnel's office, get an answer, and get it back. So we had all these things, and just the mail alone and telephone calls were fantastic. Every congressman or member of his staff who wanted to call wanted an answer and he wanted it pretty quickly, so we had two liaison officers who literally handled 1,000 telephone calls a day, some of which were easy to answer like, "You should call the army" or something of that sort. Those were not generally recorded, what the congressman wanted, get the answer and get back on the telephone.

If somebody made a mistake, of course, they wanted to talk to the chief of the legislative affairs, right now. I'd get frequent calls from congressmen and their staffs, saying they hadn't been able to get what they wanted from the liaison office and would I please ask the secretary right now so and so.

In addition to the annual run of things, which was dictated pretty much by the budget cycle and other normal hearings that we'd have every year about personnel and so forth, we had extra hearings on a particular subject that came up such as the Arnheiter affair and you had to straighten out all the witnesses on the Arnheiter affair and get the appropriate congressmen informed. There was always something going on like that which you had to do, but your main job was keeping the chairman of the House Armed Services Committee and the Senate Armed Services Committee happy, because they controlled so much of what the navy did that you just had to keep after them.

Rickover was a force unto himself. He didn't want any help. He would never allow anybody from our office to help him. We were allowed to have an observer in the room when he testified. We never knew what he was going to say until it was all over.

Q: And no control over that?

Adm. M.: No. The secretary got to the point where he didn't care. He liked to see what happened and what the testimony was in writing later, but he didn't much care about what Admiral Rickover was going to do.

Q: How did that get out from under the secretary?

Adm. M.: Well, Admiral Rickover always appeared in his AEC hat. He was a member of two organizations in the navy, the then Bureau of Ships, where he was the nuclear reactors' chief, and he had a position in the Atomic Energy Commission. When he went before Congress, he appeared as that position and then he was asked navy questions, so he never appeared as a navy witness, he was an AEC witness all the time, although he was asked navy questions. So that, although it would seem to be very difficult, was rather simple because there was nothing you could do about it. You just sat back and watched it happen.

There were other problems in the Congress. One, for instance, when Admiral Connolly decided to change his testimony and feeling about the F-111B. I was there in the room when he did it, and I knew that when he told the Congress - it was my responsibility to tell the secretary what he had testified to - that there would be fireworks, so I told Admiral Connolly:

"I have to tell the secretary what you said but I'm

having a little trouble finding a cab to get back to the Pentagon, so why don't you go on back and tell him first," and he did. So that was much better to have him tell the secretary himself. Then I went back and told the secretary, "I understand you've heard what happened," so by that time it was all done. It would have been much better to have him say what he said, rather than have somebody, in a sense, put him on report. So we salvaged Admiral Connolly on that one.

Those were the sort of things that went on. There were hearings all the time.

Q: That was a very interesting incident. Were you behind the scenes there? Jerry Miller was.

Adm. M.: Yes. I knew what he was going to say.

Q: And then didn't want to put Moorer on the spot, you mean?

Adm. M.: Well, that's why he said it, all on his own, without any advice and so forth and nobody knowing anything about it, but he had to tell the principals, the secretary and CNO, what he'd done. As I said before, the reason that was given to me why I was to do this job was that the FDL was in very big in the Defense Department. This was a fast-deployment logistics ship, a gigantic ship —

Q: It was a McNamara idea, wasn't it?

Adm. M.: It was — and it was to carry the equipment for an army group, not quite division-size but a large army-troop size unit, and it was to be at sea most of the time, so that when you had a problem developing you would put an FDL or two off the seacoast of that particular area. Then you would fly in the troops and the FDL would go offshore and, using landing craft and helos, would ferry their equipment ashore to the nearest airbase. A very expensive concept but one that was very popular in those days and it was, in a sense, a kind of replacement for the Marines.

Mr. Nitze was directed by Mr. McNamara that this was the wave of the future and we would join it. Mr. McNamara told Mr. Nitze, "You get all your best troops together and I want this sold to Congress."

Q: How many of these things were to be built?

Adm. M.: Oh, I think sixteen or seventeen, something like that.

Q: And they cost approximately what?

Adm. M.: I've forgotten, but in those days almost as expensive as a carrier, a conventional carrier. They were gigantic ships very expensively equipped. It was a very expensive proposition.

Q: Were you sold on the practicality of this idea?

Adm. M.: I wasn't asked. I was told my job was not to argue but to sell it.

Q: But what about your convictions, your personal convictions?

Adm. M.: Well, if the country wanted to pay that much money for it, that was fine. I must admit my enthusiasm for it was not very great, personally, but I couldn't let that show. I was given all the help I wanted and given a lot of brochures and the information and data, and my job was to sell this.

I did sell it to Senator Stennis. He bought it. He voted for it.

Q: How did you do this? Through personal contact?

Adm. M.: Yes. I just talked to him by the hour and showed him the advantages of it, what we'd get for the money, and so forth. So he finally said he'd vote for it, and he did. He carried along with him enough members of the Senate Armed Services Committee to carry it, but the House was a different matter. Mr. Rivers was dead set against it and he would not be budged by me or CNO or anybody else, although there were enough members of the committee who voted for it for a while and it looked as though we had it carried.

Mr. McNamara finally gave up when he decided he couldn't sell it himself to Rivers or Congress -

Q: What was Mr. River's opposition based on?

Adm. M.: I think Mr. Blandford's influence that it was something that would do away with the Marines, Mr. Blandford, of course, being his chief counsel.

And so the FDL finally died a natural death, mostly because it was so expensive.

Q: And even McNamara gave up on it?

Adm. M.: He did, finally, too much money, but I remained on as chief of legislative affairs for a little over a year.

Towards the end of that year I'd been saying to Mr. Nitze that what I was doing was too much of the same thing

I was doing before and that I was going to be left behind in the race for getting anywhere in terms of three or four stars. So finally he agreed that I would be released at the end of the year.

Q: This was after the project had died?

Adm. M.: Yes, and I was told indirectly but not directly that I was going to be commander of the First Fleet, which would be a natural progression to a vice admiral's job and a fleet command. I was not told exactly. This was only rumor and I was told that this was being processed. In other words, the nomination was going through the system but hadn't been signed yet.

Suddenly, one afternoon late, I was called to the secretary's office and there, in the outer office, were Admiral Moorer, the chief of naval operations, and the chief of naval personnel and they informed me that they were about ready to tell the secretary that I was to be nominated by them to be deputy assistant secretary of defense for manpower and reserve affairs, which was a routine job and had in it an army officer who was then to leave because that was about the time of the change of administrations.

I protested and said:

"I've been ashore a year and I thought I was going

to go out and be a fleet commander and get back in the swim for rapid advancement."

They said, "No, this is one of those things that suddenly came up," and they hadn't known it was coming up until about a day or two ahead of time. The navy cannot afford not to fill a bill like that because if they don't put up a nominee who can win the job, they will lose a three-star job, which it's now our turn to fill down there. So I said:

"There must be lots of other people who can do that." And they said, "No, you're the only one who can fill the billet in terms that you've had these two terms in personnel and legislative affairs and information and you've been an aide in the secretary's office. All this qualifies you to be in this particular job."

I was told by the chief of personnel that I could protest this to the secretary but, if I did and was successful, I could probably forget the First Fleet job, too, because if I would not help the navy in a sense the navy would lost interest in me.

Q: Unfair --

Adm. M.: The secretary agreed that I was the man for the job. I was told to go down the next day and talk to the incumbent assistant secretary, who would be leaving very shortly but was still in office, and he did go to Yale. He interviewed me and I had very serious doubts. Many times I thought I'd better unsell myself and tell them I'm no good and I can't do the job, I'm not qualified, but I couldn't bring myself to do it.

Q: Your record stood there, anyway!

Adm. M.: So I just told the truth and did the best I could, and the next day I was told that I'd got the job and to get on down there as soon as I could and they'd get me a relief in due course. So for a while I did that job and my old job, one in the morning and one in the afternoon.

Q: Looking back to the legislative affairs job and others of a similar nature, it takes a unique person to handle such a diversified job. The navy doesn't train people for that.

Adm. M.: It doesn't.

Q: It's just happenstance that a man develops the background for a job like this?

Adm. M.: I suppose so. I never sought it, never liked it, and never wanted to have any of these jobs. I wanted to be either in strategic plans or in a command position of some kind but I kept getting pushed into it.

Q: Isn't there wisdom in shaping a man's career to handle a job like that, which is so important?

Adm. M.: Yes, there is, and it's something that should be done. On the other hand, you can't put the person in those kind of jobs and then suddenly tell him he's no longer in the running for CNO or some other job because he hasn't been a strategic planner or he hasn't had enough command time or he hasn't had a fleet command or something else. You have to protect him, if you're going to do that. And while I found myself protected at times, there were other times, as in this instance - it was fine, I think that's one of the most interesting jobs I ever had when I got down to Defense and I'm glad I did it, but, on the other hand, had I been out in the fleet I would have been in contention for the CNO's job along with Admiral Zumwalt at that time, but I was left behind my contemporaries by taking this job. At least, that's what I was told.

But the navy needs people like this. I was told at one time that I was the only person who ever bridged the gap between public information and legislative affairs. There were lots of people, at least when they were looking for people to do jobs in Defense and so forth, lots of people who'd been in public affairs, but who knew nothing about legislative affairs, and lots who had been in legislative affairs and knew it well but didn't know anything about public affairs. Strangely enough, when they found a person like this, he was scared to death of the other side. He would say, "I'm glad to stay in public affairs but don't let me get anywhere near the Congress. These guys are all dishonest people who do so and so and such and such." And the congressional affairs people didn't like the press system because they were afraid that they would have their statements taken wrong or make a mistake for which they would be fired. No one could bridge this gap between one and the other. Admiral McCain came the closest, but he was never in legislative affairs, except indirectly. He knew congressmen personally but he was never in the business of managing the affairs of it.

There was nobody like this that they could find, and this helped me a lot in terms of when I was getting ready to retire, because it made me very saleable to a lot of companies if I wanted to take a job, and it should have been something the navy could have used, but it never did.

Q: Is it in the cards at any time in the future that the navy will actually train people and change the system to the point where they can protect the man's career?

Adm. M.: Yes, it has changed it. At one time when I was in the Defense Department I was loaned to the navy to take part in a study of subspecialties, which is what the navy now does. It's been decided that no one person can be an expert in everything, and so each naval officer will become a subspecialist in one or more areas. He may be a subspecialist in education and training, and now public affairs and legislative affairs, certain kinds of materiel business like gunnery, electronics, radar, and so forth.

My part in this study was to insist that legislative affairs and public affairs be lumped togehter, and they are now lumped together, so that a man who wants to be a subspecialist in this sort of thing can go to public affairs office of strategic information for one tour ashore, then he will go to sea somewhere, and come back and go to legislative affairs. In other words, the billets are written the same, instead of being distinctly different, as they had been in the past. Now you will begin to develop people like this in the navy. This is one thing that I was able to do in the subspecialist program. Now, the navy has recognized officially that they should have men and officers who are efficient across the field of legislative affairs and public affairs because there's not much difference between them. Now the navy will begin to bridge the gap of subspecialist officers who will be trained in both areas, and that's necessary.

Q: But these men who are trained as subspecialists, will they also continue to be in the running for the top job?

Adm. M.: Yes, that's the heart of the subspecialist program now, foreign affairs being another subspecialty. What it means is that you will do your command jobs at sea and when you come ashore you will become a subspecialist. Before, the race was always to vary your duties, strategic planning, personnel, and one thing and another, but not to get too immersed in one job because, if you did, you got left behind. Now the navy has recognized that the navy is so complicated that you must get into one thing and stay in it, and that should be to your advantage rather than to your detriment. It has recognized this and the secretary of the navy's charge to the selection boards each year recognizes that, also. The selection process does, so now people are encouraged to stay in one specialty, sub-specialty. The name specialty in command, subspecialty being whatever you do roughly when you go ashore.

That's a change in the navy in the last ten or fifteen years, the subspecialty concept, but I was the first and I always thought that it would kill me by doing it, but I survived.

Interview #8 with Vice Admiral William P. Mack, U.S. Navy
(Retired)

Place: His residence in Annapolis, Maryland

Date: Friday morning, 6 April 1979

Subject: Biography

By: John T. Mason, Jr.

Q: All right, Sir, our chapter today begins with your new assignment as deputy assistant secretary of defense for manpower and reserve affairs, and this happened in January of 1969. You were not very anxious to go there, but you discovered later on, I believe, that it was one of the most exciting assignments you ever had.

Adm. M.: Yes, it was. I went to the new job on 19 January 1969, thinking that this would be, in a sense, a setback to my career but I soon realized that I couldn't think about personal things and I had to look at the job from the point of view of what did it mean to the navy and, perhaps, to the Defense Department and the country.

Q: Let me divert you for a moment with a question. With your experience in personnel and so forth, what percentage of men take this high point of view about their assignments?

Adm. M.: I would be surprised if it were below 50 percent. I'm constantly amazed by the wonderful caliber of naval officers we have. So many people do so many things that are unpalatable to them because they think it's in the best interests of the navy to do so. The percentage is very high. I would say it's over 50 percent. This is a characteristic of the navy, I suppose. I can't answer for the other armed services, other than the Marine Corps, but that's always to me been a characteristic of the old navy, at least. This was drummed into you, do whatever job is given to you, do the best you can, and, if you do it well, no matter whether you like it or not, you will benefit not only the navy but yourself. Do whatever you have to do and do the best you can, no matter what kind of a job it is.

Q: Personal preference is secondary to the main thing?

Adm. M.: Yes. I have never resisted a job except when I asked for a more difficult job than the one that was given to me and said I thought I could do a better job for the navy with the more difficult challenge. That's the only kind of protest that I ever made.

I'd like to add that in my many years of working in the Bureau of Personnel and other places assigning officers and men that I always found that a good man always gets a good job. The navy cannot afford to give a second-rate assignment to a good officer or a good man, and if you concentrate on being the best person you can as a naval officer, professionally and otherwise, you will get a good job. If you're put in a job below your capabilities, it will soon be evident and somebody will put you up to the next job, if you do your best at all times, no matter how much you do not like that particular job. Eventually, someone will see that problem and solve it, and put you in a better job.

Q: That's very encouraging.

Adm. M.: Well, it is but it's very difficult in this navy because the rules are always changing as to what we should have for assignments, qualifications, and so forth for promotion. The rapid-promotion system has come along and, in a sense, speeded things up to the point where you can't afford to take jobs that are not career-enhancing, so-called, because, if you do, then you lose out in the sense that other contemporaries pull ahead of you.

This, to me, was the most challenging job in the whole navy and, perhaps, in the Defense Department, that

I was going to. Yet, in the navy system at the time, since I was not going to the fleet, I was falling behind by two years in the so-called race for high rank, four-star rank and chief of naval operations, and I guess I did, but I still don't regret it. I would not have given anything for the almost two or three years I had in this particular job. It was a challenging and fascinating job in an area that was important to the country and the Defense Department, and the navy.

Q: Will you begin your talk about it by giving me a picture of the scope of the job.

Adm. M.: Yes. I went down to the Defense Department on the 19th of January and I met almost immediately with Mr. Laird and Mr. Packard, the secretary of defense and deputy secretary of defense. I had previously met with Mr. Albert Fitt, who was the outgoing assistant secretary of defense and left a few days before the 19th to go to Yale University to take over the No. 2 job in administration. The assistant secretary of defense to-be was a Mr. Roger Kelley, who was an official of Caterpillar Tractor and who, Mr. Laird informed me, could not be there for about four months, so Mr. Laird said:

"You will be the acting assistant secretary of defense for about four months," then he outlined to me his concept of the particular position. His personal philosophy, which I learned he really meant, was that he gave responsibility and authority to each person in his organization to the hilt, to the utmost, until that person proved that he or she could not carry it out.

Q: Had you known him before?

Adm. M.: No, I had not, except to meet him when he was a congressman and to know him that way. I found him to be one of the two or three top civilian officials I had ever known, and I found Mr. Roger Kelley, who was to come in later, to be on that same level. I would view them in descending order, perhaps, as Mr. Connolly, Mr. Laird, and Roger Kelley, right in with that group of three as the best I've ever know, and I've been with quite a few civilian officials in my time.

Mr. Laird gave this as his philosophy not only to me privately but to the other assistant secretaries in a group meeting, and he carried it out. That's the way he ran his organization. I think I commented once before that his particular organization - perhaps this is a characteristic of Republicans who ordinarily are businessmen - was that most of his assistant secretaries were businessmen, Robert Froelke, Bob Moot, and many others.

Q: Laird himself was a politician?

Adm. M.: Yes, but he was not an academic, and I guess I don't mean to condemn academics. That's a terrible thing to do, but an academic in the business world is a fish out of water. He's not used to making decisions. He likes to consider, to contemplate, to argue, but he prefers to make his decisions as part of a committee with a rotating chairman given the responsibility over the president of the university, somebody else having to make the terrible, hard decisions. He doesn't like to do that. Perhaps it's because that's not what he does. When you bring academics into a situation like this, and Mr. Albert Fitt was, as witness this, when I took over his desk I found a pile a foot high with documents, unsigned letters, unmade decisions, problems not solved. He just didn't like to do this sort of thing, so he just didn't do it.

But, to get back to Mr. Laird, the kind of person he had in his organization was one who made decisions easily and well, had been doing so in some business or other in a previous part of his life, and that's the way Mr. Laird ran the system. I couldn't believe this. It was just a garden of Eden to be allowed to go down to this very important job for four months and do it all by myself, with a charter to do whatever I wanted to do -

Q: He must have studied your record!

Adm. M.: I'm not sure whether he did or not, but at least he voiced confidence in what I could do and said if I didn't do it he'd get somebody else, not to worry about it, to do the best I could, and if I made a mistake let him know first and we'd do what we could to rectify it, but making mistakes was not his real worry, the only thing he worried about was making mistakes and not doing something to correct them. That was rather exhilarating.

Mr. Packard was of the same stripe. He came from a business of his own, Hewlett Packard, and his philosophy was the same. Mr. Laird let me know that Mr. Packard had complete independence from him and anything that either one of them said could be taken as gospel. That was what was to be done, and that's the way it worked.

In surveying the total of what the assistant secretary of defense for manpower and reserve affairs had to do, it was really amazing. First, his duty was, of course, to run the manpower aspects of the Defense Department, setting ceilings on manpower levels, on rates and groupings and ranks within the manpower levels for all four services, both military and civilian, monitoring and forming, if possible, the procurement policies, the promotion policies, the day-to-day administrative policies for all the manpower involved in this grouping.

That was only the beginning. Of course, it was necessary to go to Congress when things went wrong in the manpower business or when changes had to be made, but that was perhaps 40 percent of what was done in that job. Other responsibilities given to the assistant secretary were to command, in a sense, the armed forces radio and television system, which was the third largest network, radio and television network, in the world and the only one that had worldwide scope. This was an enormous organization.

Another one was, for instance, to run an entire health system for the services. There was a deputy assistant secretary for health matters under the assistant secretary, who oversaw the choosing of all medical personnel in all the services, all hospitals, CHAMPUS, general medical affairs for the entire Defense Department.

Another responsibility was to oversee the overseas school systems of the services. This, again, was the largest school system in the world.

Q: Was this for families?

Adm. M.: This runs the schools at all military bases overseas and, in some cases, in the United States for dependents. It hires and fires teachers, administrators, runs the curricula for various schools, does everything for primary-school grades through high school. This was a rather large organization. Another section handled all the equal-opportunity affairs of the Defense Department and these also were enormous, because the contracts that came to the Defense Department ran about 10 billion dollars in total value and when you look at the 1,000,000 employees of the Defense Department plus about three million in the military, a total of 4,000,000 and, assuming that to that 4,000,000 roughly another 6,000,000 are added in terms of wives and children, you were looking at 10,000,000 people who are affected by equal opportunity and by the contracts that the Defense Department let, which, again, numbered about $10 billion.

And, of course, the other part of the title being "reserve affairs," the office handled the entire reserve of all the services plus the National Guard for the air force and the army.

So, it was an enormous responsibility.

Mr. Laird told me that there were four items that he wanted solved before anything else. These were a new study on pay - this was one of the times in history when it was decided that we were paying the wrong way, we should be paying people a total salary rather than what are called pay and allowances, so much pay plus allowance for housing and all the rest of it.

Q: To modernize the whole structure?

Adm. M.: Yes. We could recruit more if we paid a total sum of money and made the man or woman pay back out of that housing, subsistence and so forth.

So I hired a panel headed by Admiral Hubbell to make this pay study. This was done about the first week I was there.

The second point was he said the president wanted to go to an all-volunteer force and, at the same time, of course, phase out the draft as soon as possible.

Q: This was at the outset of that administration?

Adm. M.: Yes. So I began preparations for forming and calling the president's council on an all-volunteer force, which was headed by Mr. Gates, at my suggestion, and the executive director was a Mr. William Meckling, who was the University of Rochester's administrator, and it had on it when it was formed many prominent citizens from all over the country and from all disciplines of the academic world, economics, business, and so forth.

Q: Who selected them? Did you?

Adm. M.: I made the initial selections and by the time it was to be formed Mr. Kelley was on hand and from Mr. Laird, then, asked the White House to procure, in a sense, the various people. It was my original idea and it was carried through.

Q: Was there a time limit on this?

Adm. M.: No, because the president was very anxious and what he wanted to do was done. In other words, Vietnamization. The problem was to use the Vietnamese, first, to augment our troops overseas in units and then to form their own units, and to have them supplied and trained and then put in the front lines, in a sense, to relieve our units, which eventually was done. The problem was to harry the armed forces to hurry up and train the Vietnamese, which was again one of my jobs, and at the same time to tell them in no uncertain terms that the draft was going to be reduced month by month, as was the size of the armed forces, by plan. I had to make manpower plans to show the diminishing numbers of manpower to be allowed to the services each month over the next three or four years, and, at the same time, to show them the numbers that would be allowed them for draftees.

This was a very difficult job because the army, of course, didn't want any part of it. They wanted their draftees in large numbers because they saw that they had a job to do and they were somewhat doubtful that the Vietnamese could be trained as rapidly as the president wanted. It was much easier for them to have unlimited numbers of draftees to fill their ranks to go out and carry out the responsibilities in a safe manner. So, we were always balancing the army's safety and desires against the president's desires to get on with Vietnamization, get on with lowering the draft, and get on with achieving the all-volunteer forces. That was a continuing battle for, I guess, the three years that I was there, and it was very difficult because here I was, a naval officer, telling the army, in a sense, what size they were going to be and what kind of draft quotas they were going to have for the succeeding months, but I managed it without being lynched and we did achieve an all-volunteer force, we did reduce the draft to zero, and we did get out of Vietnam, which I think shows that great credit should be given Mr. Laird and the president for conceiving the idea that we could do this and then following it through against very strong opposition from the army particularly, and from the Congress.

I was given another charge, and that was that the administration was very interested in equal opportunity, which meant that it wanted all its civilian contractors, defense contractors, to have what are called affirmative action plans. That is, a plan that would make them equal opportunity employers. It went all the way from having rest rooms of proper size and without any signs on them, other than "men" and "women." In other words, in the South no more colored rest rooms and white rest rooms, and that sort of thing. It had to be in the company's plan that that's what they were to do. It had to do with their hiring and firing practices. They had to hire so many black employees, so many Spanish-Americans, and so forth, even Indians and, in some cases, Eskimos. The plans of the company had to show that that's what they were going to do and they were to be required to submit affirmative action plans that would carry this out.

Mr. Packard was in charge of this and he asked me in the first week what my advice was, and I said that that was the law and the person in charge of the Defense Department was doing it and, although it would be extremely hard for these large companies to accept it, in the end, because they valued the fact that they had contracts with all these dollars, they would accept our charge and they would do what they had to do, but it would be very uncomfortable and unpopular for him and for me and for those people working for us. He asked me what my recommendation was and I said:

"I think we have to do it, and I will attempt to carry it out. This is what the president wants and the way the law reads. Let's do it."

Q: What proviso was made for overseeing all this?

Adm. M.: We had an equal opportunity section on the staff. It formulated a general doctrine and said what was to be done. Then, the services had their own equal opportunity areas where they had parallel staffing systems which actually did the work of going, for instance, in the army's case, the biggest point was J. P. Stevens and Company and three other - one Dan River Cotton Mills - large textile companies in the South that were trying to get out of doing this sort of thing. They threatened to stop making khaki-colored wool cloth for the army and, since they were the only suppliers in the whole country, the army faced a situation where they wouldn't have any uniform material if these companies did not comply with our directives, did not keep their contracts going, and so forth.

The army was told that they would have to make these companies comply or they'd have to cancel the contracts. Within about four days, Mr. Stevens was in my office berating me in a nice way, and I simply told him this was the law and was Defense policy, and that he would have to do it, and we would give them all the supervisory help we could. He went in with me to see Mr. Packard and Mr. Packard confirmed what I had told him. We all parted friends. He went back to J. P. Stevens and Company - he had previously been secretary of the army, amongst other things - and he acceded gracefully. In a few months J. P. Stevens was in conformance with the law on equal opportunity.

His was the biggest company's president and, since he performed, the others finally followed suit and we had this done. It also had to be done for U.S. Steel, Bethelehem Steel, the large aircraft companies, and most of the Southern manufacturers in Texas and places like that had to be brought into conformance, and they finally were. It was a large step and, again, one that President Nixon received very little credit for. He did, it was unpopular, and it came out all right.

The reserve system, of course, was another large point, although I wasn't charged primarily with doing that. That eventually came about as something that had to be done. What was happening, of course, was that as the draft fell off and the war began to wane, it became rather unpopular to enlist in the reserves or even to serve in the reserves or the national guard because there was no real incentive. They weren't getting ready for war. The war was winding down. So it became my problem to put together a new reserve policy, which I did and which was that the reserves were to be made part and parcel of the regular navy and the regular army and so forth. This became our present reserve policy and, again, this was somewhat unpopular at first to the regular navy because they saw themselves as having to put increasingly large numbers of dollars into the reserve system and to give the reserves increasing numbers of large weapons and so forth. They didn't like that at first.

Q: How did you go about developing this new policy?

Adm. M.: I just called the reserve component heads of the services together. I examined the philosophy of what I thought was to be the country's philosophy in the future, which was that we were stopping the Vietnamese War. The next war would be an entirely different kind, it would not have a phase-in period, we would no longer have a draft, and perhaps not even a selective service system, so my philosophy was that the reserve had to be really ready. In other words, it had to be attuned to and closely attached to the regular service, otherwise it wouldn't be any good. There'd be no time to call it up, to train it, or anything else. I presented this philosophy to Mr. Laird and he said:

"That's perfect. That's the way I feel about it. That's it, that's the reserve philosophy."

And so that's what it became and I had to call in the heads of the reserve components and they, surprisingly enough, agreed that that was the way it should be.

Q: But the regular services -

Adm. M.: Then, when I went to the regular services, they

balked initially, with, I think, the short-range view that it would cost them in terms of money and manpower and weapons and so forth, because they would have to transfer some to the reserves and spend time, effort, money that they didn't want to spend on the reserve system. But they soon came around and, in the end, it became pretty much an unanimous reserve policy and it's the same today. It's the only one we could have. For instance, if someone had to sit down and think about it in the future a little bit, plan it, how was it going to get done, and point people's heads in the right direction, and once they were pointed they all agreed that that was what it should be.

So that was another charge that I had.

The equal opportunity system went along all right and during the three years I was running that it came out all right. All major companies that had issues with it with the Defense Department finally gave in and got affirmative action plans, and we have now what you see. Nobody thinks twice about it any more. All the Defense contractors are in complete compliance and there are no problems, except little ones that come along.

Q: It's not related in any way to the idea of quota, is it?

Adm. M.: No. Quota, of course, was never a good word. We

never used it. We stayed away from it because it had bad connotations although it's a perfectly good word.

Q: You mean equal opportunity based on merit?

Adm. M.: Yes, but based also on the fact that there had been for years discrimination against certain minorities and that the minorities had to be helped in some way. They had to be encouraged, they had to be schooled, jobs had to be created specially for them so they could learn on the job and then be put up to a higher job, and the various companies had to recruit actively on the minority market, not just wait for the minorities to come to them. There were things like that done and they came out all right.

First the pay study went along and was thought to be good and was adopted by Mr. Laird and the services. As usual, Congress would have none of it, which I predicted, because they don't like change. So the pay study was put in mothballs and was brought out in later years when somebody had the same idea. But it was an exercise we had to go through.

Q: What was the main objection to it, other than the change?

Adm. M.: It required an initial outlay of dollars that Congress didn't like to see put out. They'd rather have it indirect in their budget systems. In other words, don't give a man a chance to have quarters or not, make them have them because you have the quarters there, and let's dock his pay, in a sense, and not give him the money, make him stay in the BOQ. Lots of reasons like that. A lot of them were just plain and simply that the congressional committees involved didn't like to have anybody else take the initiative. They thought that that was their particular pigeon and if they wanted to do it they'd let us know when they wanted the plan. So that's what happened, they put the plan on file.

Q: Did you do any lobbying, knowing so many of these members?

Adm. M.: Oh, yes, I was charged by Mr. Laird with lobbying.

Q: And, of course, he had his contacts, too?

Adm. M.: Yes, he did, and we spent hours and hours presenting these plans to members of these committees of the House and Senate, but in the end they decided they had more urgent things to do and they would think about it. So they thought about it and they're still thinking about it.

Q: How was it received, when first proposed, by the personnel in the armed forces?

Adm. M.: I think they liked it because it gave them more flexibility with their money. They got the same amount of money but they just got their hand on all of it. They began to realize, I think, just how much money they were getting. What we did, among other things, was to put in money terms all the benefits they were getting. Our recruiters used the data that we developed. They realized that the SPP, all the various things that they had had access to for years, government insurance, retirement systems, and so forth, were really money that they never saw. They realized how much money they were getting, real money, plus all these advantages they had, which were translated into money terms. They realized that their pay was pretty good.

We wanted this study, of course, to use with the all-volunteer force, to give to the recruiting system, so that they could use it for the all-volunteer force to recruit.

Q: How did General Hershey take to this whole idea, all-volunteer?

Adm. M.: He was very much against it. I had various problems with him. Of course, he finally retired, at White House insistence and it was a little bit difficult getting him out of his office and getting his new No. 2 man in.

Q: He was like J. Edgar Hoover, wasn't he, he'd been there so long!

Adm. M.: Yes, he was, right, and as far as he was concerned the only way to go was the way he was doing it, which wasn't the most efficient way either of registering people, conducting the exemptions, or doing anything else that had to be done. But, as far as the draft and the all-volunteer force was concerned, the presidential commission did meet. I met with it daily and, in the end, got the report and processed it through the Defense Department. By this time, Mr. Kelley was in office, but he let me continue with this particular problem, since I'd started it.

The all-volunteer- force concept had to be evolved, using the presidential commission's report as the basis, but that wasn't quite enough. What it said, in a sense, was yes, we could have an all-volunteer force but at some time in the future we would have to pay the price, which we're doing right now. In other words, you could have a lot of incentives and they outlined some of the incentives that they thought were good, extra pay and so forth, you would achieve an all-volunteer force initially, which we did, but there would come a time when a drop-off in incentives and inflation and many other things would come along and no longer could you get all the recruits you wanted voluntarily. Some time in the future Congress would have to sit down again and resurrect the draft, or some form of it, because the volunteers would dry up, in a sense.

Q: That was all discussed at that time?

Adm. M.: Oh, yes, that was part of our plan and report. And, at that time, the Congress and the country would have to decide do they want to pay people enough to join the armed services so that they won't have to go back to a draft, which might mean quite a bit of money, or do they want to go back to the draft, and what that draft really does is it assesses young men a tremendous amount of money to pay for the armed services. What you're doing, of course, is drafting a young man who doesn't want to be in the service, paying a minimal amount, and he is paying the difference between what he could earn on the outside and what he's getting paid in the army or navy. The country is, in a sense, assessing him that amount of money to run the armed service. So what you're doing is you are putting the cost of an adequate security system on the shoulders of a bunch of young men, instead of on the shoulders of the taxpayers, which the present concept is doing. The present concept is you should pay enough to recruit, like you do in any other business, enough people to man the armed services, which means, of course, that the total amount of pay goes up, taxes go up. Taxes are, theoretically, charged against each citizen fairly and so each citizen fairly pays his share of the security of the country.

Now, if you don't do that and you go again to the draft, what you're doing is taking the burden off the shoulders of the citizens and putting it on the small number of young men. That's what the draft has always done.

Q: That's a much more modern concept, isn't it?

Adm. M.: Oh, yes, but that was the feeling even then. If somebody would sit down and analyze what was going on, that's what we did in the Vietnamese War. We did worse than that because, instead of putting it on the shoulders of all the young men equally, we put it on the shoulders of certain young men who couldn't procure a deferment of some kind. We put it on the shoulders of those who couldn't go to college, who were physically able rather than physically unable, who were unmarried instead of married. It was further discrimination, and that's a terrible way to do it.

The commission and the Defense Department also said

at that time that if we ever went back to a draft system it would have to be one that didn't have any deferments at all, and, better yet, it should be a universal-service type, where each person was drafted and required to spend a year or two, wherever it was determined to be, in the service of his country. He could either be in the armed services or, if he couldn't make it physically or otherwise, he would serve in a hospital or some public service job, so that every person was assessed equally, male and female, physically capable otherwise was assessed equally one year's service, the difference between what he would be paid and what he could earn. That would be a fairer way than just to take the ones the country wanted, in other words, who were physically able and so forth, and make them pay the price.

This is the terrible thing that we'll do if we go back to the draft, it we don't do it correctly. It's not right.

Q: Was it thought that one year would be sufficient?

Adm. M.: No, the army wanted two and that is probably proper because, when you look at three months of training, then you only get nine months of service out of a person and it's not very effective and it's very costly.

Q: Was it thought that the total cost for that procedure was less than what it would be for the volunteer?

Adm. M.: What would have to go with this would be that you would pay a draftee much less than you pay a regular. What happened with the all-volunteer force, of course, was that we upped salaries tremendously, to the point where this country could not afford a 4,000,000- or 5,000,000-man army and navy and air force now for war if you paid all of them what we're paying the ones that we're paying now. The pay would be astronomical.

Q: But when we went to an all-volunteer service, why was it necessary to up it so much?

Adm. M.: Because you couldn't get the volunteers to join, and one of the problems that the Defense Department solved was that the army could not get people to go into the combat arms, that is, artillery, infantry, without a bonus, and so we put together and had Congress pass a $2,500 bonus for every man enlisting in the army who could agree to go into the combat arms. The Marine Corps didn't want it because they said every marine was a combat type, but they eventually went along with it.

The idea was that you paid people according to supply and demand. You pay doctors more, you gave them a bonus, you pay aviators more, so the army said, "We want to pay our combat arms guys. They're the ones who bleed and die in case of war, so they should be paid more."

Q: On the degree of danger!

Adm. M.: Yes, and we pay a reenlistment bonus that varies according to the skill that's involved. So it's not a new concept. We just applied this to recruiting.

As far as recruiting was concerned, the Defense Department, again using the presidential commission as a takeoff point but really using our own plans, put together, had approved, and funded a tremendous recruiting and advertising system. We called in advertisers and so forth. At that time there were many movie spots and advertising campaigns put together for all the services, particularly the army, in terms of how to recruit. The recruiting systems were beefed up. All the services were required to put their absolutely best men in recruiting. They overhauled it completely, and put their best men in recruiting. The recruit-training systems were overhauled so that they were not as bad as they used to be in terms of turning people off. They were still to be demanding and to train properly but they were not to be the old Marine kind where they tried to scare half the people away.

And, again, the services put money into barracks,

living conditions, and that sort of thing, so that the services would be a decent place to be housed and to be fed and in which to do your thing.

We explored every avenue and there was a tremendous task force put together in the Defense Department to run the all-volunteer-force program. The services at first resisted somewhat but, in the end, they also put together task forces within their own services to handle the all-volunteer-force problems. General Westmoreland resisted to the end but finally joined the system and became a vigorous proponent of it. He had to because the army was the key to it. If the army didn't do it, then it wasn't going to be done.

Q: What assistance did you get, or what opposition did you meet, in the Congress for this whole idea?

Adm. M.: Congress quite as expected said it wouldn't work. Senator Stennis said it at that time and he still says it won't work. But it did work. We got the draft down to zero, we filled the services with volunteers, and we achieved an all-volunteer force, in spite of what he said, it wouldn't work, we couldn't get there. But he reluctantly went along with all the points we asked, including a bonus, approving extra money in the budget for advertising, for living conditions, renovation, and so forth. He just kept insisting that it wouldn't work. Well, it has worked.

Q: And how was Hébert? How did he look at it?

Adm. M.: The same way. The two were violently against it, except they saw no alternative, but they both went along, as did their committees, with whatever we wanted to do because they saw that it had to be done.

Now, today, we're about to reach the point that we predicted, which was a time when the Congress and the country would have to make a decision. You see rumbles already about the services saying they can't fill their ranks and so forth. The answer is they can't fill their ranks with the present rate of pay. We're getting to that point right now, and somebody, soon, will have to fish or cut bait and decide whether they want to raise pay and all the enticements necessary to bring people into the services or whether they want to go back to a modified selective service registration and use a service concept where everybody comes in and is assigned to some branch of service, military or otherwise. The point is that down the road somewhere, whether it's one year, two years, or five years - it's hard to predict, nobody knows.

The Defense Department and the commission both predicted that the all-volunteer force would be just fine as long as we were in a state of depression or there was a depression down the pike somewhere.

Q: A safe haven?

Adm. M.: Yes. Perhaps that's going to happen in the next two or three years, with a depression coming on and continued high rate of unemployment, will force enough people into the services to fill them until the recession is over.

Another fear that was voiced was that such a service, all volunteer, would be increasingly black to the point of 25 or 29 percent. We made various studies concerning this and predicted that it would never exceed 25 percent, but so what if it did. The country was 13 percent black, so the army would be twice that percentage.

Q: That point is being made now, isn't it?

Adm. M.: Oh, yes, but still it's not over 25 percent. That's about what we thought it would be, but we didn't see anything wrong with that.

At any rate, we finally achieved zero draft, and a great celebration, and the president was very happy about this, as were all of us, of course, and we became an all-volunteer force.

Q: Do you want to make any prognostication on what is

going to happen now?

Adm. M.: I think we're in for perhaps two depression years when unemployment will go up somewhat, inflation will get higher, and that the howls you hear now from the services when they can't quite man themselves with volunteers will be suppressed or be diminished for two or three years. At that time, of course, we'll come out of the depression, the problem will arise again some time in the future, about five years from now, and the Congress will probably enact some kind of universal military training, or universal training, part of which will be military, because they will not want to put the kinds of money into pay that they would have to to keep volunteers coming.

Q: There is the question of whether we can afford it?

Adm. M.: Yes, and, of course, the ever-present question of can we afford a war, and no we can't, not with our present pay system. We'd have to have two classes of military types, professionals whom we paid perhaps at the rate now, and new draftees who would be paid a good deal less, because we just couldn't afford it. But who says what you can afford in wartime? If you mobilize and do that sort of thing, you can do anything. That was our problem, we didn't mobilize, for Vietnam. If we'd mobilized, we wouldn't have had any problem, but that was a terrible political mistake and we're paying for it now through inflation and many other things and really the death of the reserve forces. They were not called for Vietnam so they thought, well, why should we bother. They should have been called up. They should have had complete mobilization to get the problem solved, then gone back to a civilian state again.

Q: Looking at the navy, what is its situation currently? Are they falling behind drastically, too?

Adm. M.: No. The army is falling behind the worst, the Marines a little less. The air force is in fine shape because they're highly technical, have fine living quarters, do not work as hard, and have other advantages. The navy is second to the army in troubles because the navy always has good morale and technically is interesting. It drives people away by the tempo of operations and long overseas deployments, which it has.

Q: The inability of a man to lead a normal life?

Adm. M.: That's right. This will be its problem. But, in turn, the navy has certain flexibility. It could if it wanted to and the problem became tough enough, cut its deployments, cut its tempo of operations, and stop driving people out, but nobody wants to do that now. It has to again reach the point where you have to decide whether it's going to be undermanned or do these things. They'll make a decision, I hope, and take action to keep more people in and then it will not be as undermanned. This feeds on itself. If you're undermanned, you work harder and longer hours, and then more people leave or won't stay on, and it gets harder and so forth. But, sometime, the navy has to realize it cannot do all the things it's doing, cannot meet its overseas commitments, and not drive people away. That's what it's doing.

Again, the all-volunteer force continued all during my time in the Defense Department. The pay, of course, dropped off. We solved that problem. Equal opportunity continued all that time.

Q: Did you have to stay with it? Monitor the whole thing?

Adm. M.: Oh, yes. Mr. Kelley, of course, was the assistant secretary but there was so much to do that we both worked full time on all these things, and many of these things I continued because I'd started them.

Q: What was your continuing interest? To monitor and see that it was working?

Adm. M.: Yes, right, because more and more companies would come to the fore. For instance, there were contracts to be renewed and the complaint was that they couldn't accede to our equal opportunity requirements, and I had to meet with the company, or Mr. Kelley would, and convince them that they could. Finally, they would agree and they'd do it and it would be resolved.

About the start of the second year, with the economies going on and all the requirements to cut manpower we were levying on the services, we realized we had to cut the secretary of defense's office and we did by 15 percent, which again was a chore put on the Manpower and Reserve Affairs office, which was very difficult to do, not only to cut ourselves but to cut everybody else. That was done during the second year.

Q: How did you go about that cutting, just across the board?

Adm. M.: No, we cut it 15 percent and then adjudicated all the squawks that came up to give more here and take a little there. In the end, it came out about right.

Q: Was this in order to set an example to the country, or what?

Adm. M.: An example to the services, which were being cut. We had to cut them because the numbers of people in the services were coming down, had to, because of the budgetary squeezes, which were getting worse and worse.

Q: Did it impair the function of the Department of Defense?

Adm. M.: I don't think so. I think it improved it. It was just that when we could do this, we could say to the Congress or somebody else, we will no longer have an office that handles this, you'll have to do without it, and tell the services we no longer will adjudicate this particular function for you, we will give this to the army. For instance, we gave the army most of the responsibility for running overseas schools. We maintained a small staff, which just looked over its shoulder to see that they were doing the right thing and was liaison between them and Congress. What it was doing was what it should do, which was cutting down administrative overhead.

Q: This was getting back, more or less, to the original Forrestal idea, was it?

Adm. M.: Yes. We thought there was just too much administrative overhead in the Defense Department and the office of the secretary of defense, and that the way to do this was to maintain a very slim overseeing function and put back into the services, one of the services, at least, the requirement to coordinate for all services. Then we would simply oversee. That's what we've done in many areas.

Q: Simultaneously you speak of the overseas schools. Was there a cut in their budgets too?

Adm. M.: Yes, in the sense that there were less people overseas, less schools, and less people, simply because of a shrinking of the armed services. That meant some cut in budget and a little less supervision.

Q: Speaking of manpower, in that time I think I recall the senator from Montana always proposing that they withdraw the forces from Europe. Did this affect the manpower office? How did you react to that?

Adm. M.: No, that wouldn't be a problem of ours. That would be simply a shifting of army forces. If they left Europe, they'd go somewhere else, like to Fort Bragg or Fort something else.

Q: Senator Mansfield.

Adm. M.: As a matter of fact, in some ways, it would be

more expensive if we were to withdraw somebody from Korea, for instance, or Japan. The cost of supporting troops was less than it would be in the States. You'd achieve a higher expense by bringing troops back to the States than if you left them somewhere like Korea, but the manpower and budgetary experts in Congress know that the loud-talking ones will not listen or will not take it in when you try to tell them that. If you take somebody out of Europe, you don't reduce the size of the army. You simply shift him from one place to another. You have to bring him back to the States and put him in some army encampment somewhere.

Another problem we had was what was called Project 100,000. President Johnson, in his time, decided that as a social move he would require the armed services to take 100,000 what were called Group 4 mental persons. That is, they were in the very lowest spectrum of those coming in the services, many times so low that they would not normally be going in. He required the services to take 100,000, most in the army. of these mental group 4s. As the size of the services decreased, the services stated that they could carry less and less of these mental group 4s because, as a percentage of the total, they were becoming larger. So my problem was to sort of phase out this program as I could without arousing the ire of the social do-gooders in Congress and other places, with decreasing quotas for mental Group 4, particularly in the army and also in the navy.

Q: That was a pretty touchy problem.

Adm. M.: It was, but that was solved in about two years' time.

Q: Tell me a little about the rocky road.

Adm. M.: Well, it was difficult to convince certain people, including my boss, Mr. Kelley, that the navy, for instance, had very little room for mental group 4s. I asked the chief of naval operations to take him out on a two-day tour of the carriers, the cruisers, and the submarines and show him what kinds of jobs were performed by people in CIC, boiler rooms, and so forth, to show that a naval person at sea needed education and mental ability as much as anybody else, and there wasn't much room for people — you have a few deckswabbers and perhaps mess service, and so forth, but even if they did that they would never go anywhere. They'd keep that particular job, and there wasn't much at sea for mental group 4s.

So, he went out to sea and came back and he was pretty much convinced, and from then on he turned to and helped with the program. Whenever we had somebody in Congress or somebody else come in and say, "You've got to keep these high numbers of mental group 4s going," why, we would say, "See Mr. Kelley. He went out and saw it in action." That would usually convince them that we could only take limited numbers and the numbers ought to be decreased.

Q: You imply that most of the people who were opposed to this withdrawal of the handicapped were so simply because they didn't appreciate —

Adm. M.: They saw it as a social program.

Q: They didn't appreciate the requirements?

Adm. M.: Right. They saw it as a way to help the 100,000 less-than-smart young men. It was up to the services to solve the problem any way they could, and perhaps you could do that when you had armed services of 4,000,000 or so, but when you got down to less than 3,000,000, as we did after the war, you squeeze out all these nonessential jobs. These are the first ones to go and there's no place to put these mental group 4s.

Q: What was Laird's position on this?

Adm. M.: He supported my position and Mr. Kelley's.

Q: He was more realistic about it?

Adm. M.: Yes. He thought it was a fine program, but he realized that we were getting to the point where we couldn't support any more, and the services were not a social institution, except when they could be. When they were squeezed down, they got to the point where they couldn't do this sort of thing, it had to be done by somebody else.

So that one got solved.

Q: What was somewhat in the province of the HEW people, too?

Adm. M.: Yes, it was, surely.

Q: Did you get cooperation from them with this program? Did they take over the sponsorship of these people, or what?

Adm. M.: No, not directly. Their program just expanded as it could, as it had to.

Another area was jobs for veterans. As you'd expect, as the armed services decreased in size, large numbers of people left and could not get jobs and so forth, so a commission was formed called "Jobs for Veterans," which, again, I had to head. We got members of industry together, advertising and public relations and put together a program to publicize the fact that we needed jobs for veterans.

Mack #8 - 525

Q: Was that a relatively popular issue at that time?

Adm. M.: It was amongst the veterans and amongst those we recruited to help solve the problem, but it was not a popular issue amongst the companies involved or the other people who had to compete with the veterans for jobs. It depended upon your point of view, whether you were a veteran or you were somebody else competing for that same job. It was popular in the White House because it was a big social issue with them.

All three years, perhaps one of the most important things that was going on was the drug issue, the drug-abuse issue. That was, of course, a Manpower and Reserve Affairs challenge and responsibility. I got that one. As a starter, I called together a committee formed of the services, of course, and it had on it the services' drug-abuse experts, alcohol-abuse experts, personnel and manpower persons, and we met, I guess, for about two weeks at least a half a day at a time, and reviewed the problem. What was the size and shape of the problem, how many drug-abusers did we have, what facilities did we have to treat them - first, to find out where they were, what were the legal problems involved. Once we'd gotten the facts assembled, then we put together a policy that stated what drug-abuse was, listed all the policies of the services, and put together a defense policy, which was overall to be supported by the services, as to how to locate drug-abusers, what should be done either to rehabilitate them or to remove them from the services, how we would educate people coming is as recruits and so forth. In other words, all the aspects of the drug-abuse program.

Q: How did you relate it to Vietnam and service there?

Adm. M.: Well, the problem started there, because drugs in Vietnam were as available as candy bars in this country, and you had literally thousands of GIs who turned to drugs out of boredom or to alleviate fear, whatever happened to be their problem. We found that as high as 80 percent of GIs in Vietnam were drug-abusers, or drug-users. The problem was fantastic out there.

So part of our program had to do with these young men who were coming back to the States after their tour of duty was over and, in a sense, mentally and morally infecting the others they came in contact with, passing on to other young men who hadn't been to Vietnam the drug habit, taking it back to the civilian world, to college where they went, and so forth.

So, our problem was the services' problem, but the overall problem was the country's problem, and the White House, on the president's direction, had a drug-abuse committee, also, headed by Mr. Egil Krogh. This met once a week and I was the Defense member for it. The Immigration Service and many other departments and agencies had members on it.

Q: Customs?

Adm. M.: Yes - oh, about fifteen different Washington organizations had members on this committee. The president met with us several times, the vice president quite frequently, and the problem was to solve the country's drug-abuse problem, because at that time, drugs in schools, particularly high schools and colleges, were very bad, mostly because the habit and the actual drugs had been brought back by GIs coming back from Vietnam. There were thousands of them coming back, either after they'd finished their tours or as the sort of disestablishment of Vietnam organizations took place. All these young men were coming back. They were all college age or high-school age and going back to high school or college and, in a sense, infecting the civilian population. But at this time the drug-abuse problem, countrywide, was very bad.

So the problem became one for the White House to lead the country, and the Defense Department to do what it could to cut down the infectious source, which was Vietnam. With the White House helping, we, the White

House committee, met with the government officials of Vietnam several times and they professed that they couldn't do much about it, the reason being, frankly, because all the government officials had their hands in the pockets of the drug dealers out there, and they were being bribed and so forth, there's no doubt about that. So the government of Vietnam wouldn't do anything about it.

The army was pretty much hamstrung because they couldn't separate the GIs from the civilian population where the drug transfer was taking place. They couldn't always tell a drug-abuser. You couldn't tell marijuana at all. There was no way of detecting marijuana. You could tell heroin by urinalysis, but it had to be within twenty-four hours of the use of it. At one point we did initiate thousands of urinalyses to detect drug users and many of them were found, but there's not much you can do about it, except that if the man was too bad you'd rehabilitate him. If he wasn't, then, of course, he was suspect and was watched carefully.

The president became so enraged about all this that at one time he insisted that the Defense Department do something positive to detect every drug-abuser. Well, that meant giving a urinalysis test to every man in the service every twenty-four hours -

Q: Every twenty-four hours?

Adm. M.: Every twenty-four hours - and so I received this order as the Defense Department representative, and I was astounded, but that's what the president wanted, said Mr. Krogh.

So I went back and wrestled it out with paper and a pencil a little bit and came up with the fact -

Q: Did the president really appreciate the magnitude - ?

Adm. M.: Oh, no, he didn't at that time. I tried to present the magnitude to him. I found out it would cost at the very least $1.50 per urinalysis, that each one of about two ounces had to be refrigerated before it came to the test center, and that we could require all the refrigerator cars in the United States plus about 80 percent of the transport aircraft in the United States, warehouses refrigerated about twice the size of the White House, and that's what got him finally, when I said this is what it would cost. It would cost roughly $30 billion a year. He finally acceded and said, "Well, I guess we can't do it." All it took was a piece of paper and a few remarks as to what it would cost and the size and shape of it, a mound of frozen urine twice the size of the White House every month! He didn't realize -

Q: That was a graphic way of doing it, wasn't it!

Adm. M.: So, he finally said, do what you want to, and we went back to doing what we were doing, which was –

Q: Did you have any personal conversation with him on this?

Adm. M.: Oh, yes, that was it. I'd written this short paper, and they took me in to tell him what this was going to be. After they'd digested it a little bit, giggled, and laughed about it, I read some facts off a piece of paper and said:

"Mr. President, the Defense Department is at your service. We'll do whatever you want."

He giggled somewhat and said:

"Well, I guess we can't do it."

So I said, "Thank you, Sir," and left.

He was prone to this sort of thing. He would reach out and say do something and not realize what the consequences were, and some of the White House staff were simply afraid to tell him that, so they'd pick on some little poor admiral and make him go in there and tell him that!

At any rate, the drug-abuse system went on during the three years I was there, and I was always ahead of it.

Q: Well, this entailed setting up a lot of hospitals for rehabilitation, didn't it?

Adm. M.: Yes, it did. It also meant some research into what had been going on, for instance, what the army had been doing about LSD, which is now reaching the public somewhat. They had done some terrible things, which I stopped right away, in terms of making tests without knowing what LSD was all about. But they did also produce some good facts about LSD. The tests they made were on psychologically and physically healthy, normal people, and so they got very little result. In other words, you could take LSD if you were that way and you would recover from it in due time and you had no after effects. But they also ran some tests on epople who were not physically healthy, and particularly not psychologically healthy, and they found out that there were after effects and that the gene-damage recurrence - a man who was not psychologically perfect would have a recurrence of an LSD hallucination any time or place. He couldn't control it. So, since very few people are psychologically, genetically, and physically perfect, we knew right away that, for instance, an enlisted man who took LSD after his initial exposure to it, at any time in the future might be manning a radar, for instance, in combat information center, and the flashing lights would trigger his hallucination again. He'd have one and he'd just go berserk in the CIC of a destroyer.

So we just had to take the strongest steps to outlaw LSD for anybody, and particularly remove anybody from the aviation system, nuclear power system, who had used LSD, but we never knew of anyone who had a recurrence.

Q: These tests you're talking about were not optional things?

Adm. M.: No. The LSD tests had been made by the army. They thought about using LSD as a drug to use against the enemy and they'd use our own people to make the tests, little realizing that LSD would eventually become a drug used by the population and that the data they had would be extremely valuable to us.

I uncovered this, in looking at their laboratory reports, and used it in this drug-abuse study. We found out many other things.

The Institutes of Health, for instance, had made studies about marijuana, showing that a person could not drive a care safely for eighteen hours after using a sort of a standard dose of marijuana. We brought this out in the open, used it in our policy, saying that you should not drive a car within eighteen hours of using marijuana. That was put out to the public. I held a press conference about this drug-abuse report we put together. I took it over to Congress, presented it to them and was quizzed about it. The press had access to it, yet to this day the press has never used the fact that marijuana, by edict of the National Institutes of Health, after tests, reduces your capability of driving safely.

Q: Why? The example of General Groves all over again?

Adm. M.: I don't know. The same thing I pointed out before, when I'd pointed out to them that the press is remiss in not pushing this point, they refused to press this one, because it was not flashy, I suppose. But some day someone will discover it's in the public domain and use it. People are always talking about how marijuana doesn't affect you, doesn't bother you. The answer is, yes, it does. It's worse than alcohol in this respect because alcohol, if you take a drink or two, after about two hours, you can drive a car safely again, or two hours per ounce. But if you use the standard dose of marijuana, you do not drive safely, but nobody wants to accept that for some reason or other.

At any rate, these programs did go along and, while we were never able to achieve a satisfactory solution, we were able to cope with the problem and find out the magnitude of it, roughly, start measures to reduce it, and the reduction was only really effective after we got out of Vietnam, because there were still large supplies of marijuana in this country, particularly in the southwest of the country, around California, Camp Pendleton, and so forth, and the southern part of, say, Fort Bragg, where there are lots of marijuana-users.

Q: Say a little about the hospitals that were set up in the military.

Adm. M.: Well, hospitals were not set up so much as we used unused parts of hospitals, barracks, and so forth for rehabilitation centers for drugs and alcohol. There's a navy program now in the navy hospital in Balboa for alcoholic rehabilitation. When I said drugs, I should have indicated to you that this includes alcohol.

Q: Alcohol is a drug, as well, yes, and the one that's publicized so highly now.

Adm. M.: Exactly, that was started during this period, as a result of the program which we set up which said the services would have alcohol rehabilitation centers as well as drug rehabilitations centers. That was the navy's answer to our requirement and still, today, is worthwhile.

Q: And what's the duration of the treatment?

Adm. M.: It's varied over the years. The duration really is up to how much the person needs, how bad he or she was to start with, usually at least thirty days. You can't figure that one out. It depends on the person's psychological makeup, how deeply he or she was into drugs, what kind of drugs, and so forth.

We set up a standard of rehabilitation which described how bad a man or a woman had to be before he or she was given a discharge and thrown out of the service, or at what point do you try to rehabilitate and how much rehabilitation you would give, and once you considered the person rehabilitated, how much you would look after the person afterwards to see whether it had been effective or not. All these standards were set up by this drug-abuse task force and are all followed today.

Q: Was the Krogh Committee back of the White House conference on drug abuse for youth?

Adm. M.: Yes, that conference - there were two conferences that took place during that time, all of them put together by this White House task force and run by Krogh. Also, the State Department and the Treasury and several organizations were at that time trying desperately to get Turkey to stop their citizens from growing poppies. We finally did so for about two years, but it didn't last long. They went right back to doing it surreptitiously. Now it's not as bad as it was, but it's still pretty bad.

That was a fascinating aspect of that particular job, the drug-abuse business.

Q: Is there any reason for optimism about that whole problem?

Adm. M.: I don't think so. It's under control fairly well in the country. If you didn't have that, they'd turn to something else, as you see now young school kids are turning back to beer and wine from drugs.

Q: It's cheaper!

Adm. M.: Yes, and easier to drink. They're both bad.

Always we had the problem of, well, what are you older people doing, who use alcohol.

I remember one occasion at a Defense Department staff conference during the course of the morning, it was held at the National War College, this was not just drugs alone, but I was given twenty minutes to discuss drugs and it so happened that my twenty minutes were right after the morning break. As I remember, I started the session by saying I hoped that all the conferees had enjoyed their drug break - you'd either had nicotine in the form of cigarettes or caffeine in the form of tea or coffee, and I know you're looking forward to your alcohol break when this lecture is over. So when you start criticizing young people in this country, just realize that you probably have had three kinds of drugs in the space of three hours. So, be careful how you criticize the young people of the country, because this is just as bad. That seemed to bring them up a little short.

Q: Would you relate it to the affluent society, or what?

Adm. M.: No. There are various reasons for it. One is the breakup of the family. It used to be that families kept their youngsters under better control. They came home from school and didn't run around in automobiles to drive-in joints and find things to do. They were kept busy at home. There were grandmothers and grandfathers in the family who'd take up the slack when the parents couldn't oversee youngsters when they came home. The whole family system has just gone downhill. For these young people in school, drugs are just one symptom of the problems they have. They have psychological problems, a very high suicide rate, many things have happened because the family has broken down, the control of the family, the church, and higher family organizations, such as you shouldn't do some wrong because your aunts and uncles and grandfathers would hear about it, and that was terrible for Chinese and Japanese parents.

Now, families move around so much and so many mothers

work and there are so many divorces, the family is so limited in size - in other words, there are no grandmothers and grandfathers any more. Control over children has just gone, and this is one reason they turn to drugs. They're looking for something to fill the void. There are many other reasons for it, but this is one of the big ones.

Q: It is not peculiar, however, to this country?

Adm. M.: Oh, no. If you go to other countries where it's happened, you find the same things going on. You won't find much of it in Japan and China. The family system still is very large there and the block concept. For instance, a young Japanese boy will live on a block his whole life and if he takes drugs or does something wrong, the whole block knows about it and he's, in a sense, outcast. It's hard to say that that's true of drugs, which it is in Japan, but alcohol is accepted by almost anyone there. It's not considered a drug, not considered bad. Everybody uses it to excess, but the family system does control this in China and many other places, but not in our country. They move too much and the old extended family system has gone, what you used to have.

Q: What has that done, in an overall sense, to the effectiveness of the military posture of a country like ours?

Adm. M.: Well, it's made it very difficult. For instance, you'll see frequently large numbers of nuclear submariners, not large numbers but significant numbers, discharged from the system for using marijuana under the concept that you cannot use that sort of thing. Security guards at SAC bases, for instance, when they do it they're thrown out right away.

You see many cases where, you don't know about it, but it's happening. Young men are thrown out of responsible jobs in destroyers and carriers and so forth because they've used LSD. What we consider military readiness of all the services because we have to look out for drugs and drug-users and take care of these things.

Q: We do this in advance of whatever penalty comes?

Adm. M.: Yes, but it doesn't seem to bother them at all. Young people just don't tailor their actions to their fears any more, they do it, anyway.

Toward the end of my tour, in the last few months of it, an event occurred with the selection of the new chief of naval operations with which I was involved. One of my jobs was to carry personally all the three- and four-star nominations to Mr. Laird from the service secretaries, and so I was astounded one day to find that one of the ones I had to carry to him was Admiral Zumwalt's.

Usually, what happens when a CNO is selected the secretary of the navy, by custom - it doesn't necessarily have to be that way - he interviews all three- and four-star officers in the navy to find out whether they are proper candidates or not, at least, the majority of them, the ones who would be eligible by age and so forth.

Q: This is a direct interview?

Adm. M.: Yes.

Q: And it's known why they're being interviewed?

Adm. M.: Oh, yes, because it's the season for it. In other words, so many months before the CNO is to change, normally he is interviewing and talking to the leading officers of the navy who would be candidates, in order to make up his mind which one he would want to choose. This was done very quietly and almost surreptitiously, and I found out Mr. Chafee had apparently not interviewed much of anybody. He was set that he wanted Admiral Zumwalt, and suddenly the nomination came down so I had to take it to Mr. Laird and say, "This is all I know about it. It's a piece of paper, and here it is."

Mr. Laird, I think, looked into it and found out that this was probably true. Mr. Chafee had not done much of a selection. He just assumed that he wanted Admiral Zumwalt and that was the way it was going to be. Mr. Laird talked to him at some length but finally acceded, and the nomination was put through.

Q: This was setting up a new system!

Adm. M.: Yes, it was. What happened, of course, was - and I had to give my opinion from the manpower side of it, although my responsibility was only in very general terms, it was the navy's problem to take to him anything they didn't like about it. My point was that in taking such a young officer, Mr. Chafee, in effect, was taking out of the navy system about six or seven years of officers who had been coming along who would be eligible to be CNO, and who would, therefore, not have a chance at it. What would happen would be that large numbers of senior, experienced officers would either voluntarily leave or would, in a sense, have to be forced out to speed the navy up to get in tune with Admiral Zumwalt's contemporaries. You would almost be forced to do this, and when you do you're upsetting a tremendous number of the senior officers in the navy, and was that what was really wanted. This was a problem I had to present to Mr. Laird, and he took it in and talked to Mr. Chafee, and in the end he decided to go along with the nomination. I don't know the reasons why.

Q: Did you know the reasons why Chafee was so insistent upon this new CNO?

Adm. M.: No. Apparently - I have no personal knowledge of this, I didn't talk to him about it, didn't feel that I could - Admiral Zumwalt, of course, was in Vietnam doing a marvelous job out there in a very difficult area. He was in charge of all the navy's operations in-country in Vietnam. Apparently, Mr. Chafee felt that doing this good a job showed that he could handle an organizational job of any size, although Admiral Zumwalt had not had a large fleet command and had not had certain other jobs that you expected a CNO to have before he took over the position. Mr. Chafee, for reasons unknown to me, decided that this was what he wanted to do, so the change was made.

  I welcomed it in a sense because I knew Admiral Zumwalt and always liked him very much. I'd served with him at various times and was among the first to congratulate him when he came back quietly, unknown to anybody else, to be told he was to be CNO.

  So he eventually took over and a few months, I guess, after that he talked to me about my future and said that he had hoped to put me in a four-star job quite rapidly but that I had not had a fleet, and it occurred to me that that was a rather odd thing to say because he hadn't either. But I grinned a little bit and said:

"Well, that's fine. How about a fleet?" And he said:

"I'm going to break the barriers of the system and put you in command of the Seventh Fleet, which heretofore had always been an aviator's command. You're to be the first nonaviator to command the Seventh Fleet."

That was, to me, the best job in the whole navy, including that of CNO, and I was very happy to be told that that's where I was going next.

In due course, an air force officer, General Tabor, came in to relieve me and I went on out to command the Seventh Fleet.

Q: Would you go back to the job in the Defense Department? There was a special blue-ribbon panel set up by Secretary Laird. Were you involved in that? It was to streamline, I guess, the chain of command, so to speak, within the Defense Department and to the White House. Admiral Moorer, as chairman of the Joint Chiefs, was to be responsible, I believe, by the findings of this panel, to the DOD, rather than the president.

Adm. M.: As you say, that was a panel that, theoretically, was made up of people outside the office of the secretary of defense.

Mack #8 - 544

Q: They called it blue-ribbon.

Adm. M.: Yes - and I knew, as it was going on, what was going on and watched what it did, but I had no personal involvement with it.

Q: What was back of it? Do you know?

Adm. M.: No. I think just a feeling that the secretary of defense should be a more powerful person than he was, that he should not have a parallel source of information going to the White House, because Mr. Laird's idea was that if he was going to be responsible for the Defense Department he should be responsible for all of it, operations as well as procurement and the administration of it. It's never been that way and it never will be, I guess. But it's a rather awkward system to have one side of it here, as I say, the chief of naval operations being a chief of staff to the secretary of the navy, which is what he really is, and he's called that in the army, of course, and the air force, but with no operational responsibility at all. And yet going down to meet with the chiefs, where he does have a say in operations. It doesn't make any sense, in some ways, and Mr. Laird said:

"This doesn't make any sense. Let's have it all in one system."

Q: But the other side of the coin is that the CNO is answerable to the commander in chief, isn't he?

Adm. M.: Yes, he is, certainly, for operations.

Q: And this was putting a block between him and the president.

Adm. M.: Well, Mr. Laird's position was that the secretary of defense should be answerable not only for administration and everything else, as he is now, but also for operations. Right now, the chairman of the Joint Chiefs is answerable for operations to the president, but the secretary of defense, as an adviser to the president, sits in on all operational decisions and throws his weight around somewhat, but without true responsibility. Mr. Laird said, "If I'm going to have to do this, then I ought to have responsibility for what goes into the system as well as sit around and advise the president on it."

It's an awkward thing, the way it's done now. There are reasons for it. It's a checks-and-balances arrangement and it's theoretically to make sure that there's direct military advice available to the president. But it does cause some problems at times.

But at least the commission met and came up with its findings, which were duly turned down, as would be expected. Congress wouldn't have passed them, anyway, if they'd been proposed as legislation.

Q: I think you should augment your previous remarks on the streamlining of action through the Department of Defense. Perhaps you should do it be telling me how you dealt with this report on drug abuse in order to get it through, to get it approved.

Adm. M.: Well, maybe I can make a point for any future generations or anybody else who has time enough to read this history. My feelings for the navy over many, many years of serving in headquarters and many other places always were that it was thought by navy officials, officers, that you really weren't working right unless you worked at least ten hours a day, seven days a week, that if it wasn't done you weren't doing it right. And when you wrote a paper or a speech it had to be nitpicked to death, each word had to be looked at several times, and rewritten and rewritten and rewritten, that that's the way paper work and administration were done, particularly in the Navy Department. I'd been through this for years, and I didn't think it was the way it should be, so to me it was quite a clean breeze to come to the Defense Department and find, as I said before, that it was staffed at the very highest level by businessmen who didn't believe this, who thought that if you couldn't do your work in eight hours a day on five days, perhaps occasionally six, you weren't doing it right. In other words, you weren't delegating responsibility properly and you weren't doing you job if you couldn't do it in such a span of time. That's the way the Defense Department was run.

Mr. Laird was very seldom there on Sunday, hardly ever on Saturday, and always quit about six. He always got things done. You could always get to him if you had a point. He would call you anywhere for a short answer about something. He never gave you deadlines, he just gave you the general idea of how urgent something was, and you always seemed to be able to produce what he wanted when he wanted it. He always accepted papers from you, letters, you would write for his signature, studies, and so forth, and he'd never change them unless there was a real reason for changing them.

A case in point is the drug-abuse report, which I put together as chairman of the committee. After two weeks of meeting with various members of this committee, all with differing opinions, it became evident that no subcommittee could write this report and someone had to sit down and do it. So I did. I wrote about six hours one night, got it done, typed, brought it back to the meeting, and, with a little bit of horsepower, got all the members to agree to it, put it in final form, signed it, brought it to Mr. Kelley the next day. He went through it fairly rapidly and said, "That's fine."

I couldn't believe it. This was a very important document that was going to affect the future of the whole Defense Department and all the services, as far as drug abuse was concerned. It meant the spending of millions of dollars and the diversion of many, many people to handle the drug problem. Yet he had trusted my judgment and the judgment of the committee implicitly. He decided to change nothing and said it was fine. He, in turn, took it to Mr. Laird, who did exactly the same thing.

It turned out it was fine. It did the job. It was never quarreled with. There were no mistakes in it, and it was an indication that you can run things that way if you give people the necessary authority, trust them, and then back them up.

So, to me, this was a very exhilarating three years to serve in an organization like that, where I think I did more work and probably did more good for the navy in the Defense Department with less inhibition than any other job I ever served in. I think this is just a testimony to the good leadership of Mr. Laird and Mr. Kelley that the Defense Department did so much during this period. You look back on it and, to have achieved an all-volunteer force in this era, to have pulled all the troops out of Vietnam, and to have solved the equal-opportunity problem, mostly in the Defense Department and a large part in the country, and done so many other things is a great credit to Mr. Laird and, in a sense, to Mr. Nixon. I think history will bear out that he pulled this country out of Vietnam, out of the war. Nobody remembers that. All they think about it is what happened in Cambodia and so forth, which is really a red-herring sort of thing. What he did was really a great task that is not appreciated enough by this country yet, but will be as history goes along.

Nobody knows the risks he took, but I participated in them in terms of cutting draft sizes, cutting the size of the armed services, requiring the army to bring people back from Vietnam early, and so forth, in order to get on with reducing the draft to zero and getting the all-volunteer force formed. He took substantial risks. Nobody knows about it and nobody seems to perceive that yet, but I'm sure historians will.

Q: You talked about that whole period in the Defense Department and all the things that were undertaken and accomplished, but you haven't said anything at all about the corollary, which was the building up of resentment against the war and involvement in Vietnam and all that among the populace. This must have had some bearing on your job.

Adm. M.: Oh, yes, and this brings to mind an entire facet of this job that I should have talked about. That is, of course, when I said we were in charge of the education program that included under that and also in the reserve part of our responsibilities the administration of the ROTC programs of the country.

There was building resentment on the various campuses on which we had ROTC units.

Q: Almost to the point of lynching?

Adm. M.: Oh, yes. What was happening was they were burning down armories, assaulting ROTC students - there was great trouble on the campuses.

Again, a group was formed, of which I was the head - I seemed to get all these problems where something involving violence or something of that sort happened - but a grouping of university presidents where there were ROTC units on campus was brought back and went to work to put together an ROTC policy. We did so, and it was decided to cut out a lot of ROTCs where the production was subnormal, when there were just a few candidates being produced each year, and to put ROTC units in universities where there was thought to be potential. Examples are, we took the ones out of Cornell, Princeton, and Harvard, the Ivy League places where we were getting very few long-term naval officers and where the opposition was the strongest to ROTC, and simply told the universities, "If you can't keep order and you don't want ROTC, we'll take it out." So we took them out and have never put them back. We put them in places like Prairie State and other state colleges where there were large numbers of black students and immediately began to produce good ROTC officers.

This was quite a change, a radical change, in the ROTC policy brought about because of the troubles on campus and so forth, and those schools today have ROTC units and very few changes have been made since that time.

Q: Some of them began to go back —

Adm. M.: Some of them went back at the strong insistence of the Ivy League schools, but only with reluctance on the part of the departments involved because they don't produce long-term naval officers.

But that was quite a change in the ROTC system at the time, which gets me back to the question you asked, which I haven't answered. I've forgotten what the question was!

Q: It was was there any effect on the development of all these policies in the Department of Defense because of the build-up of resentment.

Adm. M.: That's right, and I told you of the ROTC change, which was a most significant one.

The other was, in general, the feeling in the country, particularly on university campuses, that war was improper and the part of reserve units where resentment was building up because they hadn't been called as a totality, which they thought they should have been, and, of course, they should have.

From the point of view of young men resisting the draft, this, of course, was the concern of the manpower part of the Defense Department and the total Defense Department. There were general indications of it. For instance, one time a group of young law students, about twenty in number, came down to the Defense Department and insisted on seeing Mr. Laird because they wanted to protest Defense policies and the country's policy with regard to the justice of the war in Vietnam. Mr. Laird quite properly said he wouldn't see them, and so, of course, that came to the manpower place. Mr. Kelley had gone, so I talked to them for about an hour and, at the end of it, a young man said:

"I trust you believe we should not be in Vietnam."

I said: "That's correct, and we never should have been there. We should have gotten ourselves out a long time ago. That's a political question, not a military one.

From the point of view of the Defense Department and my own personal view, once the administration got us in there, it's up to the Defense Department to do the best we can to carry out national policy which, at the present time, is to fight in Vietnam."

There was a little silence. Then one young man said:

"Well, if you are against this, why do you stay here?" and I said:

"I'm against it. I've made my views known, they've been considered, but national policy is not what my views are and I am sworn to uphold national policy and I'm going to do it as best I can. If I were to leave and somebody else would come in here, I have to think that, since I was chosen, if you put the second choice in here, he would not do as good a job as I'm doing. So, all considered, I think I have to stay here and do my best, whether I agree with national policy or not."

They accepted that and all marched out.

Q: Muttering, perhaps!

Adm. M.: No, that was a new concept to them and I think maybe I did some good. But this is the kind of thing that went on.

Mr. Kelley, for instance, when he first arrived said that he wanted to know why we were in Vietnam, what were people being told about why they were going out there, being sent out to die in some cases in Vietnam. I had to tell him that, frankly, I didn't know and I didn't think they were being told anything. So he made a trip out there, expressly to find out what was being done in the processing centers, where they were sent out from various California depots for the army and the fleet center in San Diego, to find out what young men were being told about why they were fighting in Vietnam.

Then he went out to Vietnam and he quizzed, I guess, hundreds, of soldiers, sailors, and marines as to why they were there, and he came back and said:

"You're right. They don't know why they're there. Nobody is telling them anything. All they know is they were ordered to go out and that's it."

So we began a campaign to try to find out what the political policy of the country was, as to why we were there, and put together a system where we would try to inform all members of the armed services as to why they were out there, what they were doing, and so forth, which eventually came about but it was very difficult to come upon the reasons why we were there. They were not very apparent. We'd go to the White House and ask them and they didn't know.

Another thing Mr. Kelley did, which I think was very fine, was he evolved a set of what's called human goals of the Defense Department. This was a one-page document which eventually was signed by the three service secretaries, the four service chiefs, and, of course, the secretary of defense, and Mr. Kelley, and was placed in every office, almost in every service in Washington and was on the back of the telephone book. It was a simple statement of the human goals of the Defense Department. It was a fine document and something that he personally produced. It still exists today. It's updated every time the administration changes.

Q: He sounds like a humanitarian.

Adm. M.: Oh, he's one of the finest people I've ever known, Mr. Kelley.

Interview #9 with Vice Admiral William P. Mack, U.S. Navy
(Retired)

Place: His residence in Annapolis, Maryland

Date: Monday morning, Easter Monday, 16 April 1979

Subject: Biography

By: John T. Mason, Jr.

Q: I want to revert today, before we go to the Seventh Fleet, to the last interview, in which you talked about the reserves and the setting-up of the system as it exists today. I wonder if you'd discuss this a little more in terms, for instance, of how do you deal with reserves and the sudden calling up of reserves such as we saw in the Berlin crisis and other such things, the disruptions to their personal lives and disruption to the economy of the nation. How do you deal with that factor?

Adm. M.: The way it should be dealt with, to me - I think this is the consensus of all reserve commanders and those who deal with higher echelons is that the reserves should be called up only if almost all are called up and only if the country is about to mobilize or should mobilize or does mobilize. What happens is if you call up reserves selectively for short periods or if you fail to call up the reserves and use the draft, the reserves feel that their reason for being - and their morale is very high - is no longer there. As in Vietnam, we did not call the reserves and used the draft to expand enormously the armed forces, and the reserves sort of atrophied on the vine, they were not used and their morale suffered. That was under the old system. One reason given for it was that they were equipped with old airplanes, old ships, although the ships could have been used - as a matter of fact, anything could have been used in Vietnam - they didn't fit in with a modern carrier for instance. That's why the concept of the reserves was changed somewhat, to make sure they had absolutely modern equipment, as good as the regulars had. This was a bone of contention between the chiefs of the armed services and so forth and the Defense Department, who did not want money to go into equipping the reserves with expensive equipment. They wanted the regular services to hand down their equipment, their aircraft and so forth, to the reserves as it became old or used. That was a way of saving a lot of money.

The trouble there was that, when you got ready to use the reserves, particularly in a first-class type war, they were not compatible with the rest of the navy. Their ships didn't have modern communication equipment, their aircraft were not compatible because they didn't have the right spare parts in the carriers and so forth for the older aircraft, and it just became pretty obvious that if you were going to have reserves and you wanted to use them in a hurry you'd better make sure that they were using the kind of aircraft that you could use immediately in active ships.

Also, it made sense to have the men in complete units that could be brought into effect, such as a boat group, and this should be a reserve unit that was near water and could use its boats, for instance, landing craft.

Q: So they wouldn't be dispersed?

Adm. M.: That's right. For instance, you should have a landing-craft unit in Alexandria and you should have an APA unit in Norfolk, and that APA unit could go immediately and man an APA either in the fleet or in the reserves, pick up its boat unit in Alexandria, and go drill with it for a two-week period. Then, you'd have an almost active unit there that could be used within two weeks or so to augment the regular fleet.

The reserve resented being piecemeal, that is used to fill in regular units.

The new reserve concept was to have a really ready service, have them ready with first-class equipment, and when they were called up, have them all called up and have it all done in one piece and not frittered away, as was done in the Berlin crisis and other places.

Q: Is that true today? Are they introduced to new ships and up-to-date ordnance, and all that?

Adm. M.: They are, yes. You ruin the morale of the reserves if you don't keep them first class, and, of course, you hurt the morale of the regulars because you must take some money and some equipment away from them. That was something we had to rectify and I think was rectified by all the chiefs of staff concerned and they soon became, if not fans of the new reserve concept, at least they joined the party and made the reserve the best they could.

We had to avoid ever doing again what we did in Vietnam, which was not to mobilize the reserves and to call a draft and the draft people were sent overseas fighting with the reserves sitting here, who were paid to do that but were not called up. Of course, the whole political leadership of the war in Vietnam was incorrect. That's just one of the many errors that were made.

Q: Well, during World War II, of course, it was an entirely different situation, but the reserves were interspersed in the fleet, almost in every ship there were more reserves than there were regulars, and it worked very well.

Adm. M.: It did, but that was known to be really a world war and a long-time affair. You knew that you were going to have reserves on active duty in the various ships and aircraft as long as you had them. Of course, they went right to the regular ships and right to the regular aircraft but, again, in those days ships and aircraft were not as complicated as they are now. You could bring a reserve officer in and put him in a destroyer and teach him his job in a very short time. Now, a reserve officer without CIC school, radar school, or some kind of school is kind of useless in a destroyer or a carrier, unless he'd had this advanced training and advanced education and so forth. The same with the enlisted men. They don't get too much of that in the reserve. So we have a little different navy now than we had then.

Q: What is the attitude of the regular versus the reserve? At times, there's been quite a hostile attitude in the past.

Adm. M.: That's right. In World War II, the first time the reserves came on active duty in peacetime, and then they fought with us, of course, during the war and were a major part of the navy. In the process of going through World War II, the attitude toward the reserves changed completely. He was recognized and you couldn't tell the difference.

Q: He won his spurs, didn't he?

Adm. M.: Yes, he certainly did, and ever since World War II there have been reserves in varying numbers on active duty. They are right now, some are on active duty, officers. So the idea there was a difference sort of faded away, and today nobody really cares much or knows whether an officer on active duty is a reserve or not - if he's on extended active duty. Of course, if he's on for two weeks, it's a little different, but even then the regulars go all out to help that young reserve, particularly a young officer, to get his status of training up and so forth. So the feeling toward reserves is completely different now. It's very healthy and that's the way it should be.

Q: I want to cite an illustration and ask you whether this is just an aberration on the part of one man or whether it's more general. At the time there was a crisis, and which one I can't recall, in the Middle East when President Nixon put the whole nation on the alert and it looked like he was going to call up the reserves, this young man who had a reserve commission in the navy was terribly resentful, resentful toward the president, and it seemed to be related to the fact that he personally was going to get involved. Is this an unusual reaction?

Adm. M.: Not widespread and the press being what it is today the reaction of one person who's vocal seems to be the reaction of a lot of people when it really isn't. All the reserves want is, if they're going to be called up, call them up good, all of them, and get the thing done, don't just piecemeal them to death. That's what they hate, being piecemealed, having a few of them go, then their bosses don't like that. But if everybody goes and everybody knows it's an important affair, they all go, get the job done, and come back, then they're all in the same boat and their bosses do not hold it against them when they leave.

Q: Yes, it's the piecemeal thing that is so disruptive to the economy, isn't it?

Adm. M.: That's right, but it's not only the economy, it's disruptive to various companies, for instance, for which the reserves work. He doesn't like to work for General Motors or somebody and then have to leave his place in the production line, or the executive suite, or wherever, and go off to a very limited war where just a few of them go. His boss says, "Well, if this guy's going to do that and

and go off for six months' active duty, I'd better promote somebody else in his place, or we don't need him around."

But if a whole group goes and it's a well-known fact that all the reserves are called up, then the company, GM, for instance, is likely to take a more patriotic stance and say, "Yes, we're contributing our guys to the effort. Let them all get out there and do this, then come back to a hero's welcome." But piecemeal, if a few of them go, the parent company seems to take an attitude of why me, as well as the person called up who has the same feeling and attitude. That's something you really have to look at these days.

Q: You touched on the fact that in a future war apparently there wouldn't be much warning or much time for any kind of training.

Adm. M.: Not navy training, certainly.

Q: And that, of course, remains a problem and has to be with reserves.

Adm. M.: That's why the reserve concept is a really ready reserve. In other words, you have to be ready to do something within two weeks or you don't do it, and it should be with modern ships and aircraft, if you can. Most of them can't.

Also, it's very difficult to run ships these days with less than say 90 or 95 percent complement. In the old days you could run a ship such as a battleship with half the battery manned and then, if you had to, you'd call up reserves and fill up the manning level. Nowadays, a ship is so complicated and it steams so much and operates so much that it's very difficult. You've got to have three watches for almost everything and you've got to have the whole ship manned. You can't have half a radar manned. You don't have multiple batteries any more. You've got one gun or one Asroc or whatever it is on that particular ship, and it has to be 100 percent or almost 100 percent manned. You can't do the old concept, or if you have, it's got to be ready to go right now. As a matter of fact, it almost fights. It has to be ready to fight. I'll talk about this some more in the Seventh Fleet operations to show that these days you don't pull the trigger but you must be completely ready to fight all the time, and we are. All our ships are everywhere, the Sixth Fleet, the Seventh Fleet. No longer can you afford to have half a battery manned or have two watches and then anchor somewhere and sleep at night, the sorts of things you did between World War I and World War II.

Q: I wonder also if you'd say something about some of the outstanding men who were in the Department of Defense at that time. You've spoken a little about Mr. Laird. Perhaps you could say something more about him.

Adm. M.: Yes. Secretary Laird, as everyone knows, was a congressman before he became secretary of defense, very much involved with the budget and with general defense matters, very knowledgeable. He came to the job knowing more about it than almost anyone who had preceded him. It was evident to me not only that he knew his new job but he ran it in a way that was certainly the way I like it run. That is, he gave people responsibility and then he held them accountable, but he didn't heckle them. If you had a job and something went wrong, you could come back and ask him about it and get some help. But, otherwise, he wanted you to do the job and come back and tell him when it was all over or if something needed to be changed, do that, but he gave you a great freedom of action, and that was a wonderful way to do it.

The second man, Mr. David Packard, came from Hewlett Packard Electronics, his own company. He had been in politics in California besides -

Q: Oh, he had a political background?

Adm. M.: Yes.

Q: I didn't realize.

Adm. M.: Not in the sense that he ever ran for office. He raised funds and he was active in the party. That sort of political background. He didn't run for office out there, but he was a businessman and, like Mr. Laird, used the broad, long view. He operated exactly the same way. He gave you absolute carte blanche to do your job. He told you what he wanted, what the job was, and you went and did it. He wasn't afraid to take a chance. He was a fine person.

Mr. Laird attempted to use him as an alternate. In other words, either one could make a decision, and this was always the way they were, even though Mr. Laird was still in the building, if Mr. Packard made a decision, that was it.

Q: They worked in tandem, then?

Adm. M.: Yes, but that didn't always work because you couldn't run an operation like that all the way, but that was what they tried to do. He, again, was one of the finest civilian secretaries that I've run across. He was very fine.

Mr. Roger Kelley, who was the assistant secretary for manpower and reserve affairs, my boss, again was one of the finest civilian secretaries that I've ever run across. His background was that he handled the public affairs, not the publicity idea, but the relationships with countries and people for Caterpillar Tractor based in Peoria, Illinois. He was an officer of the company, vice president. He was a student of Peter Drucker and Drucker's business methods and he soon instituted classes for his particular section in business procedures, computer logic, and so forth, and tried to educate all of us at the same time he was doing his job, which turned out to be very well done.

Q: That's a rather unusual approach, isn't it?

Adm. M.: Yes, it was. Like Mr. Laird and Mr. Packard, he was a businessman and he gave authority freely. As a matter of fact, I was constantly amazed how much authority he gave me and how he had no compuntion about walking away from the office, leaving anything that was going on, and telling me, "You just do whatever you want to." I made major decisions sometimes when he was gone, with no thought of waiting until the boss got back, I just did it. I knew his philosophy and I think he knew mine and we never differed on anything that I know of, except perhaps places where he was uninformed at the moment, such as he thought that everyone knew why we were fighting in Vietnam and I kept telling him they didn't. The Defense Department and the political leadership had never really informed people why they were out there and what they were doing, and he went out and found out that was true, so as soon as he found it was true, why, he agreed, and that was it.

Our disagreements were never disagreements in principle, only where he lacked information about the Defense Department to make a proper decision. As soon as he got the information we generally came right together on what was to be done and how to do it. He was also a fine person.

The assistant secretary for comptrollership, Mr. Bob Moot, was probably the finest comptroller type that the Defense Department ever had. He likewise was a big man but he was there and stayed on.

Q: Was he from business, too?

Adm. M.: No, his background was mostly in accounting and finance. He'd been in business in the banking business or something of that sort, not in manufacturing and that sort of thing, so he was from the business world, but the accounting end of it.

Mr. Robert Froehlke was assistant secretary for installations and logistics for a while, and Mr. Barry Shillito took his place.

Q: He was also ordnance, wasn't he? Research and

Development, Froehlke?

Adm. M.: No, he was not. Mr. Johnny Foster had that job. They were all leaders in their areas. Froehlke had an insurance background but again this was just a broad-gauge business background that he brought with him, and he was certainly a fine person. He made a fine secretary of the army. Shillito was from the studies area of the Logistics Management Institute. He was also very good.

The old department that Dr. Enthoven headed when he was in the Defense Department - they had various names for it, Analysis Department or Studies Department, it depends upon what era you're talking about, was headed by various people. It was downgraded and during the time I was there there was a constant fight by the services and the assistant secretaries to downgrade the studies system, or whatever you want to call it -

Q: Was that because it was primarily associated with McNamara?

Adm. M.: That was a major part of it. The other part was that they all felt that they knew more about how their departments should be managed than someone down there studying a piece of paper.

Q: That must have meant, then, that they didn't call in Booz-Hamilton or anyone like that?

Adm. M.: No. As a matter of fact, the department was not run by an assistant secretary all the time I was there, but since then it has been upgraded again and now has an assistant secretary. The fight was on all the time, from all the assistant secretaries, to downgrade that particular grouping of people.

Mr. Sylvester, when I was first there, was the assistant secretary of defense for public affairs and he had been when I was Chinfo, but he was replaced by Mr. Phil Goulding, who was a newspaper reporter.

Q: You merely mentioned him before. You mentioned Sylvester to some extent, at some length, but you just mentioned Goulding and you thought more favorably of him.

Adm. M.: Goulding was, of course, an expert in his field, which was reporting. He carried this over and we found that he had the ability to make a big decision and wasn't afraid of doing things. He was a good one.

About mid-point in this time, General Chappy James came in as an assistant, and I found working for him very stimulating. I got along just fine.

Q: Is he army or air force?

Adm. M.: No, he's a black air force general who just recently retired.

Q: Oh, yes.

Adm. M.: He was a big man physically and otherwise and he fitted right in with the grouping of people working in the Defense Department.

Q: Going over to the navy, what about Secretary Chafee?

Adm. M.: I was chief of legislative affairs when Mr. Chafee came to the Navy Department. I had just completed about two-thirds of a briefing for the former secretary of the navy for his annual posture hearings, which are very important, and then Mr. Chafee was announced as the secretary, and it was necessary, then, to reschedule and replan all the briefings for him.

When he came into office he said he wanted to see me, the chief of information, and the chief of naval operations when he got there, his first day. He came in the office carrying a squash racket and a small envelop. We all said hello and he sat down. The chief of naval operations said that this posture hearing was coming up and the first thing he had to do was get up a speech for that and, if necessary, he'd have to be briefed night and day. He said:

"No, I'm not going to do that. You're going to handle that. I'll go over it with you, but numbers I don't have time for. I won't handle it."

Then he turned to the little girl secretary and said:

"Would you get me an appointment to play squash? And the next thing is that I don't want anybody making my phone calls for me. I'll dial the telephone myself."

So he picked up the envelope he had, took some numbers out, and said:

"Just a minute. I've got to call some of the congressional leaders."

He dialed their numbers and we sat there for two or three minutes and nothing happened while he was in conversation. Finally he slammed the phone down and said:

"All right, you can make my calls for me."

What had happened was, of course, he called the congressman's secretary and she'd have none of it. She wanted him to wait while she got the congressman, got him off the floor and so forth. He didn't seem to realize that you don't just dial a congressman and talk to him. There are some preliminaries that have to go on. Your secretary's got to call his secretary and find out when he's going to be in his office and then get the call ready and, no matter what you think, even if you're secretary of the navy, you're going to be on the telephone when the congressman gets on there, period. It took him a little time to learn that. He did learn how to get a squash game. He never learned anything about the budget, paid no attention to it, ever, which meant the chief of naval operations had to carry a very heavy load.

That was my introduction to Secretary Chafee.

Q: Had he been governor or was he governor after?

Adm. M.: He was governor after. No. I beg your pardon, he was not. He was governor before and he lost the election, then he was made secretary. That's the way it was.

Q: He hasn't raised his head very high in the Senate since he's been there, has he?

Adm. M.: No. He was a lightweight as secretary, very seldom involved in anything that was very responsible. Undersecretary Warner carried most of the load for the time that Chafee was there and he was thought of much more highly than was Secretary Chafee by Mr. Laird and Mr. Packard. When they wanted something done, they went to him. That's the way it was.

It was too bad because, after all, a long line of

very fine secretaries, starting with Secretary Thomas and Gates, Franke, Connolly, Ignatius, Nitze, Korth - they were fine secretaries. They all knew their job and they all worked hard. They did a grand job, and, all of a sudden, we ran into zilch, and the navy suffered quite a bit as a result. The arguments for the navy were not carried in very strong fashion in the Defense Department by Mr. Chafee. What the chief of naval operations didn't do didn't get done.

Q: What about the chairman of the Joint Chiefs? That was Admiral Moorer at the time.

Adm. M.: Yes.

Q: He had a tough time, did he not?

Adm. M.: Yes, he had a tough time because of some outside things that had happened mainly when he was chief of naval operations at other times in the navy and that carried over a little bit. He had some tough times, of course, with the problem of his relationships with the White House and some of his staff, the well-known business about theoretically spying on -

Q: Oh, Drew Pearson, you mean that?

Adm. M.: Yes. So he had his troubles, but he was a fine chairman, one of the best naval officers of the century, I think.

Q: Did the department have much trouble with Drew Pearson in that time?

Adm. M.: Oh, very little.

Q: He was a gadfly type.

Adm. M.: Yes. Phil Goulding handled him very well and simply gave him the information he wanted when it could be given to him and refused to give him anything, as he said in meetings, that was wrong. He acted very properly and that's the way he pulled his teeth - answer his questions if you can, and if you can't, you tell him why not. Then when he says something, come right out and say no, you're wrong, and he was willing to recant, in a way, stop talking about it.

Q: What about sources of information that he had and which his successors seem to have? How do they get this information they broadcast?

Adm. M.: Well, it goes all the way from the small dissenter

who knows something that happened in a ship or station or somewhere who gives it to somebody who's a malcontent in, say, the budget section of the navy or some other section of the Defense Department where he or she has access to papers or hears conferences or hears phone calls.

Q: Is there any recourse, any action that can be taken, against these men when they openly say that they're revealing certain things from classified documents?

Adm. M.: Oh, yes. As long as you can pinpoint the document, you can prosecute them under the law. But you have to pinpoint the document to prove it in court, which is difficult sometimes.

Q: Well, shall we go into the Seventh Fleet, where you went in June of 1971? As you said the other time, you were the first nonaviator to take this job, which is a very interesting fact. Did you have any problems as a result of that, being a nonaviator?

Adm. M.: Not at all. I had no problems with any person. Nobody criticized the fact, at least not to me, that this was a change. There's no requirement to be qualified as such out there. You don't fly, obviously. Of course, the guts of the Seventh Fleet is aviation, that is, the navy's aviation, but the Seventh Fleet has no more aviation than the Sixth Fleet or anything else.

Q: It was a sort of tradition that came about as a result of World War II, wasn't it?

Adm. M.: Right, it was, and there's been an historical division of four-star and three-star jobs. The aviators got these and the nonaviators got those, submariners got those, and so forth. Admiral Zumwalt decided he would change them all around and there wouldn't be any more of this business because no longer was aviation a requirement to be put on certain jobs and that everyone is supposed to be, at that stage of his life, qualified enough in the strategy involved to be able to do the job. You don't tell an aviator or a carrier skipper exactly what to do, you just tell them in general, which is the same thing an aviator would tell them, and you should be able to tell them to do something simple like operate a ship, where to go, how many sorties to fly. If he doesn't think he can do it, he'll tell you and you change your orders accordingly. So the business of command of the various units such as that has changed. That was the beginning of the change.

I had no hesitancy about going out to command the fleet. I'd flown a lot, had always wanted to be an aviator, but couldn't qualify physically because of my knee, but otherwise could do anything except make a carrier landing. I had done so with naval aircraft and had completed all my pilot-license requirements in naval aircraft, flying when I was chief of information and other times.

Q: In effect, you were a flier!

Adm. M.: Yes, but I hadn't got my license because to do so required several hundred dollars' worth of flights with an FAA instructor, going over again the same things I had done with naval aircraft so that I could demonstrate to him that I could take my license, and there wasn't any point in doing that unless I wanted to fly privately. I could always fly naval aircraft any time I wanted to if I could find a pilot who'll let me. So I found no problem here.

For about two weeks before I left, I was briefed extensively. I got very little political briefing because one of my subspecialties had always been political science. I thought I knew more about the politics, leaders, and so forth of the Asiatic countries than the desk officers in the Pentagon, so there wasn't any point in going through that. But I did get an extensive briefing in electronic warfare and intelligence-collection. The intelligence-collection portion, of course, I was not privy to before because that's very highly compartmented just for security purposes. And I was briefed on what we do to collect information with sensors in submarines and aircraft and ships and so forth, and what flights were being made out there by Seventh Fleet units to do this sort of collecting.

Electronic warfare had always been an interest of mine and I didn't need too much of that except to find out what the latest Soviet developments were and to find out what we had been doing out there in electronic warfare.

Q: What section briefed you on that?

Adm. M.: Various sections of OpNav that handle this sort of thing. It's divided up into three or four areas. They've got some here, they've got some at Fort Meade, some at the intelligence center down near the beltway, and some when I got out to CinCPac and CinCPacFlt headquarters. I did go out there for about three days of talking to Admiral Cleary, who was CinCPac - rather talking to Admiral McCain, who was CinCPac, and Admiral Cleary, who was CinCPacFlt - and with the various type commanders who were in Pearl Harbor.

Then I flew on out to Japan via commercial aricraft.

Q: Commercial aircraft?

Adm. M.: Yes. I didn't think I merited taking an airplane

for me and my family, as most people apparently did before and after, to fly out there. In retrospect, I should have because the baggage problem was bad and I had to have my sword for the change-of-command ceremony.

Q: Did you pay your own fare?

Adm. M.: No, no, it was paid for by the government - so I had to carry that and every time I got on an airplane I had it checked as a firearm, which caused some consternation.

Q: I wonder they didn't take it away from you!

Adm. M.: Oh, yes, they did, they took it away from me all the time. When I got to Japan, I couldn't get it out of the airport because the Japanese wouldn't let me import a weapon into Japan. Finally, the liaison officer, after about an hour of sweating with the customs group, had it declared an antique and not a modern weapon and I was allowed to carry it with me, so I had it for change of command. That's another reason why you should take a naval airplane.

Q: A rather humorous occasion.

Adm. M.: It was. It wasn't very easy to do.

I found when I got to Japan that the change-of-command had been scheduled, after several calls on the Japanese minister of defense and other defense personalities, which I did in company with my predecessor - then the change of command took place on a carrier deck below the flight deck in Yokosuka. It was attended by literally hundreds of Japanese officials of all kinds. As a matter of fact, Officials from many of the Asiatic countries, and I was amazed by the importance given to the Seventh Fleet by Asiatic countries. They all wanted to be there for the change of command and they all wanted to get to the commander as soon as possible to make sure that he realized how important their country was.

Q: That had some connection with SEATO, did it not?

Adm. M.: Yes, it did. What happened was that the Nixon Doctrine was what governed there, and the Nixon Doctrine said that, in a sense, the U.S. would have a nuclear umbrella under which SEATO would operate, and the Seventh Fleet was the main weapon to go to the defense of any SEATO country if it was attacked. So they understood very completely that the only thing keeping the Soviets from overrunning them, that is Japan, Taiwan, Hong Kong, and many other places, Singapore, was the Seventh Fleet.

The Seventh Fleet had tremendous importance in their eyes, so that whatever the Seventh Fleet did, and particularly the commander of it, was extremely newsworthy out there. You couldn't move or say anything without having four or five countries write up what you'd said. Of course, Korea was another such country.

Q: Had that significance dawned upon you prior to going out there?

Adm. M.: I would say I knew about 70 percent of it. I knew it was going to be that way but I wasn't prepared for the full 100 percent impact of how that sort of thing happened. I was frequently with the ambassador and high-level officials in Japan, including the prime minister and lots of them, who at the slightest change in the political climate wanted to see the commander of the Seventh Fleet. I had to fly back to the South Pacific occasionally to confer with them.

As soon as I could get organized, I made trips to Korea, for instance, and met all the highest officials in Korea who wanted to be reassured the Seventh Fleet would be there again in case they needed it.

Q: Let me ask you - this, I suppose, is a sort of a tangent - but, in the light of that, was that a healthy attitude for these countries to entertain at that time?

Adm. M.: I think it was an attitude which, if they wanted to remain healthy, they had to entertain. It was not good for Japan, for instance, to rely forever on the Seventh Fleet umbrella and then have only what they call a self-defense force.

Q: That's what they're facing today?

Adm. M.: Yes, it still is. However, they're getting stronger and stronger in the self-defense area, particularly in the maritime self-defense force. It is literally a navy which is small but very efficient now. Of course, they don't have much army nor is their air force very large, but what they have is very good. But they have no concept at the present moment of defending themselves.

Q: The gradual realization seems to be coming to them that they can't rely on us any longer?

Adm. M.: It is in some areas, and I'll go into that when I talk a little bit about the so-called Young Lions and the navy and some meetings I had with them.
After the change of command and during the next three or four months I made trips to Korea, to Hong Kong,

met the governor there and so forth, and again the British group there is very small, as it is in Singapore, where I also visited. They rely upon the Seventh Fleet and they'll just give you anything you want in terms of support, help, hospitality.

Q: But there are Royal Navy units there, are there?

Adm. M.: Yes, very small ones and very few ships, frigates and so forth, no carriers or anything of that sort.

I went to Taiwan at an unfortunate time, about a day or so before I arrived for really almost a state visit it was announced that President Nixon was going to China. The ambassador sent us a message saying that there was consternation there and he doubted that I should continue coming in to visit.

Q: Who was the ambassador?

Adm. M.: I've forgotten what his name was.

Q: McConaughy?

Adm. M.: Yes, McConaughy, and Vice Admiral Baumberger was commander of the Taiwan Defense Force, which was not a force, really, it was just a name, a grouping, and the group was such ships as I happened to give them from time to time or ships that passed by the strait, and that particular ship came under his control for the passage of it and he counted that as one of his patrol ships so that he could tell the Taiwan government that he was patrolling the strait and so forth. So I had a requirement to send a certain number of ships into the strait when they were going north and south so that they could temporarily be part of the Taiwan Defense Command.

Anyway, Admiral Baumberger convinced the ambassador that the visit should go on and it did go on, and I called on the president of Taiwan.

Q: Did you see the generalissimo?

Adm. M.: No, the generalissimo was not at that time the president, his son was.

Q: Oh, his son had assumed the command.

Adm. M.: Yes, and I talked to him. I'd met the generalissimo before when I was aide to Secretary Franke and offered to call on him again but they said he was too old and too ill to see anybody.

I was able to go all over Taiwan and see the Taiwanese navy and the various landing beaches and so forth which we might have to use in case we needed them. I made an extensive tour of Taiwan.

Q: Were you impressed with that situation?

Adm. M.: Yes, they had a very good navy. They had, of course, many ex-U.S. ships, a fine Marine Corps contingent, and I thought the economy was certainly booming, and the island was, I thought, completely capable of self-defense against anybody. I think even today, at least if we helped in terms of giving them air defense and perhaps some help in the straits, I don't think anybody could land on that island.

Q: What did you glean at that time about the emotional shock?

Adm. M.: Well, it was very much anti-Nixon. It was my job to explain that whatever was done at that time the Nixon Doctrine still was in effect, as was the SEATO Defense Treaty. As long as that happened the Seventh Fleet would be there and here we were. So we sort of turned our visit around to point out to them that this was a demonstration to them that the Seventh Fleet was there and would be there in case they needed it. So, in the end, they were very friendly, and I think mollified.

Q: Did they feel that they'd been betrayed, or what?

Adm. M.: Oh, yes. They thought the next step was going to be the abrogation of the mutual self-defense pact, as was done recently, but, of course, it didn't happen then. One of my jobs was to reassure them that that wasn't going to happen, that here was the Seventh Fleet flagship in there to reassure them.

Q: Is this something that you assumed as commander of the Seventh Fleet, or did the State Department step in and advise you in this area?

Adm. M.: It was a combination. Whatever I said had to be checked in essence with the ambassador to make sure that it was U.S. policy, but I had no compunction about it because I knew what U.S. policy was. It was announced and stated in the Nixon Doctrine as what it was and I didn't go beyond the defense aspects of it, to state that the Niexon Doctrine remained in effect, which I'd been told, and the Seventh Fleet was charged with carrying it out and would be there. That was all that they wanted to know.

These visits that I had to make within the first few months to orient myself with the various governments took place —

Q: It included the Philippines, I take it?

Adm. M.: Oh, yes, it did. Of course, the problem there was fairly stable and the business of having the Philippine president trying to get more and more money for the use of Olongapo and Clark Field had not come up at that time.

Q: Was Marcos there then?

Adm. M.: Oh, yes, but he hadn't started his really big drive to get more money for these two units.

The two biggest problems I had, or I'd been told I would have, when I went out there were that it was contemplated at that time to change the home port for the Seventh Fleet from Yokosuka to Sasebo because there was a little bit more housing down there and it was thought that they would close the Yokohama housing area and close Yokosuka. The Japanese wanted it back very badly because they wanted to have it not only for their naval base but ship manufacture. So the Japanese government was pressuring the U.S. government to get out of Yokosuka.

Q: Were they thinking then in terms of building warships, or was it still mercantile?

Adm. M.: Mercantile. They built large tankers and things

like that.

The other point that Admiral Zumwalt had pressed me to do something about when I came out was to homeport a carrier and a squadron of destroyers at either Sasebo or Yokosuka. This was part of his program to homeport overseas in order to cut down transit time for dependents and ships and so forth and try to economize and also to raise the morale of the men involved.

Q: Similar to what he did in Greece?

Adm. M.: Yes.

The uncertainty about Yokosuka lasted about three months, then, as the war began to heat up a little bit, it was evident that it was not the thing to do, and that was called off. As a matter of fact, Yokosuka was beefed up a little bit, as was the housing area in Yokohama, which we used. We did go forward, though –

Q: Let me ask, what did the Japanese do vis-á-vis the building of ships, then?

Adm. M.: They just didn't build them. In other words, they wanted to expand and they didn't make their expansion plans come true. They just built ships at the rate that they could in the building ways they had in Yokosuka and other places, Kure and others.

We did homeport a squadron of destroyers, which was quite a chore to prepare the various areas for housing for destroyer families coming out and to transport all of them.

Q: How many people were involved in that?

Adm. M.: Roughly fifty families per six ships. That's 300 families, and that was about 1,000 people to be brought out, mostly in ships but some were flown out.

Q: And find housing for them?

Adm. M.: Well, we had the housing. It was a question of allocating it properly, without too many squawks.

Q: Housing that we had built or - ?

Adm. M.: Some housing was in Yokohama, some in Yokosuka, and other housing was contract housing. In other words, we would go out and lease Japanese houses, civilian houses, in the surrounding area. In some ways these were good and some bad. Those who liked to get out and live on the Japanese economy found them delightful. Those who didn't like to cook on charcoal braziers and freeze in the winter didn't like it. It was a question of what you

you wanted. If you wanted to live like the Japanese, it was a great opportunity, and lots of people liked it very much, others thought it was terrible.

Q: That became a real problem, though, didn't it?

Adm. M.: Yes, it did.

Q: Not too many of the young American wives wanted to?

Adm. M.: No, it was the exceptional one who wanted to do that. But the exceptional ones loved it. They really felt they were living on the Japanese economy, which they were, and those who liked it really like it.

Q: Seizing the opportunity -

Adm. M.: The question was to sort out those who did and who didn't, and sometimes the initial choice was bad and we had to change them around, and it was quite a chore to get all this done.

Q: Was there any kind of an educational program initiated to teach them to be absorbed into this world?

Adm. M.: Oh, yes. We sent representatives back to I think

it was San Diego, where the previous home port had been to lecture and inform them all we could. They had brochures and we got them to make their choices back there, and then these representatives rode out with them and took them to their places of living and so forth. A great program was put on to educate them, and about 90 percent of it was great, but 10 percent, as always, wasn't great, the person who didn't bring enough money or who made the wrong choice as to where he or she was to live. It's always the 10 percent who make all the noise and cause the trouble, and require all the care you put into it. The 90 percent just got on fine.

Q: When you view it in retrospect, was that program a successful one?

Adm. M.: Yes, I think it was. I think it was a fine thing to do. The carrier was homeported there. After I left, I understand, there was more difficulty with that, and the destroyers, but I think it was a fine program.

Well, all this time the war was rather low-key. It was prior to April, the time when the Seventh Fleet had two carriers, a cruiser flagship, about sixteen destroyers, and half a dozen submarines, a time when we only had one carrier on the line most of the time and the war was rather dormant, most of my effort was toward intelligence-collection, patrolling the Japanese Sea, and handling several submarines that we sent up there for patrol. It was secret and I won't say much about it, except they were intelligence-collectors in close to the Japanese shore.

One of the most critical things was running intelligence-collection flights in the Sea of Japan, off the coast of Russia, the Soviet Union. We, of course, remembered the troubles we had before of having aircraft shot down and ships sunk. Therefore, when you sent an intelligence-collector up there, you had to do so with a complete communications plan and with ships standing by in case the aircraft were attacked or the ship were attacked. You had to have all this thought out in advance and even with a routine, it was still time-consuming and very carefully done things so that you wouldn't have a problem like we had before with the loss of intelligence-collectors.

Q: Did you have Pueblo-type ships?

Adm. M.: No, the collectors were either aircraft P-2Cs specially configured or normal destroyers that have a capability now, with the electronic equipment they have, of collecting anything, plus the black boxes that were put on whenever they went on these trips. That sort of thing was going on all the time.

Q: Did you have access to the Sea of Okhotsk?

Adm. M.: We very seldom went up there. We could have.

Q: You could have?

Adm. M.: Yes, if we'd wanted to, but we never wanted to.
We talked a little bit about the Japanese self-defense force. My contacts were mostly with the Maritime Self-Defense Force, which is the Japanese way of saying their navy. I became very close with the CNO, the vice CNO, and the senior officials of the Japanese navy, which I'll call it from now on.

Q: Did you have something to do with Okubo, too?

Adm. M.: No, I don't recall him at all.

Q: He's the one who started the Maritime Self-Defense Force.

Adm. M.: Oh, I'm sure by that time he must have been long retired. What happens in the Japanese Navy is that the CNO changes every year and there's a succession of people who take the job. Then, as a CNO retires, by that time he's probably never owned an automobile. The pay is very low, and he's taken into industry, either aviation or otherwise. He's given a good job and he makes a good deal of money in the first few years of his industrial career. That's the way he's taken care of, so the succession goes up every year. The CNO I knew only lasted a year and then, of course, he left and the DCNO took over.

Q: What value is that to the growing fleet?

Adm. M.: Well, I think on that level, where they just have destroyers and minesweepers and submarines and aircraft that it can be handled that way. When the vice CNO knows he's going to be CNO next and he's sitting there in that job, he, in a sense, has a contribution to make over a two-year period, when he's vice CNO and CNO. It worked very well for them and I think for their purposes it was fine.

Their problem, of course, is making sure they call it a defense force and still wanting to be, as you would expect, the old navy. Something more than that. They were constantly coming to us to get the flavor of a true navy. They liked the American navy and they liked the Seventh Fleet, its flagship and our staff. So we were very close to them. We had many social events with them.

Q: Were some of these men leftovers from the Imperial Navy?

Adm. M.: Only a few and they'd been junior officers. One of them, Admiral Uchida, the first CNO, had been in a destroyer fighting against me down in the Java Sea, so we were rather close.

They have a group called the Society of the Young Lions, which is not young anymore. They're junior officers, junior flag officers, really, and of course then they suddenly become senior flag officers and they're no longer Young Lions. But they asked that I and a few members of my staff meet with them for a day-long seminar, which we did. What they were really asking was our advice on what they should do to change their navy. They wanted advice, but, of course, to save face, they didn't want to appear to be taking it, probably just wanted our ideas.

The ideas I gave them were that they would have a problem in the years to come involving oil exploration. Already at that time there were many U.S. exploration vessels off the coasts of China and Vietnam, all up and down the Asiatic coast, exploring. China had claims, Taiwan had claims - as a matter of fact, there was one place just north of Taiwan where there was known to be oil, just south of Okinawa also, and the Taiwanese claimed it, the Okinawans claimed it, the Malays and Chinese claimed it, and the Japanese claimed it, since they, of course, were at one time in Okinawa. So here was an oil source that was claimed by four different countries. My idea was that the Japanese Maritime Self-Defense Force was going to be heavily involved in this sort of thing, with oil-exploration vessels being captured by one country or another, and this was very important to them and they, as a navy, should begin to be very aware of where these places were and should have plans for what to do in case either, say, a U.S. vessel or one of their own or somebody else's was taken into port by any of these countries up and down the coast. They should study this very carefully, as to what the law was regarding oil-exploration rights at sea and so forth.

Q: They had no hope of finding oil in Japan anywhere?

Adm. M.: No, there's no known source of it, although there's no reason why there couldn't be. The geology is such that it's possible. They just haven't ever found any.

Q: Did they feel hamstrung by the constitution - ?

Adm. M.: Oh, yes, of course.

Q: How did they hope to deal with that?

Adm. M.: They didn't have any idea how many years it would be before they could throw off these fetters, as they called them. They do have, of course, some fine aircraft. They have the only seaplane in the world today, patrol seaplane. They have good destroyers, fine submarines, fine young naval officers, a nice naval academy, and some of the nucleus for a fine navy. It's just a question that it's pretty small and limited in what it can do. It doesn't have any big ships.

Q: They're also limited by the constitution, are they not, in the money they can spend of defense?

Adm. M.: Yes, right. So they saw no hope for doing much. They had plans for small amphibious forces and how to defend against what they foresaw perhaps as Soviet Union incursions on their northern islands and, in order to defend against amphibious landings. They have a very excellent SOSUS-like network in various places, openings surrounding the Sea of Japan and so forth. They were very cooperative with us in telling us when Soviet submarines went through various straits since they could detect this.

They have the beginnings of a fine navy. The only problem is when they will get to the size that would help them defend their country.

Q: Do they seem to stand apart from the populace as a whole in this attitude?

Adm. M.: No. I would say they were very conscious of the fact that they couldn't afford that, that World War II was something that should never be repeated, and that the navy was never going to stand apart from the country anymore, ever. They were going to try to lead and advise the civilian government but they were never going to preempt it.

Q: Yes, but I meant the attitude of these men that they had plans for building up their navy and so forth, even though it was small, was this something that they would have had backing from the populace for?

Adm. M.: No, they don't have. They were not sure how many years it would be before they ever would. They thought that they'd have to go through provocation from the Soviet Union or the mainland Chinese or somebody else before they would be allowed to do this sort of thing. In other words, until there was provocation, they didn't see that the average populace would permit it.

Q: Have we given them that provocation now?

Adm. M.: I'm talking about capturing a fishing vessel or sinking a ship or shooting down an aircraft.

Q: But I meant in a much more subtle way have we given them provocation by convincing them that we can't afford to man their defense.

Adm. M.: No, and until we do, until we withdraw the Seventh Fleet from Asiatic waters that'll never happen. They just think that as long as there are any ships out there and any people living out there we're going to stand by our SEATO commitments. The Nixon Doctrine hasn't changed any of that.

Q: It's a kind of unhealthy dilemma, though, isn't it?

Adm. M.: Well, it is, but, knowing the Japanese temperament and their general feelings, I don't see any way out of it for years and years. Again, like I said, until there's a provocation that makes them change their mind.

Q: That must have been an interesting phase.

Adm. M.: Yes, it was. During my time there, they became noticeably friendlier as the months went by, and along about Christmastime the chairman of the Joint Chiefs of Japan, who was an army officer and a very straightlaced, unhumorous person, never known to associate with American officers at all and certainly not with naval officers, suddenly expressed a desire to come down and have lunch aboard the Oklahoma City, the flagship. I'd seen him on various occasions, talked to him, and I think perhaps the Japanese naval officers had unfrozen him a little bit in our favor.

He came down with an interpreter. He understood

English but he didn't want to speak it. We had a very nice lunch and then we took a tour of the Oklahoma City, which impressed him very much. We showed him things that nobody had seen before in terms of -

Q: She was a modern command ship?

Adm. M.: Yes. She's a cruiser and has a Talos system on her stern and, up in the bow area, she has an 8-inch turret and a 5-inch double mount. The 8-inch turret being on the main deck and the 5-inch double mount just above it.

At that time we were decorated for Christmas, which meant that the 8-inch guns had long protusions made out of papier maché and scaffolding and they looked like candy canes, so that the candy-cane area was bent down toward the main deck. It looked like three candy canes sitting up there. When we got to the bow area, he was amazed at this and wanted to know what that was. So I said:

"Well, we understand Japanese psychology and that those lower guns are used to shoot down aircraft and if we miss then we shoot ourselves with the second mount, hara-kiri."

He doubled up and the Japanese CNO said that was the first time they'd ever seen him laugh.

It was, I think, a change in his attitude and everybody was much happier and friendlier after that. This

Mack #9 - 602

seemed to meet his idea of humor.

Q: A macabre sort of humor!

Adm. M.: Yes. Not much for Christmas but that's the way it worked.

After Christmas the Seventh Fleet continued pretty much normal operations, although there began to be a buildup, which was pretty evident, and in January and February I spent more time down on what's called the line, taking the Oklahoma City down off of Vietnam -

Q: This was in 1972?

Adm. M.: Yes, and we had gunfire support groups. The Oklahoma City would go in and join a gunfire support group and relieve some of the destroyers and other cruisers down there and render fire support for the Marines ashore and the army troops ashore, off the coast of Vietnam. At that time, I would be free so that I could go over to a carrier and visit carrier operations and so forth, occasionally visit Danang to see the Marines and go down at least once a month and call on General Abrams, who was in overall command.

As March came along we spent more and more time down there and went back to the Philippines, to Subic Bay, for an occasional rest period.

Q: Did you have any contact with the riverine people, too?

Adm. M.: Oh, yes. As a matter of fact on one such trip - I made a trip on which I rode in eight different aircraft in one day flown by five services plus the air force of South Vietnam, flew in two combat missions, and did this all in one day. What happened was I left the Oklahoma City by navy helo off Danang, flew into Danang, the airfield, got into an air force transport, went to Saigon, called on General Abrams, went back out to the airport, got in a South Vietnamese helicopter, went down to a delta airfield, where I got in an OV-10, which is a small aircraft used to rocket and bomb and so forth. That particular group down there, the squadron, was supporting a riverine group which at the present moment was working on the side of a mountain. There were pockets of VC up in the side of the mountain, and these little OV-10s - they were dual-control aircraft - would go in and rocket and bomb these caves in the side of the mountain. The pilot found out that I could fly and he let me fly the OV-10 over to the area. He made two runs and he allowed me to make two runs on the VC pocket, so I got to make two rocket attacks and that constituted a combat mission.

Q: That was a day to remember, wasn't it?

Adm. M.: Yes, it was. Then we went back to the airfield and I got into an army helo, which took me to Saigon, where I transferred to an army transport aircraft, flew back up to Danang, where I got into one of our P-2Cs, which was under my command. The P-2C is a large patrol aircraft that carries about fifteen men. It's an electronic-warfare type aircraft. It used to go up off the coast of North Vietnam and listen to transmissions and try to find out what kind of aircraft they were flying, who was flying them, where they had radar sites, and so forth. It was an electronic snooper. I went on a mission with them and got to fly that aircraft on about a four-hour mission. I flew that half the time.

Q: Any enemy - ?

Adm. M.: No, nobody came out. We always had a backup of two fighters with us so if anybody ever came out -

Q: Any SAMs?

Adm. M.: We stayed enough off the coast so the SAMs couldn't reach us, and we were way up high. We could tell from electronic emissions what was going on ashore but nobody could fly that far out and never did bother us.

Then I went back to Danang in that aircraft, got

into a Marine helo and he rode out to the Oklahoma City, thus completing a busy day for a fleet commander who was not an aviator. I think that was more flights and more services more aircraft and more missions than most non-aviators commanders ever made. It was a very fascinating day.

Q: What kind of restraints were placed upon the navy in naval operations at that time from Washington?

Adm. M.: At that time we could not go above the DMZ, which was right at the end of the northern level of South Vietnam. That was a military zone that was being used as a division mark between North and South Vietnam. The North Vietnamese regular units, of course, were not south of that, only the VC was south of that. We had U.S. marines in Vietnamese units right up against the DMZ - there was a demilitarized zone there and they were right up as far as they could go. That was the demarcation line. No North Vietnamese unit could move into that area, so we were not allowed to shoot, shore bombardment or anything else above that line and had not been for about six months, so we were very deficient in knowing where the targets were. We couldn't go up even to take pictures of the place, so our target folders were pretty much out of date, and that concerned me because if we'd had to do anything we wouldn't have known where the targets were. They would change the locations of their guns and depots and so forth.

Q: How did General Abrams feel about the whole thing?

Adm. M.: He thought the North Vietnamese were building up and there'd be an attack. That's why he had us down there most of the time in February and March, because he thought there would be an attack at any moment. I kept saying we could get down there in forty-eight hours in the Oklahoma City and I didn't want to sit down there on the line forever. We had other things to do. We had to go to Hong Kong, Korea, and so forth, and try to convince some people up there that we were on their side. I couldn't spend all my time sitting down there, and I couldn't get away from the Oklahoma City very far because the communications system for the Seventh Fleet was in the Oklahoma City, and it was a very involved communications system. We had satellite communications, rooms full of decoding systems and encoding systems. I could never get more than twelve hours away from the ship at any one time because I had to be where I could be contacted by CinCPacFlt or the White House or anybody else, or, if something happened, I needed to be on the scene. So it was a very confining business.

Having General Abrams keep the Oklahoma City down

there so close to the line made it very difficult for all of us to work, to do our whole Seventh Fleet job.

Q: Did he feel terribly frustrated by all these constraints put upon him?

Adm. M.: Very much so. Here we were, the VC was coming down, the North Vietnamese were building up just north of the zone, they were bringing supplies down, we knew it -

Q: Yet they were in command of the situation!

Adm. M.: Yes, Sir, that's right.

Finally, I got permission to take the Oklahoma City back to Yokosuka for a short period at the end of March.

Q: From CinCPac, you mean?

Adm. M.: No - well, CinCPac was the one who delivered it to General Abrams. I had to get CinCPacFlt to ask General Abrams to do it, to let us go. He couldn't control me, since I was not under his command, but he could control me by going to CinCPacFlt and requesting that CinCPacFlt not let me do something, in which case I wouldn't do it.

So I finally got permission to bring the Oklahoma City back to Yokosuka for a short period. I think we'd been in port just a few days - this was just before Easter, which, as I remember, was the 1st of April - and, as I remember also, I was at a sunrise service on the flight deck of the carrier that was in port that day, when I was told that the DMZ had been breached and the North Vietnamese were pouring south and there was a big attack going on.

Of course, the Oklahoma City left immediately and we were down there within, I guess, thirty hours.

Q: You mean in the Tonkin Gulf?

Adm. M.: Right off Danang, which was just south of the DMZ. At that time, of course, it was evident that there was a very strong attack there, and we immediately began to take steps to reinforce the Seventh Fleet, knowing that this was going to be a long-term affair. The Oklahoma City was in there firing straight for, I guess, until all the ammunition ran out, and the other cruiser that was with us was doing the same thing, supporting the U.S. Marines and the Vietnamese Marines and other units that were just south of the DMZ and being overrun.

This became almost a shambles because we were right off the beach, so close that with binoculars you could see tanks going up and down the beach, the problem became that you could no longer identify whose tank was what because the North Vietnamese had captured so many U.S. tanks and

South Vietnamese tanks that they were using them with the same markings on them. If you saw a tank with a white star on it, you didn't want to shoot at it because it might be ours and it might be full of North Vietnamese.

Q: Wasn't it equally confusing to them?

Adm. M.: I'm sure it was, but here we were off the beach and we couldn't get any contact with our gunfire liaison units, which normally would have controlled our fire and told us what to shoot at. It was very seldom you fired at something optically, just looking at the beach, seeing something, and shooting at it. But this was such a disorganized situation ashore and the Vietnamese, many of them, had just cut and run so General Abrams himself didn't know what was going on. I kept asking him what I could do to help, should I shoot at some of these things I saw on the beach, but I couldn't get a reply out of him because he was so busy down there. I don't think he thought we could do any good, anyway. He just thought that this would have to run its course and the North Vietnamese would soon run out of fuel and ammunition and, at some point below the DMZ north of Danang, this would all be stabilized and that then we could fight our way back, which is roughly what happened.

In the month of April the Seventh Fleet continued its buildup and, towards the end of that time, we had seven carriers -

Q: They coming from where?

Adm. M.: Well, all the ones that the Pacific Fleet could spare plus some from the Atlantic. I had a force of seven carriers, five cruisers, about thirty-five destroyers, and ten or fifteen submarines, and enough amphibious lift for at least two battalions of Marines, and some left over for anything else I wanted to use. In other words, we had a division on Okinawa and I could have lifted the whole division if I'd wanted to but we only had two battalions embarked.

Q: Were the constraints lifted somewhat?

Adm. M.: At this time we still could not go above the DMZ. We didn't need to because we were preoccupied down there. After about two weeks, the fleet had built up again to this gigantic size. We had been told to make all kinds of plans, plans for landing behind the Vietnamese force, plans for landing up north. The plans were just out of this world. Some of them were obviously impractical but had to be planned for, anyway.

Q: Was this coming from General Abrams or where?

Adm. M.: No, this was coming right from Washington. I

would say it was instigated by the White House. It was coming from JCS to CinCPac and CinCPacFlt to us. We would have to make our plans, go down to General Abrams and get his concurrence, send it back to Washington and it would be sat on for a while.

I would say in about three weeks, in the latter part of April, there was an indication that when we got all these ships out there we were to begin what was called the offensive. In other words, we had contained the attack and then the president finally decided that we would try to drive the North Vietnamese back into North Vietnam and we would attack North Vietnam. So we were told we could not go one degree above the DMZ, and fire on targets ashore that we could reach with our ships and, of course, then with aviation sorties, and I was given a date. This was in the middle of the night, and I think it was at eight o'clock next morning we would go in and shoot, take targets of opportunity in the one-degree area above the DMZ.

I protested and said:

"Well, other than targets that you can see, I don't know what to shoot at. I have not been allowed to fly up there for six months. I would like to have morning flights go up for reconnaissance, bring back and develop pictures, make target folders, and get them to the ships, and the next day we'll make our attacks."

The answer came back no, it's to be done right now.

Q: Fire blind!

Adm. M.: Yes, we did literally. We'd go in and fire at a beach and we couldn't see anything. We didn't know what we were shooting at. We just laid down barrages along roads up there, so we would lay down barriers along the roads and did all these sorts of things. Then we went about getting our reconnaissance and the next day we began to shoot at specific targets.

In about three days, and I suspected it was coming, the barrier was lifted one more degree, and the same thing happened. We had not been allowed to go above that degree and look for targets —

Q: How many miles were involved?

Adm. M.: Sixty miles. So we literally walked up the coast doing the same thing, just throwing hundreds of rounds of ammunition over on the sand and the roads, just wasted because the president apparently, I found later, had decided that's what he wanted. He didn't want any argument, and, of course, the chairman knew there was no point in arguing so he just told us to go ahead and do it.

Q: But the rationale of increasing it constantly without permitting any overflights?

Adm. M.: Well, this was part of the old syndrome of trying to control the war from Washington. That happened all the way through, the whole business. It went back to President Johnson. President Nixon was pretty good about it, but President Johnson was terrible. Even then, President Nixon apparently tried to do this degree by degree, and it was not the thing to do. He should have told me to do what he wanted in general and let me do it. At any rate, it all got done and in about four days, I guess, we'd been expanded about three degrees, almost up to Haiphong and Hanoi. The fleet had gone up and what was called Linebacker began in earnest. In other words, we'd been doing a Linebacker operation for some time but now it became a major campaign and we had sometimes raids by as many as three cruisers going in at night and at various places along the coast shooting up port facilities, as far inland as they could reach, roads, concentrations of troops, and I was given quotas again, which was silly, so many raids on each degree per day and so forth, rather than letting me plan where I knew targets were, what the ships' capabilities were and where they were. We had to conform to this business of doing what Washington wanted.

Q: Did you wish at times that you had the New Jersey back out there?

Adm. M.: Oh, yes. For instance, we literally had to fly

8-inch guns out. A cruiser would go through the liners and, in some cases, the guns, shooting every day, all day, and we had to send them back to Subic Bay, where they would either reline or rebarrel, and to get the guns out there, they were literally flown out in airplanes. That's how much we could have used big-caliber guns. The Oklahoma City sometimes would fire a complete load of ammunition in three days, and when you're trying to run a war from your cabin and office, outside of which is an 8-inch turret or a 5-inch turret going off every thirty seconds all day and all night, it gets a little wearing. That's what it was. That's where our office was to run the whole war, the flag plot and so forth were right inside the bulkhead. You'd try to write something and every twenty-eight seconds you'd stop writing because you couldn't write when the bang went off because the paper would jump right up and you'd feel the bang. You'd write some more and off you'd go.

So it was quite a long and harrowing time.

This was not without answer from the beach. All during this period of at least a month, we would be fired on by guns ashore, and it was not uncommon to go up and pick up a bucketful of shrapnel off the main deck of the Oklahoma City after we'd been in for a night raid and come back out.

Q: There was no danger from the sea, was there, submarines or anything?

Adm. M.: No, none at all. The only danger was we were afraid they'd suddenly get the range somewhere and they'd hit us because the Oklahoma City had very little armor, only around its turrets and its vital organs and the C.I.C., but in the outside area where we were there wasn't any armor at all, and a shot would have killed lots of people. There were many hits on destroyers, some on the cruisers, but fortunately the Oklahoma City was never hit directly.

Q: Wasn't Linebacker in coordination with some of the big bombers coming out of Thailand also?

Adm. M.: Well, out of Thailand also but mostly from Guam and other places as far away as Guam. The B-52As were marvelous to watch. They were quite a show. The Oklahoma City was only three or four miles off the beach and some of these raids were within five miles of the beach. When we knew they were coming, we all looked topside and watched these B-52s carpet-bombing raids –

Q: They were pinpointed, weren't they?

Adm. M.: No, they were area bombs, and at night, of course, there'd be fantastic raids toward the end of this period, in May, on Hanoi, which had to be coordinated very carefully with our carriers. We were flying as many as 300 sorties a day from the six or seven carriers on the line. These were all carefully coordinated to make sure that the aircraft didn't hit in the same place at the same time. There were many requirements for search and rescue in all these sorties. Someone was always falling in the water and there were search-and-rescue operations going on simultaneously, so this became a very complicated war effort.

All the time, you could look out astern of you and see at least one or two merchant ships a day going up the area behind you and into Haiphong Harbor carrying weapons, antiaircraft ammunition –

Q: To come back at you in a day or two?

Adm. M.: Oh, yes, and we knew exactly what was happening, that this was going to happen. They would carry them in and they would come right back at us, and that's what did happen.

Q: As a political-science person, knowledgeable in that area, were you watching the coordination between these attacks and what was going on in Paris?

Adm. M.: Oh, absolutely.

Then about the middle of May or whenever it was, I've forgotten the exact date, we were given orders to be prepared to mine Haiphong Harbor. We had a plan for it, very simple —

Q: It was a longstanding plan, was it not?

Adm. M.: It was, but it was our plan, a Seventh Fleet plan, in spite of the fact that it's been written in certain books that this plan was made in the CNO's office and so forth. That's a bunch of baloney. It was not. It was made right there by the Seventh Fleet staff. All it called for was some A-4s to cross the harbor from a certain navigational point and drop mines sort of angling across the harbor entrance, which is about 150 yards wide and effectively close the harbor. Thousands of Mk-36 mines were dropped in all the other harbors up and down the coast, but we were told to be prepared to mine the harbor —

Q: How deep was the water in the harbor and did you have all of this knowledge?

Adm. M.: This was only the channel, not the harbor itself. We knew exactly what we needed. It was, I would say, fifty feet deep and subject to silting.

We had the plan, it was all set. I told Task Force 77, which was the aircraft carrier commander, to be prepared to do it, how many mines to use and where to put them —

Q: How many mines did you anticipate using?

Adm. M.: Oh, I think we only used six or eight. They were very small, just a string right across the harbor entrance. The outer entrance, of course, is quite far from the harbor and couldn't really be observed by the North Vietnamese so they didn't know what had happened. When we dropped these mines, they didn't know whether we dropped three or four or five hundred or whatever. The threat was what stopped them from going out through the field, not the number of mines.

Q: If they'd only known they could have sacrificed a few minor ships and -

Adm. M.: They might have jammed up the entrance. You see, these were all third-country ships, and they didn't want to take a chance on being sunk, so they just wouldn't leave.

Again, I was told to be ready to do it. We got all ready, then the count down began. We were told this was to be done at nine o'clock on whatever morning it was and the president was to make a simultaneous speech. There's twelve hours difference of time, so his nine o'clock in the morning was our nine o'clock in the night, but it was still light out there, but we were to do it. He wanted it mined exactly when he was making his speech, so it had to be done according to his time, again a political business.

Generally, what happens, of course, is when you're told to execute a plan like that, the word comes down, the president wants it executed. He tells the chairman of the Joint Chiefs who, in turn, tells CinCPac, who tells CinCPacFlt, who tells me, and I tell my aircraft commander. I knew that the president had told the Joint Chiefs because it appeared in this information message traffic about twenty-four hours before time and he wanted it done at nine o'clock. I knew that the chairman of the Joint Chiefs had told CinCPac he wanted it done. Then the message traffic stopped. We waited and waited and waited and nothing happened. I guess it was about two hours before mining time and I still didn't have any information from my titular boss, CinCPacFlt, to do it.

Q: Up to that time when had it come to him? I mean how much before?

Adm. M.: I didn't know. All I knew was that CinCPac had been told to do it six or eight hours before. What had happened was that CinCPac was in an aircraft down somewhere, which he usually was - this was Admiral McCain - flying around and the aircraft he was in didn't get the message. CinCPacFlt kind of got perturbed in the end so finally he took it upon himself to query CinCPac and finally got the message to him and it came back to CinCPacFlt, yes, go ahead and mine. CinCPacFlt got ready to send me the message.

Meantime, time was critical. I knew the president was going to make a speech at nine o'clock and he wanted to mine on time or else. So I told my aircraft carrier commander to launch his mine group and to make this mine drop, without having any authority whatsoever to do it.

After the aircraft were in the air, I got authority from CinCPacFlt, who finally had gotten CinCPac to send a message. Before the drop, I had authority, but I launched the attack and told them to go ahead and do it without any authority whatsoever. I knew that if I didn't, the president would want me out of there quickly. If he changed his mind and I still did it, then I'd get out, anyway. So I had no choice.

Q: It was a gamble, wasn't it?

Adm. M.: Yes. I think I'd rather be known as having done it because I wanted to do it, anyway. The navy had been wanting to do it for a long time. We did it, and it was simply done and the fifteen or so ships that were in harbor never left. They didn't want to leave. The North Vietnamese made no attempt to sweep. If they had we would have mined it again. Literally, what happened was that all traffic into Vietnam, except across the Chinese border, stopped. Within ten days there was not a missile or a shot being fired at us from the beach. They ran out of ammunition, like we always said they would.

From then on, Linebacker was a cinch. You could go in there and shoot anywhere and nobody would shoot back at you.

Q: So they had no reserve in terms of ammunition?

Adm. M.: No. It was all coming up in these ships behind us, which we knew.

Then things began to taper off. After I was relieved and left, of course, then the massive bombing raids were allowed on Hanoi and peace eventually came about.

Q: Did you reveal the story to Admiral McCain?

Adm. M.: No, I've never told him that.

About the last few days in May, I've forgotten when it was, I was to be relieved and I was relieved.

Q: By whom?

Adm. M.: By Admiral Holloway. What happened here was that roughly in January I had received a message from Admiral Zumwalt - this was a letter first - saying that he regretted to do so but he was going to relieve me in June to be superintendent of the Naval Academy. He would tell me why when I got back, and I was not to think that this was anything but a temporary stop, he said, on the way to four stars. He had told me before that, once I'd had a fleet command, I'd probably go to a four-star job.

Q: Was he thinking in terms of CinCLant-SacLant?

Adm. M.: I hope he was thinking about CinCPacFlt. I thought Admiral Clarey would leave and this would coincide with the time of my end of tour, which would be, say, eighteen months. But it didn't happen that way because he took me out early. My orders came and they read to be detached when relieved and report to the Naval Academy by the 1st of June, which was the time of June Week.

So I said I'd forego my thirty days' leave. I was fighting a war and I didn't want to go off and do that, so Admiral Holloway agreed and he arrived there just in time to relieve me in the last week of May, I guess it was. To do so, we had to pull the Oklahoma City off the line while he flew down and landed on a carrier and came across by helo from the carrier to the Oklahoma City while we were ceasing fire. When he was aboard, we went back and started firing again and spent about forty-eight hours going over the usual relieving data. Then, two days later, we pulled off the line again, assembled some of the crew back aft and had a relief-of-command ceremony. I left by helo and he went back on the line and started shooting within fifteen minutes. So that's rather an odd way of being relieved of command.

I found this rather strange. Here, I'd been shot at when I was a first-class midshipman and, here, I'd spent about three months as a vice admiral being shot at daily, fortunately never hit, but it was a good way to end an active career in some ways, but not a very healthy one for vice admirals. It's the strange way the navy has of doing things. In the army, a three-star general never sees a shot, he's so far back of the lines, but in the navy the vice admiral is right up on the front line along with the cook and the gunner's mate and everybody else. Anybody can be shot, any time, and that's just the way it is.

Q: Somehwat peculiar to that particular -

Adm. M.: That kind of war.

Q: Yes.

Adm. M.: I'd like to take a moment now to talk about that kind of war.

Although when you've got this number of ships people think you're concentrating on fighting the Vietnamese, not so. Half the ship is, or almost every naval ship was at that time. The other half of the ship is doing something else. For instance, all these cruisers and destroyers, even though their guns were being used for shooting in Vietnam, we had a war going on behind us. We were never unconscious of the fact that the Soviet Union had a large navy, aircraft, submarines, electronic sensorships right off our stern, in some cases. We always had to be aware of what was behind us, and so we had certain weapons loaded to take care of it. The Soviets at this time had a large surface task force just south of the gulf, sitting there for about two months. We always were conscious of the fact that our main enemy was not the North Vietnamese, but the Soviets. And, as the Seventh Fleet commander, I was still running these electronic sensor patrols, submarine reconnaissance, shadow patrols on all of their major surface ships, and making sure that we knew where all their submarines were.

That was my main concern every morning, where the Soviets were and was I in a position to counter their attacks if they started any, and not what was going on on the beach. Although we were shooting from the front end of the ship, the after end of the ship, the radar, Talos, and so forth, was all concentrated on being ready for the Soviets. That's the way the whole Seventh Fleet was.

Q: Material for schizophrenia!

Adm. M.: Yes, exactly. While we had seven carriers there all loaded with iron bombs to drop on the North Vietnamese, certain numbers of aircraft had to be repositioned, loaded, and ready for nuclear attacks, reconnaissance against the Soviets, and so forth.

Q: And they had a contingent of submarines with their fleet?

Adm. M.: Yes, they did. There were some down there and in the islands just below the Tonkin Gulf.

Q: What about the other old bugaboo that Red China might be involved?

Adm. M.: Well, we never bothered much about them because their navy really was second rate.

Q: They had submarines, however.

Adm. M.: Their submarines were never seen off the coast of Vietnam or even of China. They have them but they're just not very capable of operating off the coast. We never detected any of them off the coast.

So that's the kind of war it was. It was an iron-bomb war on the front part of the ship and a very complicated war, electronic warfare and so forth, on the other end of the ship. Many times we had to be in position to say go, and go bomb the coast with nuclear bombs that we had. We were confronted by Soviet aircraft coming out against our reconnaissance aircraft, we had ships in the Sea of Japan shadowed by Soviets. Many times the ships had to be completely ready for war, and the only thing for you to do was say, "Commence firing." We never knew what was going to happen.

Q: What effect did this have on the crew?

Adm. M.: I think it's rather exhilarating for them.

Q: Over a short period of time.

Adm. M.: That's why you have to be completely manned these days, and the reserve concept is a little bit out of date because you can't have a ship that isn't completely manned out there and completely ready. It has to be ready to fight. You never knew from one day to the other when it was going to happen.

It was rather an interesting tour and I left it with great regret.

Q: I would think so.

Adm. M.: I'd given up my leave, so I had to fly back to Japan, collect my family, jump into a navy airplane this time, and fly right back to the United States and directly to the Naval Academy.

Q: That's a good place to stop.

Mack #10 - 628

Interview #10 with Vice Admiral William P. Mack, U.S. Navy
(Retired)

Place: His residence in Annapolis, Maryland

Date: Thursday morning, 26 April 1979

Subject: Biography

By: John T. Mason, Jr.

Q: Well, Sir, we begin a very interesting phase - as though all of them were not interesting, because they are - but this is especially interesting, I believe, your assignment as superintendent of the Naval Academy. This occurred in June of 1972, when you were snatched away from the Seventh Fleet to become superintendent. Do you want to take up the story at that point?

Adm. M.: Yes, and I'm going to talk about some personalities but before I talk about them, the first thing I want to say is that I admired the personalities I'm talking about - Senator Stennis, Admiral Turner, perhaps Secretary Warner - I have no personal animosity toward any and I like all of them and am strong, close friends with them. I'm only relating what was told to me and what happened for historical purposes.

When you say I was snatched away in June, actually it may be the last few days of May, the snatching process started back in January, when I received a letter from Admiral Zumwalt saying, in effect, that he regretted to do so but he was going to have to assign me to be superintendent of the Naval Academy in early June and he wanted me to be there for June Week so that I would see what went on. I was not to consider that this was a stopping point on the way to four stars, since he had told me that when I left the Seventh Fleet I would either go directly to a four-star job or as soon as vacancies would occur I would go in one if I had to go to an interim job. He also said that my tour there would be about one year and then he would assign me to a four-star position.

This all seemed a little strange to me but I didn't want to question it in official traffic for all to see. I did talk to Admiral Clarey in Baguio in February, at a conference we had there, and explained to him that I wanted to send a message to Admiral Zumwalt pleading that I not be required to be there in June Week. In June I would complete twelve months and could I, please, stay on a little longer because I felt it was extremely important that the Japanese be present at the change-of-command ceremony for Commander, Seventh Fleet, since I had found this to be an extremely important event when I took over and it was attended by practically every Japanese official of high standing, except the emperor, from the secretary of defense on down to the speaker of the House, the CNO, and many high officials from all over Japan. It was their way of showing the United States how much they considered the Seventh Fleet to be of importance in their defense, and not to have that change of command there, roughly in June, when they could all attend would be a politically wrong thing to do.

I also pleaded that I wanted to be able to find out why this was happening. I didn't think it was in the best interests of anybody concerned. Admiral Clarey said he would take this under advisement, and he called later on from his headquarters, Admiral Zumwalt, and found out what I later found out. He then told me by scrambled radio message that he couldn't tell me all the details now, that I was not to communicate with Admiral Zumwalt, that the chief of naval personnel had said this was in concrete, I had to be there for June Week, I had to be there and that was it.

So I marched off as I should. I did say that I intended giving up my thirty days' leave in order to extend my time in command through the month of May. Originally, my orders read to be detached about the 1st of May and have thirty days' leave and report on the 3rd of June, I believe, or something of that sort.

Of course, events then changed. The breakthrough

by the North Vietnamese across the DMZ occurred and the flagship then went down and was almost all the time on the line off Vietnam, from April 1st on through May and June. It became evident then that the flagship could not, in any event, be in Yokosuka in May and what I should do was to extent my time in command to the last possible date and be relieved down there, and come on back as fast as I could to Annapolis to be present for June Week.

Q: Some of those nuances, since they pertain to a foreign government, are lost on our high command on occasion.

Adm. M.: That's right, that's exactly right, and when I went back to Yokosuka, where my family was, and I had one day in which to pack and get on an airplane and start back, I did find that the Japanese military, particularly the navy, was concerned for me and very kind and had suddenly arranged a dinner with all the chief members of the Japanese self-defense force there, the high-ranking ones. They were extremely kind to me and enthusiastic in their praise, and we parted on very close terms. However, as has been customary, when the change of command was about to take place, the old Seventh Fleet and the new Seventh Fleet commanders go to Tokyo to call on the minister of defense and the CNO. At that time, the outgoing commander of the Seventh Fleet has traditionally always been decorated by the Japanese government and there's a social affair, and so forth.

I was asked not to call. The Japanese, of course, are very discreet and don't like to tell you the exact facts, but the facts were that the Japanese government was unhappy with the American government for taking large parts of the fleet out of Japan, going down to Vietnam and mining Hanoi and Haiphong approaches.

Q: Did they feel insecure at that point?

Adm. M.: I think that was part of it. They were unhappy, of course, that we would expand the war, really. What they were trying to do was keep peace with the radical elements in Japan, which were at that time demonstrating because we had these ships out there with all their nuclear bombs aboard, they thought, and the government was rather unhappy.

Strangely enough, I was kept down in Yokosuka and they asked me not to go to Tokyo. This part of the change-of-command business was carefully controlled, so I left Japan without seeing the persons in the government I was supposed to call on.

Q: Did they subsequently give you an award?

Adm. M.: Oh, no.

NOTE: Pages 6̶2̶3̶-4-5-6 have been marked CLOSED by Admiral Mack. They are deleted from this volume - but will be added at some later date when Admiral Mack decides that is proper.   (JTMjr)

This, further was compounded by the fact that in June, then, late June, the flagship did come back to Yokosuka, as the war began to calm down a little bit, as I thought it would. And I was further unhappy about the fact that if they had let me alone and let me stay into June, when the Naval Academy is quite dormant, I could have achieved this. We'd have had a change of command and perhaps would have been able to get the Japanese government back on our side and so forth. But, again, I was not able to get this through Admiral Clarey to Admiral Zumwalt because I was just told the CNO was adamant, that was what he wanted, and not to rock the boat. So I had to sit there and watch this happen and know it was wrong.

Then, finally, I went back through Pearl Harbor, and I spent a day or so with Admiral Clarey. He still could not tell me all the reasons why I was going to the Naval Academy, but he did concur when I explained what was going on out there that this was a terrible thing to have done, not to me personally, but to the relations with the Japanese government and fleet relationships with the Japanese Maritime Self-Defense Force.

I went on back to Washington –

Q: Did you suspect at that time what the situation was that you were walking into?

Adm. M.: No, I didn't, I knew nothing about the real

reasons for it.

As soon as I could, I went to call on Admiral Zumwalt. He explained to me that what had happened was that in January the secretary of the navy, Mr. Chafee, had proposed to send Admiral Turner to be superintendent of the Naval Academy. Admiral Turner had just been in the process of shaking up the command he was then commanding -

Q: What was he? Second Fleet?

Adm. M.: Yes, and Mr. Chafee thought that this was a fine thing that he had done. Admiral Zumwalt on the contrary was extremely unhappy and was sure that that was not the kind of a person, although he expressed, as I did, the idea that Admiral Turner was a splendid naval officer and person, it was just that he wasn't right for that particular job.

Admiral Turner, apparently, had proposed to Secretary Chafee that when he went to the Naval Academy, he had extreme ideas of changing the curriculum radically, changing the way midshipmen were instructed, administered, and, in a sense, doing to the Naval Academy what he eventually did to the War College. Admiral Zumwalt felt that the Naval Academy was a place where you did not do that kind of thing, that if you made changes there, they had to be evolutionary rather than revolutionary for two reasons. One is you couldn't change the life of these young people that radically without changing the whole flow of what went on in the officer-procurement system, and secondly, if you did it, you would meet a tremendous storm from the alumni who wouldn't like these changes, and you would just be bucking quicksand, trying to get these changes made with everybody against you.

Q: Admiral Zumwalt was already meeting a storm from the retired community.

Adm. M.: Yes, he was, that's right, but he didn't see that any changes had to be made. He said the curriculum was roughly what was wanted, the midshipmen were doing well, the Naval Academy had a high reputation, its cost-effectiveness was reasonable. He said:

"Frankly, I don't see why Admiral Turner thinks these changes have to be made. I think many of them are being made just because he likes to make changes. I proposed twenty or thirty officers to be superintendent and Mr. Chafee would only take you. So my hands were that tied and I had to put you there."

I said:

"Well, the timing was really terrible because I don't have to be there for June Week. June Week is a simple process that goes by rote. I don't need to see a parade and so forth, and what's happened is that I've had to leave the Seventh Fleet at a critical time - not that I'm personally critical for this command, but the Japanese are now unhappy and they could have been made happy if we had waited one more month."

When he learned that, he said:

"That's terrible. I'm sorry it happened. I didn't know anything about it."

I said: "Well, I tried to get this through Admiral Clarey and I presumed through the chief of naval personnel."

Apparently what happened was that Admiral Clarey had presented this problem to the chief of naval personnel, who was then Admiral Guinn, and Admiral Guinn had met so much flak on this whole problem about Admiral Turner, the Naval Academy, and the War College that he had simply said:

"I know what the CNO wants and I will not present this problem to him. He's already told me not to shake the tree, that this is what's going to happen and he wants it to happen."

Q: Not appreciating the difficulty -

Adm. M.: No, and apparently Admiral Clarey did not present the diplomatic side of the picture to Admiral Guinn, or Admiral Guinn didn't appreciate it, but at least this happened because of a failure of communications on a high level. As a result, Admiral Holloway had a very difficult time restoring amicable relationships with the Japanese government over this problem, but finally did, of course.

I went down to the Naval Academy and thought June Week was a bust. All I did was sit and watch a couple of parades. I couldn't talk to the superintendent because he was busy eighteen hours a day conducting the normal affairs of June Week. So I simply sat in my set of quarters, which had been assigned to me behind the parade ground, and watched the parades and enjoyed life.

Q: Difficult for you.

Adm. M.: It was.

As soon as June Week was over it took about two days, I guess, to do the turnover with nobody else there. There were no midshipmen there and most of the instructors had gone and so forth, so we sat in our office and did the turnover.

Here I was feeling quite frustrated because this had happened.

The other point at issue, which I talked to Admiral Zumwalt about - and, incidentally, this was the only point that he made to me concerning how I should run the Naval Academy - that was that he was going to change the chain of command. Previously, the superintendent of the Naval Academy had been directly under the vice chief of naval operations -

of course, really the chief of naval operations, but he reported to and did his business with the vice chief. This made it very simple, as far as budgetary problems were concerned. If you had need for money or if something happened, you'd go right to the vice CNO or call him or talk to his budgeteer and the problem was solved. Or, if you had a problem concerning personnel, either midshipmen or otherwise, you could be in touch with him immediately, or with the chief of naval personnel, if it concerned curriculum or admittance or something of that sort. So you were directly in communication and only forty-five minutes by car away from the people you had to deal with.

Now, he proposed to change the chain of command so that the superintendent of the Naval Academy, along with the superintendent of the War College - the president of the War College, rather, and the other major persons in command of educational training centers were to report to a chief of naval education and training, who was about to move from Washington down to Pensacola. That meant that there was one step to go through to get to the persons in controlling budgetary affairs and admittance affairs, and you were required to compete, for instance, with the training centers and flight-training, also, and the War College, and the postgraduate school for funds and attention, really.

It became extremely difficult, as I knew it would, but Admiral Zumwalt asked me could I do this because he wanted to do it very much. I said: "If you want to do it, I'll do my utmost to make it work, and I'll never say it won't work until I've exhausted every possibility."

Q: And his reason was the consolidation of education?

Adm. M.: Yes. His idea was to get these things out of the VCNO's purview so that the VCNO would be relieved of the requirement to communicate with the superintendent.

I pointed out that the superintendent, as far as I could see, didn't communicate with him very much, but when he did he had to right now. If a congressman wanted something with regard to a constitutent or there was a drug fiasco or something of that sort, the CNO wanted to know right now what was happening. He didn't want to have to wait for me to report to somebody in Pensacola or to have that person report to him. He said that that didn't mean that I couldn't come to him or the VCNO when things happened, but that for normal, everyday affairs, including the budget, I was to go to CNET.

I also pointed out that the Naval Academy was unique. I could not change the numbers of people there. There were a set number of midshipmen, 4,300, and that was dictated by the number of bunks and the number of spaces and things, the dining hall and so forth, and I could not cut the number.

If I were required to take a budgetary cut, the product we had, which was midshipmen, would remain the same. The only way I could cut the budget was either (a) by being more efficient, or (b) by cutting the efficiency or the quality of the product, that is, cutting down the number of instructors, the number of courses, and that sort of thing, and you couldn't do this indefinitely, but I would do the best I could, and I would hope that CNET could be persuaded that this was so and that we could make this all work.

To pursue the same subject, over the three-year time, the Board of Visitors, as soon as they learned that this had been changed were adamant, 100 percent against it, and they wanted me, in effect, to say that I couldn't make it work, they would put this in their report, and, hopefully, we could get it changed. I had to say no, I had told the CNO and I would continue to tell him that when the day comes that I can't make it work, he'd be the first to know, that I would do everything I could to make it work because that's what he wants, and I continued for three years to do that.

Q: Who were the naval personnel on the board?

Adm. M.: Admiral Felt was the naval person and General Krulak was the Marine general involved.

Q: Both of whom were very cognizant.

Adm. M.: Absolutely. They didn't like this at all. In every report in the three years that I was there, they placed an article or a little discussion in their report saying they were very much against this, but each time I asked them to say that, although in principle I was against it, I was doing everything I could to make it work. It was working and if it didn't work, I would say to the CNO as soon as I found out that it didn't work.

What happened was just what I suspected. A cut would be put upon CNET, a budgetary cut, say, 10 percent, and the budgeteers at CNET, without consulting their boss, would immediately proportion this cut to every sub-activity. All of a sudden we would get in the mail a notation saying we were being cut 10 percent in personnel across the board in money and so forth. Then we would have to reclama this at great length and expense in time and money to us to go back to CNET and say, look, we can't do this. What do you want us to do? How many midshipmen should we cut out?

I think the first year we took the cut, we tightened our belts, everything we could, and found out we could take about 8 percent of it and still make the place run and not look too shabby. But the second year they tried this sort of thing it was obviously impossible. You can only get so efficient, and you can't work people overtime any more than you already have. You can't work the civilians overtime, anyway, and you cannot work with fewer instructors after you get to a certain workload. You run up against certain requirements that you cannot change. So I had to go back and reclama this one and, eventually, with great time and effort, it was removed, and I pointed out if you want to cut something you're just going to have to cut the number of pilots or the number of PG students, or something of that sort, where you can change their load. You can't change my load and won't, so don't try to cut me any more.

At one time I had to go directly to CNET himeself and complain and finally -

Q: Who was he at that time?

Adm. M.: That was Vice Admiral Wilson, who was my senior in command, in the command chain, but my junior in terms of years as a vice admiral. So we had a very good relationship.

The third year I even had to write to the VCNO and say I can't keep this up. I'm just on the verge of having to say that this is no way to run a railroad.

Q: Were there any rumblings in Congress? They were looking

NOTE : Pages 643-47 have been designated as CLOSED by Admiral Mack and so are deleted from this volume. They will be added at a later date when Admiral Mack gives permission. (JTM jr.)

over your shoulder, too.

Adm. M.: Oh, yes, that's right. There were congressmen on the board.

Eventually, the year after I left, the command relationship was changed back again to the old system. Admiral Holloway changed it, so eventually it was shown that you just couldn't run it that way. It was a good idea but impractical. So that completed that subject.

To come back again to what I was told when I got there was that I was to be there one year. At the end of one year, Admiral Zumwalt called me and said that he was issuing my orders to be Commander in Chief, South, to be Admiral Colbert's relief. This was a little earlier than he had thought and it wasn't exactly the job he was going to put me in, but Admiral Colbert had found he had cancer and a short time to live and I was to get ready to go on fairly sudden notice to go and relieve him. He said:

"I'm sending your nomination to the secretary of the Navy and then down to the secretary of defense, and it should be announced shortly."

I waited - I wasn't allowed to say anything - but I waited for a couple of weeks and finally I got another call and he said that Admiral Colbert had flown back and had persuaded the secretary of the navy that he should be left in his position as an act of courtesy to him until he could no longer function. Rather than be cut off from his job at the end of the year, what he wanted more than anything was to stay in that job, regardless of what happened to his health.

So I was told to go back on hold and that my nomination had been withdrawn, although it had been signed by the secretary of the navy, signed by the secretary of defense, and was just about to go to the White House. Admiral Zumwalt retrieved it and apparently kept it in his desk.

Q: Colbert actually died in office, didn't he?

Adm. M.: No. He lasted one more year, then he came back to the States at the end of his second year, then died about a month later. At that time, Admiral Zumwalt called me and said, "Okay, get ready again. Admiral Colbert is coming back to the States and I'll let you know what to do and when."

Then, about two weeks later, he called and said he was having difficulty with the nomination. He had sent it to Secretary Warner, who had taken Secretary Chafee's place as secretary of the navy, and Secretary Warner had said, "What's this? I've already promised this job to at least three other people, one of whom is Admiral Johnston, and I've done so in exchange for Senator Stennis's vote for

Trident."

Admiral Zumwalt didn't tell me that part on the telephone, but he flew down in a helicopter and talked to me for about an hour about this, apologizing profusely for what had happened, and said he didn't want to talk about it on the telephone and that was why he had come by helo. He was so unhappy about it that, rather than send for me, he'd come on down to the Naval Academy to apologize to me in person. He said what had happened was that he'd sent the nomination down already signed by Secretary Warner and Secretary Warner said:

"Well, that's all history now."

Q: It was signed by Secretary Chafee?

Adm. M.: Yes, I'm sorry.

"That's all history now and meantime I've promised this job to several other people, the chief candidate of which is Admiral Johnston" - who was then the chief of legislative affairs and a constituent and very close friend of Senator Stennis. And he, as I said before - this is what Admiral Zumwalt told me - he'd in a sense traded his nomination to Senator Stennis for Senator Stennis's vote in favor of Trident.

Q: Is this an unusual procedure, for the secretary to

promise an operational assignment without consulting the CNO?

Adm. M.: Absolutely, the first time I ever heard it happen, and I think it's probably the last. Obviously Admiral Zumwalt was extremely unhappy and told Secretary Warner that it was in his purview to recommend, at least to the secretary of the navy, those persons who were to take jobs like this, and the secretary of the navy did not have that kind of expertise and it was not right to put people in high office for political reasons, they were supposed to be competent in their field and a political reason was not to be considered, except perhaps in making a choice between two people or something of that sort. Furthermore, he said, he didn't think that Admiral Johnston was qualified to take this job for various reasons. He was then a rear admiral and had been one only a short time. He'd never been to sea as a rear admiral and here they were about to make him a four-star admiral right from chief of legislative affairs, and that was not right.

Q: And to deal in diplomatic matters!

Adm. M.: Yes.

This went on for a time, so I sat back and Admiral Zumwalt said:

"Well, we'll put you in some other job eventually. This has to be resolved first."

Then later he told me that the nomination, with his objection, had gone down to the secretary of defense, who also objected strenuously and said that he didn't think Admiral Johnston was qualified - this was Mr. Schlesinger. Mr. Schlesinger said:

"No, you have a qualified man, qualified in all respects, put him back in the system and cancel out Admiral Johnston."

But then the pressures on Secretary Warner at that time were so great that he had to keep on pushing for Admiral Johnston, and the process took about three months.

Q: The pressures coming from the Senate?

Adm. M.: Yes, the pressure was coming from Senator Stennis to do it, and pressures coming from other members who said he wasn't qualified, and pressures coming from Secretary Schlesinger, who didn't want to be in the position of recommending this particular nomination. So eventually it was resolved by Admiral Johnston being appointed, or nominated, rather, and approved by a committee that was headed by Senator Stennis, which made it very easy, and Admiral Johnston went to the job.

I add, as an afternote, he was relieved early. I

will not characterize why, but history will show, I think, that there was a problem there in terms of his ability to do that job. But that's not my problem.

So I stayed on as superintendent of the Naval Academy.

Q: You'd lost your opportunity for four stars?

Adm. M.: Well, I don't want to say that. To me, if I were qualified to be a four-star admiral and should have had four stars, I would have had them and it wouldn't have made any difference, they'd have found some other job for me. So I have to conclude that I wasn't, and I make no claim to being qualified.

Admiral Zumwalt then, of course, left and Admiral Holloway came in as chief of naval operations, and I stayed on as superintendent for a period.

Secretary Warner came down to the Naval Academy on one occasion, shortly before Admiral Holloway was chosen, and said that he wanted to nominate me as one of four or five candidates to be chief of naval operations and would I submit to him a précis of what I thought the duties of the chief of naval operations should be in general and specifically at this time. I did this and presented him with a three- or four-page summary of what I thought could and should be done. If my sources are correct, this was one of four nominations, I think, sent down to the secretary of defense, from which Admiral Holloway was chosen.

Q: At that point, who was secretary of defense? They change so rapidly.

Adm. M.: I think it was still Mr. Schlesinger. I'd have to look at the system to see, I'm not quite sure.

At any rate, three or four months later, Admiral Holloway called me to Washington and said that, in view of my age and other considerations along with his desire to get on with sending younger people to three- and four-star jobs, he could not at that time see putting me in a four-star job and, since there wouldn't be any openings anyway for over a year or so, stated that he'd like to have me retire, which I said of course I would do and did so in August of 1975.

Q: You still had possible -

Adm. M.: I would have had three years, since I was then 59 in August, but that's not enough for a four-year term as CNO. I told this to Secretary Warner and he said that didn't make any difference, it was not a legal requirement, it was only a customary requirement and, if if were chosen by the secretary of defense and the president, he would say that there was no reason I couldn't stay on for a fourth year, even over what was then the customary retirement age, stay on until 63. So that apparently was not a bar for that, although it appeared that if I were not to have that job, it was a bar to go to some other four-star job because that would be using up a four-star job for somebody who, if he had it at a younger age, could then be a candidate for chief of naval operations, because by that time they realized that it's best to demonstrate that you're a candidate for CNO by performing in a four-star job. Admiral Zumwalt was the first, I think, to recognize that that was a good idea.

So that's what happened in the saga of command that I went through. I relate this because I've had to say some things that I would not want made public now concerning Senator Stennis, Secretary Warner, and Admiral Turner, and perhaps Admiral Zumwalt. But these are the facts as they were presented to me, and I relate them because I think they have some bearing on history and perhaps the futures of Admiral Turner and Secretary Warner and somehow show that the things they did were maybe improper if not wrong, and so I complete that section of the history.

Q: A sad story from your point of view.

Adm. M.: No, I don't feel sad about it at all. I enjoyed being at the Naval Academy for three years, rather than the one year that I might have had. I enjoy being retired. I'm glad I retired young enough to do some other things that I wanted to do, I'm very happy doing that. I think I'm lucky to have gotten to three-star rank. Again, I've always held that if you're good enough they'll find a place for you, and all I can conclude is that I wasn't good enough to become a four-star admiral, although twice I was considered for chief of naval operations and didn't make that, but that's the way it goes.

Q: Politics.

Adm. M.: Well, I was involved in politics, too, I guess, but I was on the wrong side.

Q: Well, having been catapulted into the situation at the Naval Academy, you probably didn't have time to formulate any specific ideas as to what you wanted to do once you assumed command?

Adm. M.: That's correct. I gave very little thought to it. As a matter of fact, when I first heard I was coming I was somewhat nonplussed and really didn't want to come because I thought it was a place where very little change could be made and all I would be doing was be a caretaker because Admiral Calvert and Admiral Kauffman before him I thought had made the only changes that the Naval Academy could have stood in ten years, namely those involving the curriculum.

I knew the difficulties with Admiral Rickover that I would face and I could see nothing positive really that I could contribute to the Naval Academy, except I knew lots of things I didn't like about it. If I could have changed those that would have been fine.

Q: You did have in your background the administration of the little naval academy up at Bainbridge?

Adm. M.: Oh, yes, and I'd had much to do with it as chief of legislative affairs and chief of information by having to go there frequently to check up on what was going on for explaining to the public what was happening and, in the case of chief of legislative affairs, intervening between the Naval Academy and congressmen in certain cases. So I was very well informed as to what the Naval Academy had been doing and how it had been changed because it had to be, and, of course, the Naval Academy was one of the institutions in a sense under the assistant secretary of Defense for manpower and reserve affairs. Frequently, in that job, I'd had to compare the Naval Academy with West Point and with the Air Force Academy in terms of strength of instructors, budgetary positions, and policies regarding one thing and another. So to do that, I'd had to keep abreast of what the Naval Academy was doing and, in a sense, the Naval Academy was under Manpower and Reserve Affairs as an educational institution.

Q: Incidentally and in the nature of a footnote, did the Coast Guard Academy enter into the picture, too, I mean as a little academy?

Adm. M.: Oh, yes. When we had superintendents' conference, for instance, the Coast Guard Academy was one of the four there. They always participated in that sort of thing and they always were quite close and were considered as one of the "four service academies."

Q: Well, and they did some innovative things under Admiral Smith?

Adm. M.: Yes, they did. Some things we didn't like to do, really.

To continue with the idea of what I thought about going to the Naval Academy, I gave it very little thought, except to begin to remember many of the things I didn't like from past history, all the way back to being a midshipman to observing these sorts of things over the years in various positions I held. So when I actually got there, all I could do was, again, sit during June Week and watch, and being there really was a waste of time. Then, of course, the two months of the summer were very placid and simple. There wasn't much to be done then, other than to become acquainted with what was going on, to read all the manuals, and look through the various curricula, which I did.

Q: Did you approve of all the changes that Calvert had made?

Adm. M.: Yes, except that I thought they'd gone just a little too far toward the liberal arts field. I agreed with Admiral Rickover in terms of the fact that I didn't think each midshipman should be nothing but a student, and a student of science and mathematics and so forth. I thought that the curriculum as far as mathematics and science and engineering should be returned a little bit toward the stronger position it held years before.

Two or three of the points at issue that I felt were wrong were I thought that the plebe indoctrination system was still somewhat immature in the sense that it should be changed and strengthened and made more professional. I thought that the professional training was a little behind times and not sufficiently strong. That's one of the reasons, of course, why generally officers with recent operational experience are brought to the Naval Academy to ensure that the latest professional achievements are put into the system somehow. Whereas West Point or the Air Force Academy sometimes will bring a superintendent in from some series of jobs where he perhaps had been not even operative for ten years, the navy has always insisted that the superintendent, at least in latter years, has been an operator. When he has not been an operator it's been a mistake because he doesn't maintain the basic idea that the Naval Academy is to produce officers to be used by the fleet, and if he doesn't know what the fleet uses he can't do as well as otherwise.

Q: This is more imperative for the navy than it is for the army, is it not?

Adm. M.: Absolutely. The army does some strange things. For instance, they will take a look at the cadets coming out of their system and earmark instructors, and those instructors-to-be, as cadets, will be then told, if they agree, to go to postgraduate school from one to three years, then they'll be brought back to West Point to be instructors where they will have a master's degree and sometimes a doctor's degree. They will then instruct for four years, so that will be seven years before they ever get to troops and, as far as I'm concerned and the navy's concerned, they're dead. If the first seven years of your career are spent in instructing in English, or something of that sort, and you haven't seen a troop, then you'll be a captain and when you go out to your troops, you're gone.

Q: Don't they go beyond that even and stay on forevermore?

Adm. M.: Some of them do, yes. I can see that, if they stay forevermore. In other words, the man is not an army officer, he is an instructor, but they won't admit it. They claim that that's just great, to have a man in uniform there as an instructor. I kept asking the superintendent at our various conferences, "What do you want your cadets to see? Do you want them to think that a major is that instructor? He may be a competent instructor in English or Spanish or something, but he's not an army officer. He doesn't know a thing about the army, and you're telling me that you like the idea of having that man there in uniform because that inspires your cadets to have a uniformed officer instructing. What I'm telling you is that it's exactly the opposite of that. They will form a picture of this man as being a typical army officer and he's not at all. He doesn't know a thing about the army. I would rather have someone who is slightly less competent as an instructor but who can talk to these young men in our place from the point of view of having just come off a submarine or a destroyer or from an aviation activity. Perhaps he's a little rusty in his instructing techniques, perhaps he's not as well based in Spanish or English, but at least he is a naval officer, and if he's going to wear a uniform that's what he ought to be. If you want this man you're talking about to be an instructor for twelve or fifteen years, take him out of uniform and make him a civilian instructor. Let's have the midshipmen and the cadets know what they're talking to. Either he's a military officer, in which case he's not expected to be as good an instructor as a civilian, or he's a civilian, in which case he's respected for that. But don't try to obfuscate things by having an instructor in a military uniform saying to your cadets that this is a great example for you to see what a military person can do.

Q: You didn't make an impress on them?

Adm. M.: Never. As a matter of fact, Mr. Clements, the deputy secretary of defense in the latter two years of my time at the Naval Academy, tried to make the Naval Academy do that because he thought it was great. This, again, is a long story in terms of the machinations of Mr. Clements and the committee he headed to study the three academies - not the Coast Guard, but the three academies. When we get to that, I'll cover it in a little more detail, but back again to what I thought should be done.

Again, I was told nothing by Admiral Zumwalt, except that he thought the Naval Academy didn't need much change and whatever I did should be such that it would be in the best interest of the navy and certainly would not upset the alumni too much and would be whatever was necessary to provide operational officers who knew operations and so forth and who could technically master the tremendously complicated requirements of the modern navy, and so that's what I did.

I was always sort of caught between Admiral Rickover and his requirements of the Naval Academy were simply - he said midshipmen should have no duties other than to study. They should not be stripers, they should have no responsibility for their own administration, they should only study and recite eighteen hours a day, if that was necessary, as many hours as were necessary to master mathematics, science, a little English and some history. There should be no athletics, they should not participate in any kind of activity such as Glee Club or going outside the academy. They should do nothing but study for four years. That was his idea.

Well, of course, I didn't agree with that -

Q: What right did he have to try to impose this sort

of system?

Adm. M.: He had no ability to do so whatsoever. These were his ideas. I talked to him perhaps once a week, sometimes more frequently, regarding his ideas in general and regarding certain midshipmen in particular, and certainly regarding his selection of his candidates for the nuclear-power program, which would number about 100 each year.

Q: These were selected while they were still midshipmen?

Adm. M.: Yes. They went down to Washington to be interviewed by him.

Q: On what basis was the selection made?

Adm. M.: It was based, of course, first on their academic record. We would nominate to him all these young men who had good records, and they had to be volunteers, to start with. He would take them in groups, busloads, take them up to his office and interview them. Sometimes he would select a man with a 3.0 average who was an engineering student and reject a liberal-arts man with a 3.8 average. Sometimes he would take a liberal-arts man with a 2.8 average. You never knew what he would do. Some of it was involved with his impressions of the person, how well that man did in science, particularly mathematics, science and engineering. It was very difficult to predict the ones he would take.

Over the three years I was there, I did everything I could to satisfy the requirements that he had for one hundred officers a year, including arranging with him that if he would select some who he thought would be efficient in certain kinds of mathematics, differential equations in particular, I would arrange to have a summer school for them the year after they graduated so they would stay at the Naval Academy for two months and get themselves up to speed in mathematics, particularly again differential equations, then they could go to his schools and be up with the persons he thought were better than they.

Q: And the financing of this came out of your budget?

Adm. M.: That's right. He thought that was a good idea, I did it, and it worked out just fine. So he was able to select some who were deficient, say, they were English majors and they never thought about taking differential equations, which came in the advanced mathamatics section, so they would have lost out on his selection had they not been able to go to summer school. So he would select some provisionally if they would go to summer school and get the mathematical background they needed.

It was always proposed, I think, that every midshipman take differential equations, which came in a difficult mathematics course and take physics of a certain kind and do other things which would mean that they could not complete the requirements for their degree in English or history or something of that sort. I resisted that because I said I was not supposed to produce naval officers only for the nuclear-power program. I was supposed to produce 138 marines a year, and they didn't necessarily need differential equations. The marines would rather have a man who has a good physique, strong leadership characteristics, and so forth, and if he can't solve differential equations through our requirements then they'd rather have them without it. Also, I was required to present to the navy a certain number of aviators each year and they have got to have strong hand-eye coordination. This means rifle shooters, tennis players, golfers, men who are not necessarily big and strong like the marines want but certainly some people with athletic abilities. If they can't solve certain kinds of mathematical problems, that's all right, they can still be good aviators. We had to have a certain number of those.

Rickover always said: "I don't care about the requirements for the marines or aviators. Nuclear power is the most important thing in the navy and the Naval Academy should be geared to produce that kind of people. AVCADs can go to the aviators and the marines can produce their own marines if they want to."

I resisted this because my charge still was, by the Navy Department, to produce so many marines and so many aviators from Naval Academy sources to give to the navy a leavening of Naval Academy thought for the officer ranks and the marine corps and aviation ranks. So I guess for three years I argued somewhat with Admiral Rickover and usually won because he had no direct authority over me and the CNO made that clear.

Q: Did he, in a sense, downplay the need of leadership training?

Adm. M.: Yes. His idea was that leadership came from knowledge and that any dope, if he can master the science curriculum, he could be a leader. All he had to do was know more than his men. That is a favorite subject of his. All they needed in their education was science and engineering, English, of course, and a little bit of history. Those four subjects were all he needed. He didn't need a language, didn't need economics, didn't need anything other than those basic subjects, and I shouldn't bother to teach anything else.

Well, that would have made a fine - if I'd carried out

his ideas, a dramatic and gradual change in what was going on at the Naval Academy and I would have been drummed out of the corps by every alumnus that could reach a telephone.

Q: I suppose, in a sense, a man serving in a submarine is apart from the rest of the world, for the time being, at least!

Adm. M.: Yes, he is, but, on the other hand, you don't serve in a submarine forever. That was one of his problems. His nuclear submariners came out of submarines at some age and became captains or admirals in the political section of CNO and they couldn't cope. They were technically well qualified but they just seemed to die on the vine whenever they got into higher ranks. That wasn't only because his graduates were only then becoming captains and rear admirals and getting out of nuclear submarines and so forth, but he didn't care about that. He just thought that didn't make any difference, that the key of the navy was nuclear power, submarines, and so forth, and anything else was second grade.

So I always had this business of having, in a sense, to give Admiral Rickover as much of what he wanted as I could. When I was there the number of persons going into nuclear power rose dramatically. We did include many more candidates. He occasionally would get to one of the secretaries, particularly the secretary of defense, then I would get a requirement to increase the numbers of engineering, mathematics, science persons taking that kind of major rather than what are called the softer majors, in other words, history, a language, and so forth. When I got there the numbers that had been set by Admiral Calvert were 75-25 and eventually I changed it to 80-20. I was at one time required by a directive to make those candidates coming in sign up for a major and the acceptance was to be 80-20. That was to make sure we got 80-20, and I said:

"I won't do that because, unless I'm really ordered to do so, because it's silly, because three days after they get in, say, four science types resign in plebe summer and the 80-20 thing is out of kilter right away. So what's the point of having exactly 80-20 on the day of entry, because it won't ever be that again? I would rather get good candidates and if I have to force some liberal-arts person into science, I'll do that after they're there, rather than before."

That's what we did and, for a while, we had to say that major-choosing day would be 80-20 and some of you who are liberal-arts candidates will be required, if you are capable and qualified in our eyes, to take a heavier major. We did that and it caused some unhappiness to the midshipmen and a few resignations but, in general, what happened was that they took the major and along about their fourth year after they'd been to sea on cruises and so forth they began to realize that, yes, this is what they should do. The philosophy here was that you could teach a science major much more easily in a classroom atmosphere because that sort of thing always required laboratories and those particular qualified teachers to teach it. You could always teach liberal arts later by correspondence and learn it by reading, if you had to. You could learn history and English by reading. That could be self-taught or taught some other way at a later time, so what you'd better do as an undergraduate was take the hard subjects, which require laboratory assistance and so forth, and if you really want to be a political-science type, you have all the rest of your life to read political science and to do the sorts of thing you will do if you travel. But you will never learn physics out of a book, at least not as easily as you will in a laboratory, or electrical engineering or something of that sort.

Q: Only an exceptional person can.

Adm. M.: Right. And so that was the reason that I kept trying, by personal interview, to get these young men to volunteer, if they were qualified to take the harder majors. Most of the time I was successful. I would tell them, "If you want political science, we have a political science seminar here, you can go to that even though you're not a political-science major." On one occasion I invited two young men over to have lunch with a couple of ambassadors we had down. If they wanted to be political science, we'll make you political science in your spare time, if you will go ahead and do the hard things in your class time, and they did. They began to see the light.

That was a continuing battle, the business of how many majors we had in each general category. I think that was the only real academic difficulty I had there. That was the only real change I made from Admiral Calvert's reign. We did go far toward beefing up the mathematics part of the curriculum, and when I left we were just on the verge of making everybody take some kind of differential equations.

Q: And that was, in part, due to the pressure -

Adm. M.: Well, no, there was a need for engineers in general, for high-pressure steam for destroyers and every other kind of aircraft which we knew had computers. For instance, every aircraft has two or three computers in it and every ship has a dozen. The ships were becoming more complicated as were the aircraft, and we knew it was going to be a requirement that everybody be mathematically qualified in everything he could be before he got out of the Naval Academy.

Q: It's interesting to observe the fact that the Bureau of Personnel kept close touch with Rickover's views on education in the academy and established a study on the refutation of what he proposed and so on.

Adm. M.: Well, that was, of course, engineered by us. Admiral Rickover, in his annual presentation to the Appropriations Committee would list all the things that were wrong with the Naval Academy and I'd be required to send back a refutation of these, go back in the Congressional Record and so forth. Then he'd do the same thing all over the following year, even though we'd proved that the things he'd said before were incorrect. Apparently, he never read our refutations.

Q: Did he succeed in having a representative on the Board of Visitors?

Adm. M.: No, he never did.

Q: That was an oversight, wasn't it?

Adm. M.: We said he could send anybody any time he wanted

and we'd be glad to give him carte blanche to see anything we do or explain it and so forth. We had no problem there. We had close liaison with him and his office and the people who worked for him.

Q: Well, you'd had that prior to -

Adm. M.: Yes. Oh, yes. As a matter of fact, in the middle of all this, Rickover Hall was being built, or, rather, a complex was being built which was to be the engineering laboratory system. About the middle of the building period, when the structure was still bare inside, I received a call from Secretary Warner saying that he was going to name the building Rickover Hall. I pointed out that it was not customary to name buildings or anything else down here after a living person, not a ship even, and he said:

"I know that, but I'm going to make an exception."

I said:

"Well, I'm sorry because I have three or four names on their way up to you to be considered."

"Well," he said, "that's the way it is. I've made a commitment."

That was the second time he'd made a commitment without consulting anybody, and he said:

"What I want to do is wait a couple of weeks and then have a ceremony in Rickover Hall, which will be somewhat like the ones that Admiral Rickover has for his nuclear-powered submarines. That is, where he has the keel initialed with a welding outfit by the sponsor. What I want is to have him come down and have a ceremony, dedicate the building, and then have his initials actually welded into one of the main beams."

So I arranged a ceremony there where in the main lobby there was a big beam, vertical beam, where we had the ceremony performed. He came down in uniform. He said he didn't want to do it but if the secretary wanted him to do it he would do it. So he came down. He'd been recently remarried and he brought his wife down. Strangely enough, the day before he called me and said would I get out of the midshipmen's store a couple of little mementoes, things that midshipmen give to their girl friends, and have them there for him to give to his wife. He came down and he was absolutely charming all along, as was his wife, who was a commander in the Nurse Corps in uniform. He couldn't have been nicer or more pleasant. He had lunch in the dining hall with the midshipmen, made a short speech, and was cheered. He was very talkative and very nice. He went to the ceremony. He had his wife join him - we got two welding outfits with leather aprons, head gear, and so forth, and he had his wife help him to put his initials on this beam.

Then, later on, strangely enough, he asked me could

I send him up the welding outfits, the leather aprons and so forth and a copy of the plaque for his wife to have.

We also had him over to the quarters and talked to him a little while. He couldn't have been nicer and the ceremony was absolutely fine. So he did dedicate Rickover Hall. At one time, I think about the next week, (my wife got on with him very well always), we were at the secretary's house in Georgetown and we just happened to be in the receiving line with Admiral Rickover and Mrs. Rickover adjacent. We were talking and finally my wife said:

"Admiral we're very proud of the building that you dedicated named after you the other day." Admiral Rickover said:

"I'm not." And my wife said:

"I don't care whether you are or not. We are."

The conversation terminated and we got out of the receiving line and into the party and Admiral Rickover came up to my wife and was very charming. It just shows that occasionally you just have to talk up to Admiral Rickover and tell him what's what! He thinks my wife is just fine because she told him off!

But he always was, in a sense, a positive force because he couldn't touch me. The CNO had said that what I said would go and he always supported me and there was no problem. There were occasions when I had to do some pretty strong talking and tell him why we wouldn't do certain things. He was always after me to stop all kinds of recreational activity and just study. He said:

"Your midshipmen that I interview are not studying enough. They're only studying twenty hours a week and they ought to be studying one hundred." I said:

"Some of them are incapable of studying any longer hours and wouldn't even if we shut them in a dark room with just one light. They need certain other things to be naval officers and marine officers and aviators, and I'm not going to do what you want. I've got to do what my mission is, which is to produce submariners, some aviators, and to provide a general base for all the corps in the navy."

I had to argue this time and time again with him and eventually I won out.

Q: Again, it's interesting to observe that Steve Swartz, whom you may have known, he was a speechwriter for Admiral Zumwalt, is writing on Rickover and went and spent some time out in Chicago, where Rickover was born and grew up, and he was interested in this aspect of his opposition to athletics and so forth. He discovered that Rickover as a boy had an aversion to athletics because of his size and all that sort of thing. It was built into his youth. He didn't participate in baseball or anything of the sort.

Adm. M.: Occasionally I would invite him down as a routine

matter, to come down to a wrestling match or a football game, and his answer always was:

"Well, have they changed any of the rules since 1925?"

I said, no, so:

"Well, I saw a game in 1925 and if they haven't changed anything, I don't want to see it," and he'd hang up.

Conversations were always very dramatic. He would call up, not announce himself, say what he had to say, and then you'd say:

"Well, Admiral – " and he'd hang up. Sometimes you got a chance to answer, other times not. Sometimes I'd have to call back and say:

"Admiral, what you just said was wrong, and I'll give you the right answer and send it up to you on a piece of paper," then I'd hang up!

But we were always very friendly, very nice, and I admired him as a naval officer, and I think, as I said before, that he and Admiral Nimitz will be perhaps the two most honored naval officers of this half of this century.

Q: He seems to have lost the value of athletics as team work?

Adm. M.: To him there's no need for team work. All that team work or leadership consists of is having each man know his job so well that every other person will respect him and will do what he tells him to do because that man knows what's to be done. The fellow he's telling it to knows it's got to be done, so that's what team work is to him. No need for leadership. Just know your job better than anybody else in the world. There's a certain amount of logic to that, but there are times when it's not enough.

Perhaps another general subject to talk about there is race relations.

Q: Oh, yes, indeed.

Adm. M.: When I first arrived there were about twenty blacks in the entering class. I thought this was not correct, and, of course, Admiral Zumwalt's general philosophy was to get on with desegregation in the navy and do all you could to encourage the entrance of black officers and men and so forth, so I did that. I appointed in the Admissions Office a black officer, a superb officer, whose main job was recruiting minorities such as blacks, Indians, Chicanos, Aleuts, all the parts of American life.

As a result, the next year we brought in ninety black persons, all completely qualified and no question ever of letting down any bars or anything else, we just got every well-qualified person we could.

Mack #10 - 674

Q: How was this achieved through the appointive system?

Adm. M.: That was quite simple. We have many black congressmen and white congressmen who had black districts, who would have appointed candidates if they'd had qualified candidates presented to them. Our job was to go to black schools and so forth and to present the Naval Academy story and the navy story to potential candidates and get them to go over to their congressmen and ask for appointments. It was as simple as that, but it took a person who spoke the language of that particular group and who would know where to go and what to do. He did, and we did it, so we got a large number of candidates.

Also, the navy was getting favorable publicity in athletics and otherwise. As a result, we got ninety candidates. The next year it was down to about fifty-seven, but it's leveled off, I think, now to where we have a fine ongoing program. Also we cut out anything that could smack of discrimination in any way at the Naval Academy. I could soon see that we had problems. We were required by the Bureau of Personnel to present to each midshipman and member of the faculty and everybody else some fourteen hours a year of race-relations education. Then we were required to do something on drug abuse, on discrimination against women, safe driving. We had about ten programs which, when added up and put into the curriculum, would have taken a quarter of our time for midshipmen.

I tried to put all these together and find a common denominator in all of them, which was first you had to establish in the eyes of the midshipmen certain self-respect for himself, which was the key. If he had that certain self-respect, he would treat other people right, he wouldn't use drugs, he'd drive safely, and so forth. So, with the help of Chaplain John O'Connor, who was our senior chaplain, a Catholic chaplain, I put together a course that lasted four years and which, while it was not accredited academically at the start, was aimed at that eventually, called "The Professional Officer, a Human Person." What it did was hopefully to condense the thirty or so hours into about ten hours because if you taught a man once that he had to respect himself, whereas before we'd been doing the same sort of thing, teaching the same thing in all these five or six different programs, if we taught him once, then we expanded from that.

Q: It was all focused?

Adm. M.: Yes. We were also required then, since we had no requirement any more to go to chapel, to teach a certain amount about ethics, and teach not religion from the point of view of telling a man he should be religious, but teaching him something about religion so that as an officer if he went to a Moslem country, for instance, he would know what their rules were, what to say and do and not do, and if he went to Japan he knew something about Buddhism and Shintoism and so forth. We had to teach a certain amount of that, a little bit of it, and so this one course was aimed at, first, establishing in a man's mind that he was a worthwhile person. This is a very short way of describing something that took a major part of the course, and then teaching the things he should do, ethically, morally, in life. For instance, you respect other races and women and he should respect his own body and not use drugs, drive safely, and know the ethics and morals of other groups and the religion of other groups, so he wouldn't offend them and would treat them properly.

Q: Did this prove to be a difficult concept?

Adm. M.: Yes, it's hard to present this to midshipmen. It was hard to present it and require that instructors master this new course and use it, but it did its job and for, I guess, about three years we taught this.

Q: And this was done under the aegis of the chaplain?

Adm. M.: No, it was under the aegis of the commandant, and, of course, the chaplain comes under the commandant. He was required, like the superintendent, to train midshipmen and educate them mentally, morally, and physically, sort of amorals department, so to speak, but the commandant did it. Company officers and others under him in a professional section were the instructors. The chaplains and I and others who were involved in human relations put the course together, using the television studio we had, using Dr. Bauman, for instance, who is a well-known religious instructor in Washington, D.C., and many others, and we were able to use films, video tapes, and so forth from many libraries to put these courses together.

And we put together a textbook about four inches thick, an inch for each year. This was mimeograph paper so it wasn't all that long. It attracted a lot of attention. As a matter of fact, the Bureau of Naval Personnel came down, went through the course, took it, and used it for ROTC and parts of it for recruit training in other parts of the navy. So our course, in a sense, was used by a good many parts of the navy.

Q: In retrospect, how successful was it with the midshipmen?

Adm. M.: Well, my successor, Admiral McKee, tells me that what happened was he had to instead of making the course a credit academically, he had to use parts of it in leadership and so forth. He took the course and cut it up and put it into different parts of the curriculum. So it's not given as a single course any more, but the subject matter, the lectures and so forth are still there and are used, and it was very successful.

Q: I'd think that was watered down somewhat?

Adm. M.: It was.

Q: It lost its focus!

Adm. M.: But I think he was very careful not to make it duplicative. You don't want to teach a little bit of ethics here and the same thing in some other course. Corresponding sort of things, something that strengthens is all right, but don't teach the same thing. That's what we had been doing, we were teaching the same thing in about five or six different courses.

Q: There's something to be said for repetition, too.

Adm. M.: Right, but you can only repeat so much, though, then you run out of time. But it did create, I think, a much better climate racially and in many other ways, and certainly in preparation for women coming to the Naval Academy. I think it created a climate racially where the increasing number of blacks got along just fine. We never had any racial problems. West Point had lots of them. We never had a single racial problem. We, I think, educated and trained our midshipmen in time to accept the increasing numbers of black midshipmen.

Q: You mentioned earlier Aleuts and Indians and so forth. How many did you induce into the academy?

Adm. M.: I can't tell you the numbers, but you see the percentage of black in the country is 12 or 13 percent -

Q: Yes.

Adm. M.: We were often asked what kind of a quota did we have, and the asnwer was none, but we'll be happy when we get 12 percent of blacks at the Naval Academy. The percentage of Aleuts versus the percentage of others in the country is very small, but we had one or two, which is about the percentage it should have been. Chicanos we were somewhat below. We were never able to recruit many Chicanos. We also had, say, about twenty South Americans from various countries in South America.

Q: Now, they're being trained for their own navies?

Mack #10 - 680

Adm. M.: Yes. We had two Iranians, finally.

Q: Oh, no doubt!

Adm. M.: From Iran, but the percentage of minorities was never as high as we wanted it to be, except for some of the small groups.

Q: How do the South Americans fit into the educational picture?

Adm. M.: They have to meet the same requirements as everybody else, but not always very well. We had problems with lots of them. Some of them were political appointees who were pushed in by, say, the CNO of whatever South American navy who really weren't qualified and they didn't last very long. But it was always difficult because you didn't have a common denominator which, in this country, is the basic test, ACT or the basic college entrance board test, which we used.

Q: And the different cultures and backgrounds?

Adm. M.: Yes. For instance, they all take Spanish and get 4.0 but they wouldn't do very well in English. We found we had to bring them up early and put them in a family at the Naval Academy for a month or two so that they could learn idiomatic English, sometimes basic English, by being here for a month or two.

Q: Those were some of the problems that Admiral Rivero faced, a brilliant man like that, but he did have problems with his Latin background.

Adm. M.: Yes. Well, he never spoke perfect English even when he was a four-star admiral! But pretty close.

Q: You mentioned the Chicanos. It was simply that their background didn't permit them to qualify?

Adm. M.: That's right.

Another basic subject that you asked was I interested in and that was making sure that every midshipman who left the Naval Academy was professionally qualified. When I got there, they weren't, the accent had been on academics. I instituted a system where over the three years we improved the system of professional education and we found a method of testing for it.

Before I got there, of course, every midshipman passed navigation and passed seamanship, part of navigation, but his other professional qualifications were very nebulous. So I instituted a system where we listed all the professional requirements he should have. He had to know how to rig a ship to fuel and do this and do that, most of which he generally got on a cruise, if he were on a proper cruise ship, but if he didn't hit the right ship and went into submarines or his cruise ship didn't particularly do something, he never found out about these things, and he would go out to the real navy and the captain would ask him something he didn't know a thing about.

So we had to make a listing of all the things a midshipman should know when he graduated, professionally.

Q: How did you arrive at this? Simply based on your experience?

Adm. M.: Yes, plus we used our young officers who had just come back from the fleet and the commandant and others, which is another reason why you want to have professionally qualified officers on your faculty, and not just uninformed instructors, as they do at West Point.

The first year we assembled these requirements and told each midshipman he should be able to do all these when he left, and we made it, in a sense, voluntary. The second year, we made an examination, we tested him in his first-class year, after he'd come back from his first-class cruise, tested him in all these subjects. We did not require that he pass the examination. We gave him the results and said:

"Look, you don't know anything about this, this, and this. You'd better learn it before you go to the fleet and we will help you to learn it by having voluntary classes and so forth."

The third year, we made the test a requirement and passing it was a requirement. If he didn't pass it, he didn't graduate. He had remedial classes in first-class year where he could qualify in the things that he had not passed, so almost all midshipmen then were able to grasp the things that they had failed in or had not even been exposed to. The third year we were able to graduate midshipmen who could pass the professional requirements that we laid on them and we found that was fine, they could go to the fleet then, and they would know something about everything, even though they hadn't necessarily seen a ship fuel, they would have been exposed to it, instructed, and told about it. There were many other things. This is just one example.

Q: When you inaugurated it, what percentage were unable to pass it.

Adm. M.: I'd say about half lacked a complete professional education. So, if anything, this was one of the things I did to strengthen it. The first thing I did was to strengthen the science and mathematics curriculum a little bit, not too much to where we would fail large numbers of midshipmen, but enough so that we would certainly comply with the requirements of Admiral Rickover and also the requirements of the fleet for more professional training and more technically trained officers.

Then, the second big area I worked on was the professional business of getting every person professionally qualified.

The third area, which I did a lot on, I think, and saw as a challenge when I got there, was I didn't like the business of having plebes spend a lot of time memorizing silly stuff and doing things that did not contribute to their education. So for the three years, the two commandants that I had there and I changed slowly, not radically, plebe indoctrination, and with the help of the first class, not over the objections of the first class, we changed slowly the idea that anything a plebe was required to memorize, other than perhaps the menu for the day, would be professional. There'd be no silly stuff, "How's the cow, and how many panes of glass in this or that window and so forth." But a plebe could be required to know how many ships we had in the navy, how many destroyers, what aircraft, what are their characteristics, and so forth, so that when he went home he would have naval knowledge at his fingertips, and when he went home on leave he wouldn't appear to be non-naval.

We thought this was a good thing, to know about the navy. It's what he was doing for a profession and he ought to know something about it. The first class were enthusiastic. As a matter of fact, they had a program where the second class would take plebes in in the evening hour before study hour and actually instruct them. The second class were required to make up the curriculum and to teach the plebes all about ships and aircraft and so forth, so the second class learned something and the first class had the satisfaction of running something, and, in a sense, the pelbes were taught professional subjects. The upper class thought they were running the plebes, but they were enthusiastic. They cut out a lot of silly stuff and substituted for it professional ideas.

Q: I'm surprised that Admiral Calvert overlooked that point.

Adm. M.: Well, I don't know. He had a lot to do and he just never got to that.

Q: But it's just common sense.

Adm. M.: Of course, this met resistance. The first class

said they had to do all these things, why should these guys get away with it, and the answer we kept giving was:

"Well, what do you want to do? Do you want to sit still and do the same old thing? We'll let you have a little fun, but then let's get on this professional educational program."

Over the three years, that progressed to the point where, at the end of three years, there was none of the stuff that you hear about, except unofficially occasionally, but kids are kids and they have a lot of fun. I think they confined it to pep rallies and times when they could all have a little fun. But we finally got to the point where by the time academic year started, very little was done to the plebes. The first class were given charge:

"It's your responsibility to get the plebes in shape in plebe summer. Do it, and when plebe summer's over they should be having their noses in books."

And that's what happened. The first class took responsibility for making sure plebes had time to study, that they had their lessons done, got good marks, and if a guy didn't have passing marks as a plebe, the first class were all over him, because we said that the mark of their leadership as platoon leaders is that your platoon is sat, and if you have a bunch of unsat plebes we're going to find out why. If it's because they didn't have time to study, you're going to answer for it. So we put in the leadership system some responsibility for the first class to take care of the plebes, not just to treat them like a bunch of second-raters, but to educate them, to make them part of the brigade, and so forth, and I think it worked a lot better than it used to work.

Q: It's certainly related to what you were talking about earlier, the course in ethical standards and human reactions.

Adm. M.: So I think perhaps these are the three things that I spent most of my time on, and achieved some advancement.

Q: They were certainly innovative, weren't they? Did other academies have anything similar, had they developed anything similar?

Adm. M.: Yes and no. West Point, I would say, does very little in terms of professional education. I just can't understand West Point. They still go by the ideas of Thayer that when you go to class you're supposed to memorize a section of the text and go and recite it every day, and that's that. You do it that day and you forget about it. Whereas the Naval Academy goes on the theory that you're taking a course and you take an exam at the end of it, but that you should have a certain amount of initiative in the speed at which you study and how deeply you go into certain parts and so forth. There shouldn't be absolute control every minute, which is the theory at West Point. I don't think they have very much professional education when they leave. I know they don't, because they go on to various basic schools of one kind and another to learn.

Q: Well, they have more time for this?

Adm. M.: Oh, yes, because that's all they do. The basic difference between the army and the navy is that the navy operates ships all the time, and the army simply finds things to keep people occupied. They don't do much. At the end of the day, they can walk away, they might post a couple of sentries, but they walk away from what they're doing, other than perhaps locking up a tank, and that's all they do. Well, a ship steams day and night, even in port it steams, so the navy is always doing something with the equipment it has. Even an airplane has got to be inspected when you get through with it. But the army is unique in the sense that they spend their lives educating and training themselves and finding things to do just to keep people busy. A squad leader learns to be a squad leader and after that he can train to be something a little bit higher than that, but generally their problem is just keeping people occupied, whereas the navy's problem is keeping ships up. You've always got to scrape and paint something or repair it or grease something in order to get it ready for the next day.

So a naval officer, a naval person, is busy keeping his equipment up, and the army is just busy doing something to keep themselves occupied. This carries over to West Point. They don't try to make a finished army officer when he leaves there. We do. We try to make a person who can be what we call an instant naval officer. When he steps aboard that destroyer, he's supposed to be able to take a job and do it, not deftly, but certainly well enough to learn on the job and be a good one.

Q: And the Air Force Academy falls in between the two, doesn't it?

Adm. M.: Yes, they're halfway between. There again, the pilot brings the airplane back on a wide runway, a long runway, and it needs skill to do that, he gets out of his airplane and the crew takes over, and that's all he does. He may go back and inspect it but he has lots of riding time in an airplane interspersed with nothing. The Naval Academy guy brings his airplane back to the carrier and he might stand a watch the next day on the ship. He's supposed to be mastering the ship at the same time he's mastering his airplane because he doesn't expect always to be a pilot. So it's quite a different philosophy.

Q: To go back to my question. Did they inaugurate any courses or any directions such as you indicated at the Naval Academy?

Adm. M.: Yes, they did. We presented to them our course and General Berry, who was superintendent at the time, was very impressed with it and he used certain parts of it at West Point. The Air Force Academy did not. They thought they had a system of their own that was good, so they didn't care for it.

Q: What about the Coast Guard Academy?

Adm. M.: They looked at it, took it off, and I never heard what they had done about it.

Another general area of difference is the honor systems. We had many arguments with West Point over this. Our system says a midshipman will not lie, cheat, or steal, and that a midshipman who finds another midshipman doing one of these three things can either ignore it, in which case he brings discredit upon himself and the brigade, he can counsel the person who's doing it, and then he can either report him or not report him. Of course, if he doesn't report him, he's expected to counsel him or do whatever is necessary to see that he doesn't do it again. The idea being, again, that at the Naval Academy we're required to teach midshipmen mentally, morally, and physically, this being a way of teaching morals, that is not to cheat, lie, or steal. You get many young men coming in and that's a way of life where they've come from. They don't know the difference. You can't expect instant morality in a plebe. So with the idea of having some flexibility in the area, if a first-classman catches a plebe in an act that he thinks borders on lying, cheating, or stealing, he may say "That's wrong, you should never do it again. I'll watch you very carefully," and he'll spread the word around his classmates to see if that plebe can be salvaged. Stealing is very seldom tolerated, but lies sometimes get very close for a plebe. You don't know whether he's telling the truth, telling a lie deliberately, or whether it's part of something he thinks is funny or whatever. In other words, it's not cut and dried, so the upper class has to have some authority, we thought, and flexibility to determine what's going on and to tell the plebes what to do, and they should have a certain period in which they're being indoctrinated in this sort of thing and brought into the brigade.

A first-classman who lies, cheats, or steals, of course, always, there's no question, he's out. By that time, he should have learned this thing and that's it.

Q: He's had four years to -

Adm. M.: Yes. That was always our philosophy. Now, at West Point, they're very inflexible. They say that one man catching another in any one of these three acts has no alternative but to report him to the system, and so they have lots of honor courts and lots of things happen that shouldn't happen. The officers, in a sense, administer the honor courts much more closely than ours, so what you have is a bunch of cadets reporting things to officers who then do the administration and they throw cadets out willy-nilly for very small things sometimes, which are not really right.

We always had this argument with West Point. That's the wrong way to do it, you should have flexibility.

Q: Those standards might have been acceptable when among the civilian population there were standards, which we don't have now.

Adm. M.: I don't know how many years ago there were. Perhaps in General MacArthur's time, who established the

West Point system, but we found in our research that very few universities, for instance, Princeton, Virginia, and so forth, Notre Dame, which have honor systems, they always have some system where you can judge whether this was a real dereliction or not. West Point has very little judgment at all. We just thought our system was the best.

Q: Well, it relates to the point you made last time about the breakdown in the family because this is where a lot of this training would have come.

Adm. M.: Our system was established maybe twenty years ago by midshipmen, and they administer their own system, they change their own system. They like the one we have and the administration liked it because we thought it was right. West Point's was established by General MacArthur, inflexible, typically - if I may say so - army style. I used to argue with General Berry, saying:

"Well, if General MacArthur established this and you like it, what do you think of General MacArthur? What did he to in his career? Was he a product of it as well as being the author of it? What do you think about his lies, because we know he did? Is that wrong or right? How do you hold him up" - he kept holding him up as an example - "as an example to the cadets? You'd better be careful because the cadets have enough sense of history to read and see what happened, and they'll know as soon as they do that General MacArthur lied repeatedly in his career. Not little lies. He wouldn't lie to another person, another officer, but he lied to his president, he lied to the press, he lied to the American people, Filipino people. There's a complete concrete evidence that this happened. What do you do? Is it the scale on which you lie? You can tell a big lie but not a small one, is that an honor system? We don't teach that in our place, we teach something different."

As a result of the things I'm talking about, I come to, I think, the general subject, which was that there was formed by the Secretary of Defense during my time here a committee for education. The idea was basically sound. It was headed by the Deputy Secretary of Defense, Mr. Clements, who could see that the secretaries of the services and defense didn't know enough about the academies to be able to answer questions from Congress when they suddenly came up about the honor system or education or one thing and another. So this committee was formed of the services secretaries and the assistant secretary of defense for manpower and reserve affairs. It had initially as its secretary Colonel Dawkins, an army officer.

Q: Did this occur about the same time West Point had its great difficulty?

Adm. M.: No, this was before, in my second year. He formed a committee. He announced that he and the committee would visit the three academies twice and then after they'd been briefed and so forth they would sit down and determine what to do.

Colonel Dawkins was very instrumental, I guess, in making sure that West Point was visited first, then the Air Force Academy, and then, strangely enough, they came to our institution and were just beginning to be briefed in the morning when suddenly Mr. Clements was called back to Washington. He was there only two hours. There was no time for discussion. We were just getting to the essentials of a simple briefing. So that visit was never concluded.

Then he went to West Point again and the Air Force Academy again and about that time Commander Fitzgerald was added to the secretariat, which began to give the naval side of it some entree but not too much. Meantime what was happening was that Colonel Dawkins and West Point were completely influencing Mr. Clements's ideas. Our secretary, then Mr. Middendorf, didn't seem to be much interested in what was going on. When we did have our meetings, he would never take our side, he would never make any points in our favor, but Secretary Calloway, the army secretary, strangely enough, took our side all the time. He was a very fair person and he spoke up when somebody would talk about West Point being right and the navy being wrong. He'd say:

Mack #10 - 696

"No, I don't see it that way. These are the facts," and he'd make very good points.

So down toward the end of the time when it became time for us to be visited the second time, it was evident that Mr. Clements was making up his mind on many subjects and was having the results written out by Colonel Dawkins and the subjects were such things as honor, curriculum, administration, budget, and so forth, and that he had many ideas that were completely inaccurate and some that were just impossible. For instance, he wanted us to adopt the West Point system of honor. He said ours was no good, we shouldn't give midshipmen any flexibility, and West Point was absolutely right.

Q: Did he document this?

Adm. M.: No, that was just written as his opinion.

He wanted us to change our curriculum to that of West Point, with much more basic subjects, logic, philosophy, rhetoric, and so forth, and to cut down our engineering curriculum, and we, of course, couldn't do that. He wanted us to have a system of recitation like West Point, the Thayer system, instead of the way we ran things. He wanted us to cut down the number of civilian faculty and increase the number of officer faculty, which we've long said is not right. We don't want an officer teaching physics who has a master's degree in physics. We want a person teaching it who's a qualified civilian with a doctor's degree, who's had experience in it. These complicated subjects should be taught by well-qualified, professional professors. West Point would have these regular army officers who had a doctor's degree in physics all right, but they were just out of West Point and that's all they knew, and they were teaching physics. We didn't think that was right.

He wanted us to have many more uniformed instructors and fewer civilian instructors. We protested that there was no source of them in the navy. So he was going to require the navy to send many more officers to postgraduate schools to achieve the degrees they would need to teach at the Naval Academy.

There were several other ideas like this that we were presented with but never had a chance to refute. These had been put forward by West Point and the Air Force Academy.

Finally he did come down with his committee to the Naval Academy for our so-called second visit. It took us most of the day. We achieved, I think, most of what we wanted. For instance, we had a presentation on the honor code by me, by the commandant, and by a group of midshipmen who came over and helped carry the day. We at least persuaded him not to make us take on the West

Point system of honor. He slacked off his requirements somewhat for officer instructors, which was all right with us because BuPers couldn't find them, anyway, they didn't exist. So if he wanted to make a policy, it would be six or eight years before the navy could educate enough officers to take over uniformed instructor positions.

We were able to present to him some of the courses we had in different terms, once we could get his ear and show him that these courses were better than West Point's, and during the day finally he fell off many of his positions, the ones we wanted him to fall off on, at least. The ones he didn't fall off on were such that nothing could be done, anyway, such as the one about more instructors.

Q: Did he have qualified people on his committee?

Adm. M.: No, the committee was simply the three secretaries, himself, and Colonel Dawkins, who pushed the West Point version of everything. It was not until we got Commander Fitzgerald on the committee that we even began to find out what he was thinking about what he wanted done. Fitzgerald was able to act as our liaison and go back to him and begin to disabuse him of some of these ideas that Colonel Dawkins had given him, and to warn us what to present when he came down. That's why we were able to salvage what we did. Eventually, we were able to to live with what he decided he was going to do. He backed off on all positions that we thought were really untenable. So, in the end, we prevailed, if not without a lot of hard work.

What happened very soon after that was the West Point cheating scandal, after which West Point eventually decided to come around and use our honor system. So we were vindicated as far as the honor systems were concerned.

Q: Let me ask a more general question. This cursory kind of study of a situation, did it happen very often in the government?

Adm. M.: No.

Q: I mean to make recommendations that are of lasting import?

Adm. M.: Well, the initial concept of what he knew was sound, which was to make sure the service secretaries and himself were all well informed about the academies.

Q: Well, that's one thing.

Adm. M.: If he'd stuck to that, it would have been just fine. We would have informed the hell out of him. But he took it upon himself, as he got informed, the idea that some of the things that were being done should be done a different way.

I say again that what had happened was that Mr. Clements had visited the two academies on four different occasions and only visited our academy for about two to three hours, during which time he had very little information. So he had had a period of almost nine months where Colonel Dawkins was the only person who got to him on the subject and where the other academies twice had briefed him on their way of doing things. Of course, he saw their point of view because he didn't have ours, and I must say that when he finally was presented with our point of view he began to realize that he had made mistakes, or almost made mistakes, and backed off on many of the positions he had taken.

Again, Secretary Calloway was one of our strongest supporters. He said he thought West Point ought to change its honor system to be like that of the Naval Academy. Mr. Middendorf didn't say anything.

Q: I wonder if Admiral Moorer was helpful in this situation?

Adm. M.: No, he was not involved in any way.

Q: He was so very close to Clements as a friend.

Adm. M.: I think we could have enlisted him, had we needed him, but I felt I could carry it, and I did, as soon as I could have a chance to talk to Mr. Clements and brief him and tell him our position. Our position was actually sound, and as soon as he got the position, why, he saw that it was sound, and, as I say, in the case of the honor system, it was proved to him very shortly that West Point's was unsound, and West Point has since changed their system to be much like ours. They liked our system when they sat down and listened to it.

Q: It certainly looks like a more modern system!

Adm. M.: Well, it is. You see, it's so simple. The army is always looking for simple systems because their job generally is administrative, a lot of average people, and they need simple, sound rules that will govern a lot of average people during a big war. They draft a lot of people and bring them in. The navy's different. We try to do things the most efficient way, and if not the most efficient way, at least a way that's flexible. That's what our honor system was. It was flexible but it required people to think and make decisions. That's what we're trying to train our men to do. A naval officer has to think and make decisions. An army officer not so much. The army is run by rote, particularly when it's mobilized in wartime. A whole lot of second lieutenants, first lieutenants, and people who have to have rules and be told to do them because it's a big organization and it grows so fast that it has to be run by rules. The navy is not that way. The navy sends ships out and airplanes out where they have officers and men who have to make their own decisions, so we have to start early, at the Naval Academy and other places, and teach them to make decisions. The important thing is not exactly how honest somebody was, but is somebody else going to assess that and make a judgment and a decision. This is what we want. We want to train them morally. We want the first class to be involved. How can you train a midshipmen who lives by rote, absolute rote on the honor system, then send him out to the navy to be a naval officer and expect him to make a judgment the next day? We want him to make judgments as a midshipman, where we can supervise him, train him, and educate him, show him what he's done wrong, what he's done right, and that's what we do. We try to make the Naval Academy as much like real life as possible, and not like some monastic existence which a West Pointer leads. Admiral Rickover always used to criticize the honor system. One of the things we told him was, "You don't have any honor system out in the fleet." Admiral Rickover kept saying:

"Why do you have an honor system? When they get out in the fleet, they have to be honest out there."

I said: "Wait a minute, Admiral. There's nothing in the fleet that remotely resembles an honor system. In the fleet you may lie, except you cannot make a dishonest official statement. There are certain statements that you can't make, but you can lie to a shipmate, you can lie to the captain, if you want to, if it's something that's not an official matter. You can steal, but that's illegal. You can cheat. It happens every day. There's no law against cheating in the navy."

He was astounded. He said, "Well, they don't do that."

I said, "You'd better take a look, Admiral. It's done every day. What we're telling our midshipmen is that you have a much higher standard here as a midshipman than you'll ever have in the fleet. You should take this standard with you and make it your own personal standard. Don't you ever lie, cheat, or steal. You're cheating yourself, if you do. But remember in that ship there will be officers from ROTC, OCS, and enlisted men who have no concept whatsoever of the honor system, and it's only as good as you make it. You're an example, you have to indoctrinate these other people and make sure that the navy is a good place to be. But Admiral Rickover would never believe this, but finally I think I convinced him.

Q: But he'd served in the fleet?

Adm. M.: Well, he didn't remember. Back in the old days, you see, every officer was a Naval Academy graduate, but they had not been subject to any honor system. You couldn't lie, cheat, or steal from your classmates because, if you did, they'd take it out of your hide. The only system there you had was the company officers administering midshipmen. The midshipman officers had no responsibility. It was between you and the officer, that was it. If you made a false statement and got caught at it, that was too bad, but a lot of people did it all the time. There wasn't any honor concept in the old days. It was a cops and robbers sort of thing. It's only today we have a real honor system where you expect a midshipman to be honest, no matter whether somebody's over him or not. The only difference is we make ours flexible enough so that you can train people, and you don't do it just by rote, to differentiate from West Point. And I think that's good because that's the way the navy is. It's not a rote service. They are geared to mobilization, when you bring in thousands of people. Their system has to train its present officers and present men to take care of that system. We're not that way. We may expand but generally when we start fighting, our ships and aircraft fight right now. We have to be ready to fight any day. Not so the army.

So there's a difference and that's why the difference in philosophy in the way we train and educate a midshipman.

Mack #11 - 706

Interview #11 with Vice Admiral William P. Mack, U.S. Navy
(Retired)

Place: His residence in Annapolis, Maryland

Date: Monday morning, 14 May 1979

Subject: Biography

By: John T. Mason, Jr.

Q: Well, it's great to be with you again today and to hear a continuation of your story on the Naval Academy, when you were there as superintendent. Do you want to take up the cudgels at this point?

Adm. M.: Thank you, Jack. I would like to add a little bit about the course we talked about, "The Professional Officer and the Human Person," which was, I think, a creature of the superintendent and Captain O'Connor. I saw the need for it and put Captain O'Connor, who was the senior chaplain at the Naval Academy, to work on the text that I wanted, and tasked the commandant and others in whose area it fell to get with the program and do it. And we did put together a very fine course that lasted for four years. That is, each midshipman took that course for four years. It was not for credit. We were going to work toward credit, and it was essentially a lecture seminar series. When it was finished we showed this to West Point administration, the Air Force Academy administration, the NROTC administration, BuPers, and the chief of Education and Training's office, and to the Officer Candidate School staff, and it was used in some form by all of them except the Air Force Academy, and again I'll say at West Point.

We taught this course for two years. Each year it got better. The lectures became more professional, we were able to find better video tapes to put in the various course segments, and it became part of the curriculum, except, again, it was not a credited course. I understand Admiral McKee, who succeeded me, because of the pressure of perhaps Admiral Rickover, the chief of naval personnel, and others in the CNET chain, felt that he had to take the time that we'd used for this course to beef up the areas concerning science and engineering basically to make every midshipman, regardless of what he was doing or what he was going to do in the future, take differential equations and, in a sense, also make him take one more technical course.

Therefore, the course was put in the background and the parts of it that were necessary were put in the leadership areas and other parts of the curriculum.

I recently talked with Admiral Lawrence, who succeeded Admiral McKee, and note that Admiral Lawrence was a prisoner of war, said that he, after reviewing the Naval Academy's administration, curriculum, and method of doing business for several months, now had decided that what was needed in the way of a change was to concentrate emphasis on ethics, morals, religion in the sense that the midshipmen knew something of the religions of the world, not necessarily to be counseled on one particular religion, and, of course, various elements of leadership.

This corresponds so closely to the requirements I had foreseen, which required the POHP courses to be put together, that I was amazed to find he was going back again in the same direction that I had pursued. He thought perhaps this was because he'd been a prisoner of war and recognized the extreme importance of human elements rather than engineering and science elements in a naval officer's career. He felt that, first, the midshipmen had to be able to do anything that required strength of character, an ethics and morals base for his daily living, and if he had a strong base, then he could do anything. The requirements for engineering or mathematics or science could be met if you had the base on which to learn and a base on which to conduct your daily life, and, more important, a base from which to conduct leadership and your relations with other people, particularly the men under you.

So I was, in a sense, happy to see that Admiral Lawrence was going back toward this path which I'd started some years ago.

Q: It certainly is a fortunate thing to have a former prisoner of war add an element to the training of young officers.

Adm. M.: Yes. This, as I'm sure everyone knows, is an element in the navy now. There were many officer prisoners of war, mostly pilots, of course, in Vietnam. As a matter of fact, this is perhaps one of the most popular elements in the navy in the sense that more was done and said about POWs than about those who actually did the bomb-dropping and the rest of the war, and it's quite proper that this should be.

There was quite a publicity campaign when the POWs were brought home. They were looked at carefully, their careers in the POW camps searched minutely to find out how they behaved, and it was found that they had behaved magnificently, Admiral Stockdale, Admiral Lawrence, and Admiral Denton being three cases in point. In a sense, when one thinks about the war, the POW experience is what really comes to your mind first.

So this war introduced a new element, whereas in Korea no POW really resisted the Koreans and most of the POWs in the Korean War were young army enlisted men who were mostly draftees. In the Vietnamese War, it was quite different. Almost all the POWs were officers, pilots, all but a large majority. There were some marines and soldiers taken in ground fighting, but most of the POWs were officers, many of whom were Naval Academy graduates. This gave a strong leadership flavor to the POW experience in the war and showed what leadership could do.

Q: Certainly we did learn, however, from the experience of men in the Korean War who were taken captive, did we not?

Adm. M.: Yes, we did.

Q: And we learned from Turks who were taken captive.

Adm. M.: Exactly, and fortunately one of the things we learned from Korea was that no man could resist and no man ever did resist brainwashing, torture, and so forth, not a single person, General Dean included, not a single person resisted completely in the Korean War. I knew this because I was involved in briefing the secretary of defense on this issue and in formulating new POW policy when I was working in the Defense Department. So I was required to look at the records of all those in the Korean War and all those we knew about in the Vietnamese War, and we found that in Vietnam they were not holding up, either.

Q: But they still didn't succeed in breaking them completely?

Adm. M.: No, they didn't, but of course the question is what is breaking completely. To violate the old Geneva Convention system, which says simply name, serial number, and so forth, was violated by everybody, and our policy was changed so that that was not our policy any more.

Q: To break them completely would be to be completely subservient from then on?

Adm. M.: But, if you look back, you'll remember the incidents where some of our best POWs bowed before the cameras and made certain statements obviously to mislead the Vietnamese, but they did certain things that, theoretically, they were not required to do by the Geneva Convention.

So, how ever you want to put it, they did violate the so-called regulations. Now, did they break? The answer is probably not, in our eyes at least, not in the navy's eyes.

Q: They were able to resummon their energies and meet another onslaught?

Adm. M.: Exactly. In other words, the total experience of the POWs was outstanding, and the Naval Academy honored those POWs always. They had a pew set aside for missing in action and POWs, which became a missing-in-action pew when the POWs came back. We had campaigns for raising funds for the families, we honored them with parades when they came back, we had a place set aside with the names of all the academy graduates' names were displayed. In other words, the POWs' experience was made part of the midshipmen's experience, and we used this when the war was over to explain to the midshipmen why we were trying to strengthen them morally, ethically, and give them a strong religious base so that they would have this kind of a base from which to fight in case they were POWs. Our POWs coming back had reported that the Naval Academy training was one of the best things they had which made them able to resist their captors, not just the training but the strong moral and religious and ethical base that they were given at the Naval Academy was a great help to them.

So we turned this around and said this was the reason why we were going forward and making our own course longer and stronger.

Q: I think it's worthwhile noting the fact that the prisoners of war themselves gave the navy exceedingly high marks for the treatment they received when they came back, easing them back into society, and that sort of thing.

Adm. M.: As a matter of fact, we had an outstanding prisoner of war, ex-prisoner of war, Commander Jack Fellowes, whom I had met at the parade in Norfolk when he was one of the guests at the parade as a returning POW. Then it was proposed that he be sent to the Naval Academy and it was difficult to accept him in the sense that he did not have the teaching expertise that others had and he had health problems and so forth. I arranged to accept him as an instructor at the Naval Academy and gave him the kinds of jobs that would allow him to develop his instructive techniques, expand his knowledge from which to instruct, and also to bring his physical condition back to normal. He came to the Naval Academy and was an outstanding person. He was almost worshipped by the midshipmen, and he gave lectures continuously, three or four a week, on his POW experiences. He liked the midshipmen and they liked him. Finally, he became a football representative. He was a good influence at the academy.

Q: Yes, that was a very happy thing that he went off to do athletics because he has great enthusiasm for that.

Adm. M.: Exactly, and I tried to find a place for him where he would use his leadership abilities and not be handicapped by his lack of academic credentials, and it turned out to be a very fortunate experience to have him there.

So the POW experience totally was good for the Naval Academy, the midshipmen, and it did help us with the POHP course.

Q: Let me ask about that course as it was fragmented under Admiral McKee. What about the standing requirement from HEW, which you cited last time, for so many hours on race relations and that sort of thing, how did that fall into the situation?

Adm. M.: As a matter of fact, that was one of the reasons he put it back into the regular curriculum, essentially back in the regular curriculum, because that requirement was eased. Whereas it was fourteen hours per year, it was eased to be less than fourteen hours for the first-year students, and the Naval Academy could meet that requirement for the plebes during plebe summer mostly for racial indoctrination and so forth, and that helped him to make the decision to put it back in.

My philosophy always was, and I'm sure Chaplain O'Connor's was, that basically what requires you to be proper in your conduct racially is the same that requires you to be proper in your conduct toward any person, any women, any other minority, any person less fortunate than you, and so forth. You had to establish your own base of

Mack #11 - 715

identification and confidence that your personality was good and was going to stay that way, and if you were confident in yourself then you would be able to accept other people who were less fortunate than you and not discriminate against them. One reason people discriminate is because they're trying to push their way up and push the other person down. Historically, this is the way it's been in this country.

We thought if we could establish the midshipmen's sense of being recognized in their own worth that would be a base from which they could operate and they would not discriminate as much.

Q: In that course, you, as superintendent, must certainly have foreseen the coming of women to the academy and it happened right after you left -

Adm. M.: Yes.

Q: Did you have them put any particular emphasis on that aspect of things?

Q: No, except to say that women totally or men in minority groups, such as blacks or eskimos, or Swedes or Japanese, or anybody else who was not in their peer group, was in a sense a minority. That's what a minority is, of course, the lesser of two groups in size or strength, and women were in this same category and the same reasons should hold true for treating, say, blacks properly that would hold for treating women properly. We emphasized this. Women were mentioned frequently in this context of being a minority, that you should treat properly, and I think, if that were so, there'd be no reason why midshipmen as a group couldn't accept women as part of their group. In that sense, we did prepare midshipmen for what was going to happen but we didn't take a whole course on how you should treat women equally and so forth. Women were one of the minorities that you would treat properly if you had your own strong moral and ethical base.

Q: Well, it certainly worked out when they came because the upper classmen who were there when you were there received them fairly well, didn't they?

Adm. M.: Yes, they did. I was surprised. I'm not surprised either, or I should not have been surprised because we tried to prepare for it, and I think that's the way it came out.

With regard to women at the Naval Academy perhaps this is the time to set forth what happened in this area.

For a long time prior to the acceptance of women at the Naval Academy, perhaps a year or two, there was a drive or a push from women's groups and other areas to require the Defense Department to send women to the Naval Academy and to any other school that they'd been excluded from, such as pilot school. Of course, they had been to OCS schools, ROTC, and so forth.

The navy's position was that there was a law that prevented women from going to sea in combatant ships and aircraft, therefore it did not make sense for the Naval Academy to be used for women if they couldn't fill this kind of billet at sea, because you could train them in ROTC and OCS areas sufficiently to do the kinds of jobs they were allowed to fill.

Q: And not take a billet from -

Adm. M.: Yes. Further, the Naval Academy was a fixed size. In other words, there are 4,300 bunks, instructor billets for that number of midshipmen, that number of seats in the messhall, and so forth, and you could not expand the Naval Academy very much without overcrowding it. The problem was that if you took in women you'd have to cut out a corresponding number of men, which meant that in the end, when they graduated, you would have that many fewer men available to go to navy and marine billets, because the women couldn't go to these billets because they were prevented from going there by law.

This was the rationale we used. I appeared before Congress on many occasions, the House Armed Services Committee, to testify to this effect, and just before the series of legislative maneuvers was made which allowed women to come in, I appeared and so testified. Apparently, I thought this was received properly. I kept saying "if you want us to take women in, you have to do only one thing, that is repeal the law which prevents them from going to sea in combatant ships and aircraft."

Q: Which they didn't do.

Adm. M.: They did not. Congressman Sam Stratton conducted an end run and put the requirement for women at the Naval Academy as a rider on a bill and it passed. The House Armed Services Committee did not approve it. Usually, of course, any legislation like this has got to be approved by the House Armed Services Committee. He end ran the House Armed Services Committee and did this directly which, of course, made him in great disfavor with the House Armed Services Committee, but he did it.

Q: We might add as a footnote that it was rumored at the time that he was planning to run for senator in New York?

Adm. M.: Yes, and we all thought he did it as a political

gesture because he told me privately he didn't believe this was what should happen, but he did it, so it happened.

In the meantime, thinking something like this might happen, the Naval Academy had been preparing for women. Essentially the plan we prepared ended up by being carried out. We had thought that we would do a minor amount of change to Bancroft Hall. Perhaps we could put commodes in a room and put two or three women in a room and that would obviate the requirement for putting entire head areas for them, particularly in the first year or so when there would only be eighty or ninety women there. In the end, I think this was changed a little bit and certain head areas were set aside for women with hair dryers and all that sort of thing. But essentially, our first plan went well and it was carried out.

We foresaw that we would have to make some uniform changes, some changes in the athletic requirements, physical training requirements, really, such as doing hangs under the bar instead of pullups and that sort of thing, and that we'd have some changes in the sports area to make. We were prepared to make these and they were made roughly as planned, so that when the event happened it was not very difficult to carry out because we had planned for it and we had thought that something would happen that would require us to take women in, even though we thought that the Congress would have to change the law as they should have done. Of course, now, several years later, they're again contemplating changing the law and perhaps will change it. In the meantime, the navy's had to suffer for it and the women suffer because, as we pointed out, I pointed out in my testimony, the Congress has done them an injustice. They have required that we take women into the Naval Academy and give them the same education as men and give them the same chance at promotion and so forth, yet they deny the Navy the authority to send them to sea where they were going to learn what they had to learn about the elements of their profession so they could be promoted fairly. In other words, they'd given the Navy something to do which it couldn't carry out -

Q: You mean the summer cruises?

Adm. M.: Yes - if they couldn't go on a summer cruise they would not be equally educated and trained, and when they came to take their exams later on as officers and so forth they would suffer correspondingly with men because they had less professional training.

Q: What reaction was there to that logic?

Adm. M.: Oh, nothing. They all nodded their heads and said yes, that's right, and went right ahead and passed the law. Congress has no collective responsibility, really, just a lot of people, each one saying yes, that's right, and when it comes time to vote they forget about this sort of thing and just blithely do something like this, putting the superintendent of the Naval Academy in an untenable and impossible position.

Perhaps now, as the first woman midshipman is about to go to sea, they will change the law to allow the navy to put women in combatant aircraft and ships. As superintendent, I tried to do all I could to get around this by planning to put them in YPs and otherwise getting them to sea as much as could be done without violating the law, hoping that by -

Q: Can they serve in auxiliaries?

Adm. M.: Oh, yes, tugs and that sort of thing. Certain tenders have been set aside where they have room to go. These are not combatant ships, except in one sense, so they can go to a tender.

Q: And I was going to say they could learn to refuel ships?

Adm. M.: Yes.

At any rate, we prepared for the advent of women, and

I think the actual advent was quite calm, properly done, everything went off all right. In the meantime, the superintendent was in a bit of a bind because he was required to do something he couldn't do, which is not unusual.

Q: Now perhaps there should be an addendum on your remarks last time on the curriculum and the tightening up that you did in that area.

I recall, a year or so ago, having lunch with Charlie Duncan and he was serving and I think he still does on a Department of Defense committee studying the curriculum in various academies and so forth, and he was very concerned about the Naval Academy. He thought the tendency, and apparently the committee did, too, was to go back sort of toward a trade-school status.

Adm. M.: I wouldn't think this is so. As a matter of fact, I think it's exactly the opposite. We have not, did not, push what you might call trade-school courses. What we were trying to do was increase the academic disciplines in, we'll say, mathematics and physics, which is the basic sort of thing that you get in any university system and your undergraduate college leading to graduate areas in that same university system. We didn't push things such as the mechanics of missilery or seamanship and navigation. Those courses are fairly routine and we didn't increase these at all. It was never contemplated that we do so.

What we tried to do was to increase the efficiency and the depth of teaching in those courses that would lead midshipmen eventually when they became officers into the graduate areas where he would be competent to deal with his equals, his peers, from other systems. In other words, if a person took physics at Princeton and then went on to, we'll say, the aeronautical engineering school at Princeton, he would not be a giant step ahead of the Naval Academy graduate, as he used to be. As a matter of fact, it used to be that midshipmen had to go out to Monterey for at least a year, which was a disguised way of bringing their Naval Academy education up to the level of their university peers, so they could compete and stay in the same class with a young person from CalTech or Princeton or somewhere else. All we were trying to do was so increase the efficiency and the depth of teaching in these basic academic subjects which were not trade-school subjects at all, mostly differential equations and mathematics and teaching physics, using differential equations, which you can do and should do, and preparing the midshipman so that technically he could get into the same academic areas with people coming in from other areas into the graduate-school system.

As a matter of fact, we began to downgrade such things as ocean engineering and other kinds of courses where the major courses really were trade-school-type things.

Admiral Rickover had been after us for years to abolish completely oceanography as a major, as a general area of teaching. I resisted this and said that we were going to change oceanography somewhat to get away from the hardware and mechanics aspects of oceanography but study of the ocean areas was an area certainly for a naval officer to be expert in. You don't have to know exactly about some of the mechanics of it but the general principles of underwater physics and so forth are extremely important for a naval officer.

Q: I would think it would be for a submariner, too?

Adm. M.: Absolutely. So he never prevailed and although we did bring oceanography down in numbers, lesser numbers of students took oceanography as a major, and we did tighten up the curriculum and make it much more difficult and add differential equations again to that part of the curriculum, we never did away with it, as a major.

Q: There was a high pitch of interest in that area in 1970.

Adm. M.: Exactly, Management was another area in which he always wanted us to abolish the complete curriculum. I refused here because there was a need for management in the navy and, quite frankly, it was an area where midshipman who could not quite cope with the high-level technical aspects of physics, advanced physics, or that sort of thing leading to perhaps a more technically oriented midshipman, you had to have a place for some of them. In other words, you cannot produce in this country 4,000 young men who can deal with the complexity of advanced physics. There aren't that many young men that you can get in the Naval Academy. Rickover's idea was, well, if they aren't, throw them out, and my answer was, "Well, I can't do that. I'm required to produce so many naval officers and marine officers in particular every year. There must be some course where they can, in a sense, get through. Not lowering the standards for graduation by giving them some areas where they can cope with the difficulties of academia and get out, graduate."

So, we did need some areas like this -

Q: Was there any input because of your own personal experience in the navy when you served as Chinfo and when you served as liaison with the Hill and discovered the necessity for knowledge of this sort on the part of a naval officer? Was there any input into the curriculum in your time?

Adm. M.: I felt I'd gone through the technical revolution, I suppose, where my first experience of the navy was a four-stacker which was a Model T Ford type of ships with very little in the way of technical requirements and a lot in the way of leadership and personal athletic ability, in other words, being able to conn a ship, withstand the pounding of it, and so forth, and the dirty sorts of things was very important. I'd gone through this and by the end of the war a destroyer was an extremely technical piece of machinery with sonar, radar, electronic warfare, and so forth, and you really had to know this, and the only way to get them, in a sense, as a naval officer was to get in there and study yourself. In other words, read the manuals, go back and look at your textbooks, and so forth to learn the principles of electronic radiation and so forth, which were then parts of the machinery you dealt with.

I could see it was going to be a very technical navy in the future and that a midshipman was going to get this at the Naval Academy and not have to get it out of manuals and books, as I had to do. So, to me, the Naval Academy curriculum had to be extremely technical, there was no getting around it.

On the other hand, I could see that not every person was going to be able to master it, and still there were places in the navy where you needed a political scientist, a management specialist, and others who couldn't master the techniques of coping with radar, sonar, and so forth. What you had to do, hopefully, was instruct the Naval Academy to produce and to educate and to challenge the young people who could meet these requirements, yet you had to put places in it where you could put the people who were needed for later use as political scientists for marines, pilots, for instance. It would be nice to be a pilot with technical expertise who understood all the machinery he had in that airplane because it was extremely complicated. On the other hand, that doesn't do you any good if you can't fly the airplane and you bang it into the deck or you can't maneuver it to be on somebody else's tail and so on. There was still a requirement for the hand and eye coordination of being a pilot.

So you had to produce people who could be pilots, physically be pilots, and as many of them as possible who would be physically able to be pilots and would also be mentally able later on to gravitate into design of aircraft and so forth.

So there was a place for all of these kinds of people, and you didn't want to throw out the ones who couldn't master the academic routine as long as they could cope with it reasonably. And that's what the Naval Academy was, an attempt to produce as many as possible of the finest young men you could who would be, first, mentally able and, secondly, physically able, hopefully. And, if they couldn't, then you had to have a few who were only physically able without being mentally able.

But you couldn't just do as Admiral Rickover wanted to do, just take the ones who were mentally able and throw everybody else out, as he advocated. This argument went on for a long time.

Q: I was recalling the fact that you were forced out of the mainstream of a line officer's activities on at least two occasions when you had to take these high-level assignments having to do with Congress and then with public relations because there was a dearth of men in the navy who could do this kind of thing.

Adm. M.: That's true, but the navy didn't really recruit anybody to do that amongst line officers. They did recruit public affairs officers as specialists who were expected to go up through their system and usually get to be the deputy chief of information, but that was all. There were no flag-officer billets for them. Now, of course, there is a flag-officer billet for it and I think I had a lot to do with that because I pointed out that I had no way of becoming qualified for this billet and it wasn't right, so, as a result, one of the later secretaries said, "All right, we'll select from the PAO ranks a flag officer, put an extra billet in the system, and Chinfo from now on will be a flag officer PAO," and that's what he is, mainly because they couldn't get people from the regular navy who would do this kind of a job.

Q: That's why I asked originally; I mean while you were at the academy, whether there was any emphasis in an area like this, whether there was any possibility of emphasizing it, as these young men were in training.

Adm. M.: What we did there was – of course, there has always been a public-speaking course at the Naval Academy, an academic credit sort of thing, where each midshipman was given some essential elements as to how to organize his speech and give it, then he goes down to a special diningroom where once or twice a semester, as a first classman, in his formal attire and so forth on a formal occasion, he's required to get up and make a speech. But that doesn't really do the job. It teaches him to talk on his feet a little bit, but public affairs is a question of a little bit more than that.

As a public-affairs type, if you're going to do something like that, you have to go through the whole system of analyzing the audience, the requirement for your speech, and figuring out what they want and don't want, what you want to give them, melding the two together, and then getting up and giving it to them, sometimes ad lib rather than from a set speech. You also have to know how to find out what you can and can't say from the Defense Department, what's within national policy, what can be cleared, when it's necessary to clear - all these things are a little bit technical and they require a little bit more than just going through the public-speaking course down there.

So what we did at the Naval Academy we included in one of our leadership areas some simple elements of public affairs, what to do as a public affairs officer. About one out of eight midshipmen graduating was going to become the public affairs officer of his ship or station when he went there. They always give it to a junior officer, so we want to prepare them a little bit. What a PAO in a ship, for instance, is required to do, how do you go about it, where do you find the public affairs manual in a ship's office, just the essential elements so that when he got there he'd know where to go and get the whole information.

Q: That's something you instituted?

Adm. M.: Yes, and the midshipmen liked it. They all found it was great. They all used it when they went on to the fleet and wrote back and said it was the only thing that saved them when they had to write a story as PAO of a destroyer, "I didn't know squat, they'd say, until I remembered what I'd learned in my course at the Naval Academy, so I started doing it."

Q: Is there a more competent breed of such people in the navy today?

Adm. M.: I think so. It certainly means that a ship gets better service from its officers. That's one of the professional things he has to know, just like letting go an anchor. He's got to know something about public affairs because every naval officer, whether he likes it or not, has a duty in public affairs. By simply stepping off a liberty boat and onto a pier somewhere and going up in town in his uniform, he is part of the public affairs system of the navy and he'd better know something about it. That's one reason we tried this shift-over for the plebes. Instead of doing silly stuff about how's a cow, they were supposed to know how many ships we had, what their mission was, how many aircraft, and so forth, so when they went home on Christmas leave they would sound like a midshipman instead of just like some guy who's had his nose in the books.

Q: In effect, doing public relations then?

Adm. M.: Yes, and they came back and said it was fine,

"My parents asked me about the ships, and I was able to tell them all about battleships, why we don't have them any more, and carriers and marines and so forth." They appreciated the fact that they'd been given information like that, rather than how's the cow and silly stuff that we used to get in the old days.

Q: As I told you off tape, I was surprised by an observation that came my way today on naval officers, so I want to pose it to you. The fact that this man, who is very knowledgeable about all service people, said that in his experience, generally speaking, naval officers have a more narrow base than do the other services in terms of their interest in international affairs and what have you.

Adm. M.: I would expect this to be true, and the reason is that, when you look at the West Point curriculum, it is less technical than the navy's by quite a bit. The West Point graduate does not have to go out and become an instant first lieutenant, and if he does, his duties are so simple technically vis-à-vis that of a naval officer just astounding. In other words, a second lieutenant in the infantry doesn't have to know anything else except how to run his platoon, which is probably what he'll have. In other words, the uses of all the weapons involved and that sort of thing, perhaps the duties of the first lieutenant above him or the captain above him, something of that sort, he may go to armor or he may go somewhere else, but generally the requirements for him the day he steps into his army billet are far less than those for a Naval Academy graduate who's got to go to his destroyer and he's supposed to know something about every piece of machinery on that thing. That goes all the way from sonar to radar to extremely complicated automatic loading guns, he has to know how to navigate it, the personnel management of it, that sort of thing, and something about political affairs of any country he might be in the port of at the moment. In other words, the requirements for a midshipman are extremely complicated and he's got to know more than does the West Point graduate.

Having said that, it would fairly seem that that would broaden him. Actually, it doesn't. What I'm trying to say is he must stick to, first, mastering the technical expertise needed in the field he's going to, such as a destroyer. That gives us very little time, or did give us little time, to broaden him in the sense of giving him a mandatory requirement for language, the kind of history and geography we'd like to teach him, public affairs, literature, and all these sorts of things that we'd like to broaden and teach more of were limited by the number of hours left to give them.

Now, at West Point, since they don't have to teach

them as much professional matter, they do teach many more subjects that would tend to broaden them in the liberal arts area.

So that's what happens.

The Air Force Academy is somewhat like us, except that they again gain this ability to teach more liberal arts because every air force graduate is not going to be a pilot. Some are already earmarked to be MPs and all these silly things like that that we wouldn't waste a Naval Academy billet on. They actually send people to the Air Force Academy, take them out of the Air Force Academy and put them in nonpilot jobs and even nonflying jobs, and that's a terrible waste, to us at least at the Naval Academy, of that kind of an education. So what they do with all these people is they broaden them. In other words, they start teaching political science at the Air Force Academy and the same thing at West Point. We don't. We teach naval officers. We have no thought whether they're going into political science, even though they may major in that subject. Basically, their curriculum is professionally, technically, and engineeringly oriented to becoming an instant naval officer when he steps on a ship or into an aircraft. Every naval officer who graduates, without exception perhaps a few who can't qualify physically - goes right to a combatant billet. Nobody goes off and goes to the sort of thing that they do from West Point.

West Point, for instance, will take some of their graduates and earmark them when they're in the West Point system and tell them, "You want to be an instructor? Okay, we'll send you off to graduate school the moment you leave here for three years, and you'll get your doctor's degree and you'll come back and be an instructor in English or philosophy or something like that at West Point." So what they've done already is to take so many graduates and take them out of the professional system and bring them back as instructors.

We could no more do that than we could fly at the Naval Academy. We can't waste that kind of education on making a non-naval officer out of a graduate, and so our graduates tend to be more narrow in the sense that they have not had time or opportunity to study liberal arts subjects and that sort of thing, but they're broader professionally in the sense that they can do their job internally in that ship a lot better than a West Point fellow can do in his first billet.

Q: This observation came as a surprise to me and I suppose I have a kind of a one-sided attitude about naval officers because the ones I've talked with for tape are usually very accomplished and broad-gauged people like you.

Adm. M.: I think they get their broad-gaugedness, if you

want to call it that, outside the Naval Academy curriculum and outside the navy. You can stay very narrow, if you want to, in the navy and there are people like that. They don't always go very far and perhaps they're very happy. There's a need for people like that who just stay technically oriented and very narrow. Usually they become engineers and they don't get selected along the way. They retire as commanders or captains, and they're happy. They've done a good job for the navy, but the person you see and look at is one who has had to educate himself. He read and studied and he traveled and he asked questions and talked to people and he became a pretty broad person, which he has the opportunity to do if he'll just do it.

There are lots of things to do in a ship. You can do a lot of reading, if you want to, or you can play acey-ducey, take your choice.

Q: There are certain selectees from the Naval Academy, of course, who have an opportunity to get a much broader base almost immediately. I'm thinking of Burke scholars.

Adm. M.: Yes, the navy has a little bit of that. Of course, the Burke scholar has to go to sea eventually.

Q: He goes to sea immediately, doesn't he, after graduation?

Adm. M.: Yes, but there are variations of all this. Some of them go to sea for a year, then come back and start their Burke scholar proceedings. They're guaranteed a doctor's degree, for instance, but they may not go to it right away. A lot depends upon their particular discipline, when it starts at the school, whether it's a fall subject or the summer or whatever. Each one is pretty much individually tailored. But even the Burke scholar has got to qualify at sea in whatever he wants to do, but it is a way of guaranteeing some very top men getting a doctor's degree and that's hard to do in the navy without the Burke scholars system.

Q: Yes, there aren't many Bob Dennisons!

Adm. M.: No, there aren't. It's tough to do. The navy just won't cooperate. They give you master's degrees all right, eventually, but that's about as far as they'll go, and if you get a doctor's they want it to be in a technical subject and they want you to become technically oriented. Even for a master's degree, going to PG school, the navy requires you to serve in a billet twice after that, three years at a time. In other words, six years if you want to become a master, say, in ordnance engineering and you go to PG school. You know when you go ashore twice after that you're going to go into a billet requiring that kind of education, and it generally is a technical billet, in other words, having to do with the procurement of ammunition, design of it, or whatever, and you stop being a candidate for broadening in political science and so forth. You become strictly a technical guy who's going to fiddle with ordnance from then on. Maybe you like that, and there is a place for people like that.

It used to be in the old days that that was the way to success in the navy. You had to be a constructor or an ordnance engineer and so forth. That was the elite part of the navy.

Q: The top 10 percent.

Adm. M.: Right.

Q: Well, to introduce another subject, which is certainly in the area of training and education, that is the summer cruises. Do you want to talk about them during your time?

Adm. M.: Yes. Most naval officers remember the days when summer cruises were quite by rote. In other words, there were a certain number of ships, almost always the same ships, set aside each year for midshipman training –

Q: Battleships!

Adm. M.: Yes. In the old days it was the Wyoming and the Oklahoma, and each midshipman did the same training. In other words, all the youngsters went through a routine of standing watches, scrubbing decks, going down to the engineering spaces, and that sort of thing. As a first classman he navigated and he was officer of the deck and that sort of thing. So these midshipmen had a kind of common cruise experience and went to the same ports, perhaps.

When the old training squadron disbanded, when the two wars came along, this became a catch as catch can system of the Naval Academy trying its best to get cruise ships for the summer. What usually happened was - also I might add that the ROTC system had expanded enormously and they had requirements for summer cruises which had to be met, so the Naval Academy was struggling, and has for the past twenty-three years, to put together a satisfactory summer cruise system. What happens is that sometimes two or three ships are set aside, not always, these are usually LPDs, which have a flight capability for helos, of course, and a boating launching capability and space for troops. In other words, they're big enough to hold midshipmen, give them some flight experience and they have boats, of course, to get them ashore when they get to port, which is a good thing to do.

Q: But they're fragmented, aren't they? I mean they're smaller ships so they can't go as a group.

Adm. M.: Well, when this is ideal you get three of them and you can pretty well get the same mix again of third and first class in the same ship and, providing three of them, you can have some intership maneuvers, even though it was simple, like columns and so forth, which is a good thing to do, and you have some shiphandling and so forth.

So when it was possible to get these three ships, that was fine. When the economy wave hit the navy and the Vietnamese War was using up every ship they could get, it became common to have sort of a nonstandard cruise. In other words, you'd get so many billets in an aircraft carrier, so many in an LPD, so many in a destroyer, and you spread out the midshipmen all over hell's half acre, some of them going as far out as Japan to ride in a destroyer, which is pretty good, but it was a little difficult getting them out there and back. Unfortunately, some of them would go down to a carrier and the carrier would suddenly have a casualty and spend the entire cruise at a pier in Norfolk, which wasn't good, although perhaps the, say, forty midshipmen involved might have an instructor or two with them and be kept busy and he'd make arrangements for them to go out in other ships and so forth. But it was nonstandard and it was not the best way to train midshipmen.

Q: The same thing would pertain to other ships, too, wouldn't it?

Adm. M.: That's right. In other words, they couldn't be earmarked to do midshipmanlike things, which is give midshipmen shiphandling experience or they might be doing something which -

Q: That put an awful burden on the administrative end of it, didn't it?

Adm. M.: It was extremely difficult to do. Some midshipmen didn't make out very well at all. Also, in some cases it was good, sometimes a midshipman was allowed to go out on an SSBN cruise, but all he saw was a submarine. If he wanted to be a submariner, that was fine, but even then he missed broadening. So there were some good things and some bad things about it. Some midshipmen had great cruises, others had terrible cruises, and that experience, perhaps, kept some in the navy and drove others out, men who didn't like what was happening. And still it was nonstandard and a little difficult to administer because it is nonstandard.

Q: You would think that the top people in the Navy Department would have been more concerned about making available the proper ships for these cruises.

Adm. M.: Yes. I would say they did everything they could. The CNO, the vice CNO, and Op-03, of course, the deputy chief for operations, all expressed sympathy for my position when I went to see about it and did the best they could, I'm sure, to give the Naval Academy the ships that we asked for and to tell those ship commanders the importance of training midshipmen. That was what they had to do, either as a primary mission or as a secondary mission. They had to do the best they could to give the Naval Academy midshipmen a fair shake, and they did, but still there were times when it couldn't be done. We went through periods of fuel shortage and all sorts of things like that, economies, where hardly any ships got under way, except for combat missions and so forth, semicombat missions.

The trials and tribulations of the cruise system during the past ten years have been pretty high.

Q: With such a dispersal of the midshipmen throughout the fleet for their summer cruise, what was the overriding objective on the part of the academy, or did you have one?

Adm. M.: Yes. We knew these midshipmen should get certain training in seamanship, navigation, engineering, aviation, and so forth, so we put together cruise notebooks outlining what each midshipman should know about fueling ships or standing watch as a junior officer of the watch or as officer of the deck or an engineering watch. If a midshipman didn't have this cruise experience - in other words, if he went to a submarine, we tried to make arrangements when he got back or in some other fashion to have him instructed in how you fuel a ship. That's why I was talking the other day about we knew we had to figure out what every midshipman should know professionally when he graduates, and we had a long compendium put together which said he had to know this about navigation, take sights, bearings, navigate a ship, in engineering he had to know this, in seamanship he must know how to fuel a ship, describe the duties of the various parts of a fuel party, how to make an approach, and so forth. We listed in categories all the things in missilery, aviation, all the requirements a midshipman should be required to meet before he was considered qualified to go out to ships.

That's why it became very important, the differences of the cruise systems, where a midshipman came back and he hadn't had that cruise experience, he could ask his seamanship instructor how to do this and get extra instruction. It became the duty of the midshipman and the department concerned to meld together what he knew and didn't know so that every midshipman in the end had roughly, hopefully, the same kind of experience. I think we did very well at it. As I say, in the end my next to last year we required every midshipman to take an examination and, voluntarily then, he was helped to make up his deficiency and told the answers to the questions he missed and so forth. In the last year, it became a required course and now is not only required but is given a mark.

That was the trend. It was up and up in professional qualifications so that every midshipman when he went out to a ship would be qualified to do what he had to do on a carrier and so forth.

Q: I wonder if one of the benefits from those earlier cruises in the summer fell between the cracks with the new system. I wonder if you'd comment on that. Many of the men I've talked with indicated that the cruises on the battleships and so forth, especially when they went to Europe and the Mediterranean, gave them a broad cultural experience which they hadn't had, and how could they have this when they were so scattered.

Adm. M.: That's quite true. Drawing on my own cruise experience, for instance, I went to a battleship. I went to Rome, I saw everything there. I stayed at a nice hotel, I had an audience with the pope, a mass audience it's true, but I saw the pope, the same thing with Mussolini, who was then, of course, dictator of Italy. I went to London, to Paris, three principal capitals of Europe and I was able with the tour system to see an awful lot, and I think it was a very broadening experience in terms of seeing all the sights of London and other parts of England, the same thing in Paris and the same thing in Rome, the three principal cities. That was an invaluable experience.

On the other hand, I don't think it helped me to scrub decks every morning and do the sorts of things I do as a third-class midshipman as much as it would help a young man now to go out in a Polaris submarine for sixty days and get immediately into the system of a submarine, having to stand watches on missiles and so forth and learn a tremendous amount about the technical navy. In other words, he bypassed all the deck-scrubbing chores and so forth, but on the other hand he didn't see anything but the inside of the submarine. So he missed what you're talking about, the cultural expansion. Of course, he can get that later on, hopefully.

Q: Piecemeal!

Adm. M.: Yes. He won't get much as a nuclear submariner because the nuclear submarines don't go anywhere except Scotland and Rota. By virtue of being what they are, they don't get in to many ports. They're just not allowed to get into port. So you do miss that sort of thing, and that, I'd say, is one of the faults of the system.

Q: Did the navy ever really seriously consider keeping in commission some of the big battleships for the use of the Naval Academy?

Adm. M.: No. Of course, there's been a drive forever to keep at least one battleship, and we did need one drastically, of course, in Vietnam and should have had one out there.

Q: They did have one for a while.

Adm. M.: For a while. It should have stayed in. There are lots of reasons for having one battleship in the fleet, all the way from fleet flagship to midshipman training, and the ship and so forth being a shore-bombardment platform, but the cost is just too great.

Q: That's the deterrent, the cost?

Adm. M.: Yes. The money could keep three or four LPDs in commission, another carrier, and so it was never, I guess, pursued.

Another area that should, I think, be noted is athletics.

Q: Yes, indeed. You have never shared the opinion of Admiral Rickover who would have banned athletics completely!

Adm. M.: No. As the Naval Foundation will attest, one midshipman in four is involved in some kind of varsity athletics. That's the basis, of course, on which the foundation operates, that they're allowed to provide money for the prep school education of a number of young men, one fourth of whom can be varsity athletes, or athletes of some kind or another, because that's the ratio of varsity athletes to others in the Naval Academy. I supported to the ultimate the idea that every midshipman should be required to do something concomitant. That is, the Naval Academy should provide the opportunity for midshipmen to do something, whether it was shooting a rifle, sailing or whatever. So I encouraged and promoted and helped all I could athletics of every form, all the way from rugby clubs, if that's what midshipmen wanted, to football.

Q: They all had to participate in something, didn't they?

Adm. M.: Yes, that's right, and I think they all really wanted to.

Two areas on which I more or less concentrated because I thought all the rest of them were pretty well in shape were football - on my watch there, of course, Mr. Rick Forzano was the head coach for the first year and a half or so, then he had an offer to go to the Detroit Lions as a professional coach and did go, so it was my privilege to choose George Welsh as the head football coach. I found this a very exciting experience because George Welsh is an outstanding person in my estimation, and when I was negotiating with him together with the director of athletics, we got toward the end of it and we asked George Welsh what he wanted in the way of a contract and salary and he said:

"Well, you pay me whatever you think I'm worth and I don't want a contract. At the end of a year we'll know whether I want to stay and whether you want me to stay, and that's the way we'll do it."

Q: That's typical, isn't it?

Adm. M.: That's George Welsh. I asked George:

"Do you think you can produce winning teams at the Naval Academy? I don't think you can because the requirements for academics to get in here and stay are too stringent."

And George said, "No, I think I can do it." And, of course, he has proved that. I asked him how he was going to do this, and he said:

"I'm going to do it on a quality rather than a quantity basis."

The recruiting system there was kind of haphazard before in the sense that the general policy was get as many nominations as you can, give them all to athletes, and go out and get all the athletes you can, the best you can, we'll get them all in here and hopefully we'll get some good ones. George said that won't work. He said:

"You have to go after the really blue-chip athlete who is academically sound and is a good athlete, and concentrate on getting a few good ones in here."

Q: This is precisely what some of the outstanding universities do, isn't it?

Adm. M.: Yes. That doesn't mean you bend over backwards to proselyte some fellow who's a heck of a good football player. George also emphasizes the moral and ethical side. He wants a good man. He doesn't want a bum type of college athlete. He wants a good man, a smart one, who's athletically able, and he knows he won't get the professional type. The Naval Academy always tried to get just a little bit below that level. In other words, you don't get any 250-pounders and very few of them are any good. They all go to Maryland or somewhere else. But George thought he could get a 200-pounder who was smart and, by virtue of being smart, he would be a football player if he had talent and he could build him up to 250 pounds. So that's really what the Naval Academy does.

Q: It's a pretty limited pool, isn't it?

Adm. M.: Yes, but George felt that that was the way to do it.

Q: How did he go about discovering these people?

Adm. M.: He concentrated on the areas where he knew that kind of person abounded, I suppose, in New Jersey, Pennsylvania, Florida, New York, and California. Those are about the only places he would go because he found that people in these areas liked the navy and would come here to stay. He didn't bother to go to, say, Alabama or Ohio or somewhere like that. I guess that was because -

Q: Or the Middle West is the province of Notre Dame, anyway.

Adm. M.: That's right. So whatever he decided to do has been extremely successful. My year and a half with George Welsh was outstanding in the sense that he never once asked for anything for his football team, no special privileges, no this or that. He just told them they had to be midshipmen first and football players second. The morale of the football team was outstanding. I had a hard time changing the attitude of the brigade. The average midshipman - I'm talking about the average now - is a funny person. He doesn't like varsity athletes because he thinks they get all kinds of privileges. He doesn't know they don't.

Q: You mean they're stars?

Adm. M.: Yes, they get a lot of publicity and so forth and he thinks that they are getting away with everything. I used to get questions like this at lectures. They would ask why we did this and so forth for the football team, and I would say:

"What do you think they get?"

"Oh, they don't have to go to class, they get to do this and do that."

I said: "Well, I don't know about you. I've been a football player and I know what these football players do."

What they do is they work their butts off at practice and they get in about seven o'clock and are so dehydrated they can't eat at the special training table you're talking about. If they did eat, it would be food you wouldn't want, anyway. It's pretty cut-and-dried food. They stagger up to their rooms and try to stay awake and study. They have the same requirements academically as you do, even more rigorous because they have to miss a few classes and missing classes isn't all that good because what you're really doing is making it more difficult on yourself. They take trips where they have to study on a trip and they have to get right back and only get one night where you get to stay overnight. If you think that going out there and beating your brains against a bunch of 270-pound Notre Dames is a lot of fun, then coming right back to the Naval Academy and studying on Sunday when you're out somewhere in New York, or whatever you're doing for the weekend, you ought to try it sometime.

After I'd get through explaining all this sort of thing to the average midshipman, he would more or less say yes, he understood. But a lot of them didn't, so it was very difficult for the football players and extremely difficult for the plebe football player, particularly if he was any good because he would perhaps be given a few privileges in the eyes of the first class by being taken out to practice and so forth and maybe making a trip or two. Then the first class would jump all over him.

So this was one of the problems with athletics, trying to keep the average brigade member aware of the fact that being a varsity athlete is not really a privilege, it's a duty and a tough one. The average football player

doesn't get anything out of it at all compared to his
compatriot, say, at Notre Dame or USC, where a fellow is
given a car, an apartment, a girl friend, $10,000 a year,
and a few other perquisites that we know they're getting,
but our guy doesn't get anything. He just gets the
privilege of working his tail off day and night, getting
sores, getting banged up, and so forth. So that was really
one of the difficulties of keeping a varsity ahtlete happy.
At the Naval Academy he doesn't get anything. He contributes.
If you watch the daily life of football players at the
Naval Academy, you'll find out that it's not very much.
You can say the same thing for basketball or soccer -

Q: Or any other sports.

Adm. M.: Yes. They just work harder than anybody else
and they have the same requirements for academics exactly.
It's a tough life, but a good one and so they like it.

Q: What about the burden placed upon the football team
to bring in enough money to support a large part of the
athletic program?

Adm. M.: That is obviously a continuing argument in that
area. The argument goes that you have to have high-
class opponents because that's the only way you bring in

enough attendance to pay for the program or, hopefully, you have to have the army-navy game be a close game and it has to be on national television so that you can get television receipts, and, hopefully, now and then you go to a bowl, which certainly solves your problems for a year or two because of the added revenue.

Q: How valid is that argument?

Adm. M.: It is valid in the sense that if you didn't have a fairly good team and you didn't have the army-navy game, the athletic program at the Naval Academy would go way down. We'd have to cut out half a dozen varsity teams because we couldn't support them.

Q: Why is this, why doesn't Congress support it - ?

Adm. M.: Congress doesn't support anything athletically at all and it only supports very little of the physical training program. The funds that the Naval Academy gets to conduct physical training are very small and they only go towards hiring a few instructors who do Swedish and that sort of thing. The funds perhaps might cover taking care of the natatorium and that sort of thing, but generally the funds that are given by Congress just don't do anything.

Q: Couldn't they be persuaded to include that kind of thing?

Adm. M.: No, they're like Admiral Rickover. They just think that that's not a proper function. They know you're supposed to train a midshipman physically, but as far as they're concerned you can do that by running them around the field or doing setting-up exercises and that sort of thing.

Q: But they're like a cross section of our population, they're very sports-minded?

Adm. M.: Well, of course, the average university doesn't do any differently. Take the University of Maryland. All the money for their athletic programs comes from football and basketball. Now what's happening, of course, is that the average university is being told by Congress and others to provide equal athletic facilities for women and the women's programs don't bring in any money, except a little bit here and there. So what they're doing is telling you what to do with your funds, and the university system is getting pretty uptight about this sort of thing. The Naval Academy, of course, is a little different, but basically this is what happens. Funds from the football receipts plus basketball takes in a little bit of money and now and then baseball has one game a year where they charge money -

Q: And lacrosse a little bit?

Adm. M.: Lacrosse takes in a little bit but generally the football proceeds support all twenty-two varsity athletic systems and a good part of the rest of the system, too, the intramurals.

Q: This should be a help to the student body in understanding the position of the football team, if they understand that they're contributing to the whole program.

Adm. M.: Well, you can tell them that but they don't believe it and they don't believe it very long if they do believe it. It's just a kind of a fact of life that has to be gone into all the time.

Q: Are you going to talk about the foundation and how it fits into this athletic picture?

Adm. M.: Yes. I started talking about the foundation. Of course, the foundation is an organization that provides prep school funds, half the funds for a year of prep school, for up to ninety candidates who just fail of entering, you know, the year before or whatever criterion you want to use. They generally use the criterion if a man got close the year before and he wants to go to another year of prep school or the university of his choice, the foundation will fund half of his total fees.

Q: And he has to have athletic prowess?

Adm. M.: No, he doesn't. In the old days, the foundation was formed years ago just for that, and the only persons who went to foundation schools were athletes. Then the NCAA decided that wasn't right and so our foundation and foundations from other universities now must fund students in the same ratio as varsity athletes to total students. In other words, at the Naval Academy one-fourth of the students are members of varsity teams, so that one-fourth of the foundation's students can be athletes. The other three quarters are nonathletes.

Q: Is this supervised closely?

Adm. M.: Yes, exactly. It's never violated.

Q: And the foundation is made up of alumni, is it not?

Adm. M.: No, the foundation could be made up of anybody

who wants to become a member of it. It has 135, I believe, trustees, each of whom contributes quite a bit of money each year to become a member.

Q: That's one of the requisites, is it?

Adm. M.: Yes, a healthy contribution, and as a good strong fund where alumni and friends of the Naval Academy over the years have left in their estates considerable amounts of money to the foundation, so it has a good deal of money. It had enough money to fund, as I say, about ninety scholarships a year. Many people have established in memory of somebody a scholarship for a particular person or group of persons.

Q: What supervision is maintained by the foundation over the students when they're in prep school?

Adm. M.: The foundation has a small staff and that staff requires every member on scholarship to report his grades and keep them informed. They do pretty well in terms of monitoring what the student is doing.

Q: And is there any way of measuring his continuing attitude toward the navy?

Adm. M.: Not really, unless he happens to be in their ROTC unit. Sometimes he is and, if that's so, the ROTC will help, but sometimes the man will graduate and go off to West Point or not go to the Naval Academy, but that doesn't happen very often.

Q: I'm mindful of the fact that one of my boys in the parish up in New Jersey was an outstanding athlete and they sent him to school somewhere around Washington. He was there for a whole year, and he and five or six other boys who were in the same category then decided they weren't going to the Naval Academy. We never did discover why. It seemed to be part of that youth movement in the sixties.

Adm. M.: I was surprised that there were that many. In my knowledge now, there might be five in the whole program who wouldn't go to the Naval Academy. To have that many in one group is odd, but I guess it was probably that time —

Q: Yes, it was, just about that time.

Adm. M.: Now, as part of athletics, I'd like to talk about the sailing program.

When I came to the Naval Academy, sailing was, I would characterize it best by saying it was on the back burner. The sailing team was not given Ns as a reward for, say winning certain races and so forth, sailing competitions. The system in effect for acquiring boats was archaic. Each boat acquired by the Naval Academy was usually a gift and it had to be surveyed and the results and the request had to go to the secretary of the navy for acqusition by the Naval Academy. That sometimes would take six months, just bureaucratic stupidity in the secretary's office.

Q: This would be a yacht or something?

Adm. M.: Yes, maybe a 40- or 50-foot yawl or something of that sort. It got to the point where I just couldn't move anybody up there. Most of the time, the boat would be withdrawn by the owner. The owner usually gave it to the Naval Academy because he wanted a tax advantage or for some other reason. He wanted to get it out of his hands because he didn't want the maintenance and if the Naval Academy couldn't take it expeditiously, then he would say, well, I'll give it to somebody else. We lost many boats that way.

The commanding officer of the naval station at that time was a fine person and enthusiastically supported sailing but he had no technical knowledge of it. The naval station had help over there for keeping our boats up but not very much and not much money to keep them up with because, again, we couldn't get much money out of the Congress.

So our sailing program really was in the doldrums.

Q: You had a disparate group of boats, too, didn't you?

Adm. M.: Yes. We had fourteen Luders yawls, which were the heart of it, but these were just day-to-day boats that you would send people out in and you'd have races in them and so forth, but they didn't permit the Naval Academy to participate in international races or any big-time racing. They weren't that good. We didn't have any sailing instructors to speak of. We had no sailing center. We had a little shack down there in the Santee area. So we had a very difficult time. The director of athletics was not very enthusiastic about sailing nor in taking care of the various sailing teams that visited, since sailing teams tend to be a little bit obstreperous and sort of nonregulation and left bottles all over his visiting team area and sometimes did bad things in the middle of the night and none of the other teams could sleep. So he was very unenthusiastic, which I could understand.

So I had quite a problem and I started solving it first by the help of some of the fine people in the country who support navy sailing and who were members of a group that support our sailing system. They agreed to form a Naval Academy sailing association.

Q: Do you want to name some of these men?

Adm. M.: I'd rather not since most of them have changed. A couple of them have died, but anyway it was a changing group. Bob McWethy, of course, is a retired naval officer who was sort of the hands and feet of it. Admiral Bob McNitt was a help. Al Van Metre, who is a very prominent sailor in the area, was a keen member of it. Arnold Gay, who runs a shipyard in town, and there were four or five others in the New York area who'd been involved and interested in navy sailing, who were members of the New York Yacht Club and came down and helped us. But the membership of the group has changed over the years. Some of them have died. Anyway, it was a group of people in the country who were great sailors in their own right and who agreed to help us. But at least they did form a foundation and took the burden of financial responsibility for the foundation.

Q: Are you going to tell me what your motivation was for this?

Adm. M.: Yes. The motivation was to find a way to acquire yachts in a hurry. So, when the foundation was formed, it had the ability to accept a yacht overnight if it wanted to. So a person would offer a yacht to the Naval Academy and we'd say, fine, the foundation will look into it, and two or three of these members would come down, have it surveyed, say this is what we want, and the charter they were given allowed them to accept the yacht overnight. So just like that we'd have a yacht.

Q: You circumvented the government?

Adm. M.: We did. Then we could go through the longer process of telling the secretary of the navy that the Naval Academy would like to have this, so they could keep the papers up there for six months or a year if they wanted to. We had the yacht in the foundation's hands, we were using it —

Q: And the man got his tax benefit?

Adm. M.: That's right. And then we were allowed under the IRS system between one and two years to sell that boat, so all we would do would be to get a boat and run it for two years and then sell it and take the proceeds and keep other boats up, and also hire a sailing director. In other words, the sailing program was run from the proceeds of donated yachts to the Naval Academy, which were then used in the system, maintained with this money, and then the sailing team is instructed by instructors paid from the same pot.

I also got BuPers to send Captain Alex Grosvenor here. He was a very prominent sailor.

Q: Of the National Geographic?

Adm. M.: He's a relative. He became commanding officer of the naval station and, as such, the head of the sailing program. He was a fantastically successful person in promoting sailing.

The third leg of this triangle was the donating of money by the Robert Crown family for the sailing center which I then had designed and constructed.

Q: And what was their motivation?

Adm. M.: Their motivation was they'd always been navy minded - Robert Crown was a naval officer in the reserve in Chicago who died recently. I'm from Illinois and I knew him and his family well. He was a public affairs officer in the reserve, and that's another area where I knew him. So when it came time to look for money, the Crown family, which is very wealthy in Chicago, was contacted, and I agreed, if they would give the money, to name the center the Robert Crown Sailing Center. The Crown family did donate the money and the center was named after Robert Crown. A fine dedication ceremony was held and now you see the beautiful sailing center we have.

So now we had boats, we had money, we had sailing instructors, we had a center. Then the other things came more easily. The athletic director was persuaded that the sailing team should have an N like anybody else when they won certain races. He was also persuaded to put some people in there to police his Byzantine dormitory, and all things were solved in the area of bringing sailors down for the Kennedy Cup system and various sailing events held down here. We were able to persuade academic types that sailing was important and the sailors could go off and miss a few classes like the football teams and everything else. Finally, the sailing club program grew and grew to where now the Naval Academy is recognized as one of the top sailing organizations in the country in the university system.

Q: Quite an achievement. What has it contributed to the knowledge of the midshipmen?

Adm. M.: I think that sailing is a very important part of being a naval officer. Even if you're an aviator you've got to recognize and know what happens with water, tides, winds, and waves, and so forth on any boat or ship. Even a ship, an aircraft carrier, sails like anything else with sails and you've got to know what happens when the wind hits you at various angles, how fast you're going and how to judge the movement through the water, you're going sideways as well as forward when you're coming into a harbor. You know the effects of winds on flat planes, curved planes, and all the rest of it. You learn all these things in sailing.

Q: Was it anything that came out of your early experience that motivated you?

Adm. M.: Well, I would say in the first week I was here - that was in the summer - I guess it was not the first week but about the third month I was here when the new plebes came in and I asked a plebe one day what he thought was his most significant experience here, and he said:

"Sir, we went out in a yawl the other day. It was the first time I'd ever been on the water. Nine of us and a first classman went out in a yawl and stayed overnight. That's the most fantastic experience I've had in my life," being out there like that all by himself with his eight classmates and a first classman. He said:

"I want to stay in the navy because I want to do more

of this."

So you can bet that every plebe from then on went out on an overnight trip as soon as we could get them out, and that's what happens now. That's one of the best experiences they have, as far as life in the navy is concerned, going out like that in a boat overnight.

Q: Has the academy ever been tempted to indulge in something like the Eagle?

Adm. m.: No, the reason being that's too much of one thing. We don't sail that much, we just don't have time to send them all out for two or three months, for a summer cruise maybe, in a large ship like that. We think that it's better for them to get small-boat experience. In other words, who needs to learn how to clew up a sail and do that sort of thing as much as he needs to know how to exercise command over a small boat. He does the same thing in a small boat, but he does it rather than watch somebody else conn the ship and so forth. He gets to do everything. He puts up the sail, he rigs the sail for better drawing power, he navigates the ship, the boat, rather, and does all the things in a small boat that he would do in a big one. He does it at various times in the summer and all during his four years there.

The sailing program is fantastic in terms of the use

of boats, all kinds of boats that we didn't have before. If you go down and look at the seawall in the summer time you'll notice that we can't get the boats over from the naval station fast enough to get them full of midshipmen and get out in the water areas.

Q: I've noticed the contrast from when I came here ten years ago.

Adm. M.: They have now women's sailing teams, class sailing teams. The sailing program is about as big as football in terms of numbers of people involved in intramurals and other things that go on. It's recognized and a sailing team gets the same recognition as any other varsity team now. It's a far greater program than it was five or ten years ago. But again, as against the Eagle, we want a program where more midshipmen can get hands on in the control of the boat rather than rigging some big ship.

Q: Of course, the coast guard has used it to very great advantage, it seems to me, in terms of public relations.

Adm. M.: Oh, yes.

Q: Recruitment and so forth.

Adm. M.: I think so. On the other hand, the fact that the midshipmen sail in the Bermuda race and that they bring four or five yawls into New York occasionally for sailing races or to Newport or somewhere of that sort. That gets a lot of publicity, too.

Q: That's a very interesting phase of the athletic program that you instigated.

Adm. M.: It's changed a lot but, on the other hand, in spite of what I did for the sailing program, I never let the football end of it down because I still think that, as the varsity football team goes in the university system, so go the rest of the athletics. If you have a good football team then you're going to have a good team in everything else. What draws people to the Naval Academy is football teams, strangely enough. If you have a football team, then, all of a sudden, you'll find good gymnasts, good baseball players, and everything else, because they knew that the academy has a good athletic program if it has a good football beam. If it doesn't, they're doubtful about everything else.

Q: Do you want to tell me what your concept is of teamwork and athletics? Harry Hill was so hepped on this subject and emphasized it so during his superintendency.

Adm. M.: Well, as a midshipman I was a member of three varsity athletic teams and when I became injured I went on into several intramural teams, company basketball, company this, and company that, and so forth. I'd done this all through high school, and to me, one of the best things about it was the feeling of being part of the team. I hardly noticed the difference when I went aboard a battleship on my first duty. Suddenly, I was the coach of the football team, the baseball team, and the basketball team. I was a junior turret officer in a turret where you were in the gunnery competition for Es and so forth. Running a turret was just like, again in a division, just like part of a team. You had a team of a couple of chief petty officers and about sixty men who manned this turret and shot the competition. It wasn't anything different than the baseball team. The same thing when you went down to the communication system, you were competing with all the ships in the battleship area for communication Es, or down in the engineering department. In those days, competition for an engineering E was very high. So you went from atheltics at the Naval Academy to a different form of athletics in a ship. In a big ship like that, you had some athletics, but you had besides that the athleticlike things of being part of a turret team. You even had sailing competitions or pulling competitions, all kinds of things in a battleship.

It was the same old thing all the way through, just athletics of a different kind. Teamwork was involved. That team had better load that turret or you wouldn't get a shot off and you wouldn't get an E. So it worked all the way around. You had a boat and it had to be a better-looking boat than anybody else's boat. Each division had responsibility for one of the boats of the battleship. Your boat had to be the best one or they'd get a new boat team. I think what he said was very à propos in the sense that war is just a different form of athletics, competition, with a team. It's a loading team or it's a radar plotting team or it's a ship command team or it's a couple of guys in an airplane acting as pilot, navigator, gunner, and so forth. That's all the navy is. It's just continuing teamwork of one kind and another. That's why I think it's so important that you stress athletics at the Naval Academy.

Furthermore, one of the biggest points about athletics is that it teaches a young man to perform under stress. In other words, he's got to learn if he's going to be on the bridge of a ship, he's conning that ship, with waves breaking over it and making 28 or 30 knots, guns going off and the captain hollering at him, and all the rest of the stuff, he's learned that because that's what you do when you are playing football. There's nothing different from that and getting banged on the helmet by some guy,

the quarterback is telling you to do this and the coach is
hollering at you, you're hot and you're sweaty. And the
same thing playing basketball. That's where you learn to
maintain your cool under stress, to listen to what's being
told to you, give a command, carry something out, and do
all the things you do. It's not a bit different playing
football and conning a destroyer out here in the midst
of a war.

Q: What about the value of the army-navy game, the annual
game, as a sort of a climax to the athletic program?
It has nationally lost its stature in recent years, I think,
somewhat.

Adm. M.: Well, it has.

Q: It used to be really at the apex of the football season
for everybody, but it isn't any more.

Adm. M.: I think it's because army has slipped a little
bit. If you will notice, the years when they were pretty
close together, attendance went up again, but when one
team gets so good and the other doesn't come up to it, why,
it slacks off a little bit. We've lost in attandance the
last couple of years. Of course, we make it up in television
proceeds.

Q: I think Welsh told us at the Civitan one day that, was it two years ago, when it was really in jeopardy, the television coverage, nobody wanted to do it.

Adm. M.: Well, that was right. What happened was - of course last year the time change was made, so it was a later time, and, all of a sudden, the audience last year was the biggest in history. I think it had to do with time change more than anything else, because the television audience in California wasn't getting much out of an eight o'clock or nine o'clock in the morning game. When they could see it in the afternoon, why, they suddenly began to watch.

Q: Yes.

Adm. M.: So that indicated that it will bring back more people to go to the stadium, but television proceeds are what you want more than attendance. That brings in more money.

Q: Are there any other aspects of the athletic program that we haven't covered?

Adm. M.: I think that's about it, Jack.

Q: What about the aviation summer?

Adm. M.: Aviation summer is somewhat the same now as it used to be, perhaps even better, in the sense that each second-classman spends a week at Pensacola where, if he's good enough, he can solo. But at least he flies not only in training aircraft but he gets a ride or two in a combatant type.

Q: That's an improvement, isn't it, because it used to be entirely at the academy?

Adm. M.: Right. He didn't fly nearly as much in those days. He flew an old PBY usually for a long time, or a small aircraft out there at Lee Airport eventually. Now he goes to Pensacola for a whole week and really gets into flying full blast. Also, he goes to New London and has a week in a submarine, then he'll go to the destroyer area and have a week in a destroyer, and then he'll have a week as a marine. Totally, this is much better than the old days. He'll go to Quantico with the marines, for instance, put on a marine suit, go out in the field with them, camp overnight, and fire weapons and all that sort of thing.

Q: Did you have some input into this?

Adm. M.: No, this had been done for some time. I just thought it was a great program to continue. The only change I made, very regretfully was we had to take rifle-firing out of the curriculum. It used to be that every man qualified with a rifle, at least as a marksman, if not as an expert. In my day there was too much rifle shooting, in my estimate.

Q: You mean when you were a midshipman?

Adm. M.: Yes, we spent too many hours on the rifle range doing the same old thing. After we were qualified, we still went over there once or twice a week in plebe summer, which was too much time. Now, the plebe summer area is so filled up that we just had to make a decision and I took out, again regretfully, rifle qualification because you very seldom use a rifle in this world. You use a pistol now, and so we kept pistol in, but not rifle. Every midshipman is indoctrinated in how to use a rifle, but he just fires an indoctrination course and that's all. Just a little bit, he just fires enough so he knows how it shoots. That's one of the changes recently.

Q: You mentioned plebe summer. You might dwell on that for a little bit. It is a culling process.

Adm. M.: Yes, and it's a time when deliberate stress is put on a midshipman, perhaps more than he can cope with unless he's a pretty good person.

Q: How closely is he watched to see?

Adm. M.: Very, very carefully. The first class watch him day and night. He's watched to make sure he doesn't get overstressed physically. In other words, if it's a hot day, he's kept inside. He's not in any danger but he's just required to do something every day, every minute of the hour, of the day, from when he wakes up to the time he goes to sleep, from physical exercise to marching to sailing to all kinds of things that tend to keep him going and tire him out and see what he can do. If he can't take this kind of stress, we want to know about it in a hurry because it's better to cull him out as a plebe, if he just doesn't like that sort of thing. If he knows he has two months and hasn't the foresight to figure out, well, I'll do this for two months and then it will be a little easier physically, if he can't even figure that out, then he might as well get out now. But the idea is to find out early whether or not he can take this sort of thing or get him out, because he's going to have to take more in the academic year and more in all four years as a midshipman and more as a naval officer all his life.

Q: Some of this shows up, does it not, in the preliminary examination for qualification to the academy?

Adm. M.: Not very much.

Q: Not very much?

Adm. M.: No, it's surprising.

Q: There's no aptitude test of any kind?

Adm. M.: No, not enough.
    I guess this is about all we can do for today.

Interview #12 with Vice Admiral William P. Mack, U.S. Navy
(Retired)

Place: His residence in Annapolis, Maryland

Date: Friday morning, 25 May 1979

Subject: Biography

By: John T. Mason, Jr.

Q: At first today, this will be a continuation of your discussion of your period of 1972 to 1975 as superintendent of the U.S. Naval Academy. You've covered a number of the subjects, but you have some additional ones today.

Adm. M.: Two subjects that I would like to add to that era when I was aide to SecNav. The first one has to do with the use of a star to designate a line officer.

Prior to the present situation, where a line officer wears a star and a legal officer, for instance, wears a particular device, all non-staff corps officers wore stars. This was about, oh, in the 1960s. That caused some consternation on occasion, such as a large number of senior officers getting in a boat, some of whom were legal officers, some of whom were EDs and things, engineering duty officers, and some of whom were line officers. It was difficult for, say, a commander to know whether he was in charge of that boat or not, and if the boat hit something else or went aground when he was there and a captain legal officer was standing in the stern sheets, then the line commander was liable. But there was no way to tell because they all wore stars and there was the embarrassing situation of having to go up to a senior officer and say:

"Pardon, me, Sir, are you a line officer or are you something else?" And that wasn't generally done. This happened frequently in San Diego and Norfolk where ships were anchored out. For this and many other reasons there was a movement to differentiate line officers from those who were wearing stars but were not qualified to command.

A study was made and it was approved by Secretary Franke and by Admiral Burke, who was then CNO.

Q: Who instigated this change?

Adm. M.: It was Mr. Gates, who was secretary at the time. It was his idea and I think I influenced him to make the study. A study suggestion that differentiation should be made and that the staff, not the staff, but the non-command groups of the navy should be told to come up with their own designations in lieu of a star. For instance, the present legal device would have been at that time the legal device, and a sort of retort or a boiler system would have been put on the epaulets and sleeves of engineering duty officers only, and there were other symbols to be used in lieu of a star. And the women would have a special device, since they were not qualified to command.

This was all approved and it was scheduled to go into effect on a certain date. About two weeks before that Admiral Burke came in and asked to see Mr. Franke privately and did, and when he came out Mr. Franke sent for me and said:

"Admiral Burke has persuaded me not to do this, to put this into effect, that there should be a variation of it, and he feels, having been persuaded by the heads of the various groups who would be, in a sense, destarred, that that would be a terrible thing to do and they should be given a special dispensation that will allow them to keep their stars. A system should be devised that would allow the line officer to wear a star on the breast of his tunic, which would indicate that he is a line officer and qualified to command."

I protested to Mr. Franke and said it was fine to be so sympathetic toward these various splinter groups, but what about the large majority of line officers who felt very strongly that the star meant something. It was a symbol of command and you were, in a sense, going back and taking away from them the prestige of the star and the indication to anybody else that they were in command if they were in a boat or a ship and so forth. He said:

"I agree with you 100 percent, but Admiral Burke has apparently been persuaded by these splinter group heads to do this. I argued with him for a long time and I couldn't change him, so I can't go against the uniformed head of the service."

So I said: "All right, I will carry out your orders in that respect," so I transmitted this to the chief of Naval Personnel and it was done.

I also asked him for permission not to wear the star which indicated you were qualified for command, so he gave me a little piece of paper which said I didn't have to wear it. So I was the only officer in the navy who was qualified for command and didn't have to wear what I considered the degrading symbol, which was a little star on the breast that indicated I really was a line officer.

That was a bit of humor between the secretary and me for some time but at least I was different.

Q: Did anybody ever catch you up on it?

Adm. M.: Yes, several asked me if I wasn't qualified to command, and I said yes, I was. "Where's your star?" And I'd pull the piece of paper out of my wallet, so I don't have to wear it, which was a backwards way, I suppose, of showing disapproval of what was going on, but at least that's what happened.

Over the years, of course, the splinter groups became aware that they had a prestige of their own and they were given permission later on to wear their own symbol and now do. So this is pretty well squared away, but for a long time it was a sore point with the line that they were not allowed to wear their star unmolested by the splinter groups. But it's an interesting point in history that, of all people, my friend whom I admired perhaps most in the navy, Admiral Burke, was the one who felt he was forced by these groups to do this.

Q: But you say it has been largely resolved now?

Adm. M.: Yes, it has, and of course they have quite a new system now of wearing again a big command star on your chest. What's happened is that that now becomes a symbol that you're qualified to command by virtue of having achieved a certain status. That is, you've passed an examination, you've been actually in command of a ship, and so forth. So the only persons not wearing the command star are those of junior rank who haven't passed command qualifications yet. But it's a useless ornament to me. To me, the star on your sleeve means you're a line officer who can command. That was what it was in the old days when it was placed on the side of the sleeve, and it was a star so that in battle in the old square-riggers and so forth, where you were fighting to one side or the other, the captain or anybody else could look up and down the waist of his ship and see his line officers. He could see the star on the side of his sleeve. That's why it was placed on the side of the sleeve. If he wanted his surgeon, he'd know the surgeon because he could see his sleeve with the surgeons' device on it. The same thing with the chaplain. That's what the symbol was for, and we somehow in the navy got away from that, and I tried to get the navy back into that system, saying the star means that you're in the line of succession to command. When you see the star on somebody else's sleeve, you know that's what he is and that's what he should be known for. If a person's a chaplain or a doctor or a lawyer, he should be honored for that. It's a great profession in itself, and if you want a doctor, you want to look at his symbol to know he's a doctor, if you don't know him.

Q: It makes sense.

Adm. M.: It did, but the splinter groups were at cross purposes. Unfortunately, they were listened to and that's what happened. At least, it's a point in history that clarifies why the navy suddenly changed its policy, where Mr. Gates had directed that they carry out this new system, Mr. Franke had endorsed it, and all of a sudden it just crumbled and went away. Many people wondered why and the answer is that the splinter groups got to the CNO and persuaded him that it would harm their morale too much and he changed his mind, saying, in a sense, that this would maintain their morale and it would not hurt the morale of the line officer too much. Perhaps he was right, but it caused quite a stir at the time in the secretary's office.

The second point I'd like to make which I did not approach as an entity but the point came though in what I said at various times. It has to do with the achievements and accomplishments of Admiral Raborn.

Admiral Raborn was in charge of the strategic weapon program for the navy. This means in another sense the Polaris system.

Q: Special Project.

Adm. M.: Yes, it was called Special Project and it was given a special office with special priorities, the highest priorities in the country at that time, which were personnel, strategic materials, and money. Admiral Raborn devised a special system called PERT, which is an acronym, to maintain on a large chart going all the way round a big office the flow of information, materials, and actually scientific and engineering achievements that had to be integrated with each other to make the Polaris system work at a certain time. In other words, you couldn't have a submarine if you didn't have the ability to open the doors under water and let the missile out, you couldn't have a successful Polaris submarine.

All these engineering achievements had to be integrated, one following the other, and if he knew he was behind on the door, he would go over to the door guy and put the bee on him to speed up the technology concerning the opening of the doors so that that would be achieved in time for the doors to be put on the first submarine, so that, in time, the missiles could go into the tubes, which, of course, were closed by the doors.

What was happening was there was so much new technology involved in making a submarine this large with an integrated missile-control system, with inertial navigation systems, two or three of them, with the very careful depth control that was needed, the silencing of the machinery, and so forth, which was required, and then the missile-firing systems to let the gases out when they went off, to make sure that when this enormous weight left the boat, it would be able to compensate itself so that it wouldn't suddenly broach or keel over to one side or the other. Of course, the missile-guidance system in itself was extremely technical and complicated. The warhead, of course, was the province of the Atomic Energy Commission, whereas the back end of the submarine where the engineroom and the machinery were located was the province of Admiral Rickover. But the rest of it was Admiral Raborn's, and that was by far the most technically complicated, more so than the warhead and more so than the engineering part of it.

So, what he did in five years was to place in the hands of this country a strategic weapon of enormous significance, perhaps the most crowning achievement of this century, and I think even perhaps more prestigious and more meaningful than nuclear power. He did it on time and he did it with a minimum of overruns -

Q: Actually, it was a little ahead of time?

Adm. M.: Yes, it was.

The missile itself worked, the submarine worked, there was no gross failure or even minor failure to mar his program. It was a tremendous achievement. For some reason, it was never given the recognition it deserved. Admiral Raborn, of course, was given the Distinguished Service Medal and praised highly by the chief of naval operations, the secretary of the navy, and the Congress, but, for some reason or other, it did not strike the public fancy because, I suppose the Polaris submarine is unused, unseen, and unheard. It's just there. But what it is is vital to this country's security, has been for years, and will be for perhaps another century.

Q: Isn't it true that while the program was under way, in the first five years, there was some public interest in the project -

Adm. M.: Oh, yes.

Q: It was generated very handsomely by Raborn himself and his staff.

Adm. M.: That's right. He had a rather large public affairs staff headed by Commander Ken Wade. I watched his achievements very carefully.

I'm not saying that there wasn't proper publicity given to the project and it didn't get the publicity it needed. I'm simply saying that vis-à-vis Admiral Rickover, for instance, Admiral Raborn is not well known nor is his achievement well known. His achievement was accomplished in five years or even less and Admiral Rickover's goes on for maybe twenty-five years and, therefore, perhaps he's better known. Maybe Admiral Rickover is better known because of his personal characteristics and the way he does his business. That is, he's at cross purposes with large segments of the government and this keeps his name in the papers. A congressman now knows all about Admiral Rickover but if you asked him who Admiral Raborn is, he may not even know - a new congressman, for instance, and people in the government. This is true of people in general. Who's Admiral Raborn? Never heard of him.

What I'm trying to say is that over the five-year period, the ballistic-missiles committee met weekly. Oh, they considered Tartar and Talos occasionally, but nine-tenths of its job was with regard to passing on the merits of the Polaris missile and how its progress was going, and on each occasion Admiral Raborn personally reviewed the progress of his project. My function was to be there with three different secretaries over about a three-year period, take notes for the secretary, carry out whatever orders he wanted carried out at the end of the session. So I had a very good overview of what Admiral Raborn was doing, how he was held, that is, what the secretary thought of him. When the secretary went off to see the Polaris missile fired or would go down in the submarine or watched it launched, I was generally along with him, and saw Admiral Raborn's performance, heard the secretary's comments, and so forth.

Based on this three-year period and these observations, I just have to say I think Admiral Raborn should be considered one of the prime naval officers of this perhaps fifty-year period.

I think when history reviews all this, naval historians will probably agree that two of the most famous naval officers of the hundred-year period are, of course, Admiral Mahan and maybe Admiral Nimitz in this period, passing by Admiral King, passing by Admiral Spruance, and certainly passing by Admiral Halsey. Of the latter period, they will probably say that of the three perhaps prime candidates would be Admiral Raborn, Admiral Rickover, and Admiral Burke. Admiral Rickover will be first in naval history, Admiral Burke second, and Admiral Raborn perhaps third or very little known, and it is unfortunate because, to me, his achievement was one of the prime achievements of this fifty-year period.

But, having seen all these officers personally over a long period of time and having been in several areas where I could see officially the opinion of them by the various CNOs and SecNav, I felt I had to say that, based on what I'd heard and seen, certainly Admiral Raborn should rank very high, and Admiral Burke perhaps of the post World War II and late World War II officers, certainly an outstanding officer. Admiral Halsey will drop down the line somewhat in a historical way of rating people and I would think probably Admiral Spruance will go up, with Nimitz certainly at the top.

I just make these observations based on what I have seen and heard over a long period of years.

Q: I'm very grateful to you for having made those observations, particularly as they pertain to Raborn, because I agree with you so heartily for I know him and know what he did.

Adm. M.: Admiral Raborn never claimed to be technically competent in the sense of being an expert. He was an executive. He had enough technical competence to take into cognizance what was going on and who was doing what, but he brought together a group of people, organized them, motivated them, and kept them going in such a fasion that at the end they produced a fantastic achievement.

Q: All right, Sir. You have some points on the Naval Academy that you want to add?

Adm. M.: Yes.

The first two items rather go together. One is the five-year obligation, which means that you are required to serve five years in the navy after you graduate. This is common to all academies and it was put into effect late in the Vietnamese War by the Congress. The stated purpose of the Congress was to "make young officers who go to the academies pay back the money invested in them and the time put in."

Q: What is the current investment, generally speaking?

Adm. M.: It ranges from $75,000 for the education of a Naval Academy graduate to $90,000 for the army graduate, West Point, and almost $100,000 for the air force graduate.

Congress felt this was a large amount of money, and, of course, there was a reason for it in the Vietnamese War because it was thought that some of those going to the service academies did so to avoid active service in Vietnam. They felt that after four years the war would be over and they wouldn't be required to serve actively. So the Congress had a point when it did this, but there's no point in it now. I kept making this point for some time and getting nowhere, my argument being that you'll get better naval officers to come to the Naval Academy if you do not have this five-year requirement staring them in the face. A fine young engineer or a good athlete or a good candidate of any kind, when he sees five years at the end of his four-year education he thinks that's a lifetime at the age of eighteen to twenty, and it is a long time. He knows he has, in a sense, made up his mind at the age of eighteen that the navy in his career, and he doesn't like that. Therefore, the good young engineer, the good scholar, won't go to the Naval Academy. We've had these young people tell us that.

I kept making this point to the CNO and secretary and to Mendel Rivers, the chairman of the House Armed Services Committee, asking that they change the obligation, at least to reduce it to three years and perhaps two, my theory being that the present BuPers detailing practice is that a young graduate goes to sea for three years, then he comes ashore for two years, and these are the last two years of his obligated period. If he's going on for sure in the navy, he requests postgraduate school or submarine school or aviation training and so forth, which then extends his five-year obligation period beyond five years, but if he's not a career person he's sent, say, to a naval station and he spends his fourth and fifth year in the navy as a rather dissatisfied young officer waiting for his time to expire and he gets out. My thought was we don't need people like that. These are the malcontents, the people who don't do so well, so why need them.

I thought that if you were going to sell a young man on a naval career you could do it in three years. At the end of three years, which is a good-sized obligation, he should by then know if he wants to stay in the navy, If he does, he will. If he doesn't, why not let him out. We don't need him ashore, anyway.

Q: That's the three years while he's at sea?

Adm. M.: For three years, yes. Let him serve three years at sea and that should be the obligation, period.

I was able to make some progress, and the way I made the final bit of progress was that on another subject the use of what's called the science seminar at the Naval Academy. Admiral Rickover had made the point several times, why didn't I do all I could to get the best young brains into the Naval Academy. I said I was doing that and would search for further means, so I thought of the idea of looking at the scores of high-school graduates and sending an invitation to those who had the highest achievement in scientific subjects, mathematics and so forth, to come to the Naval Academy for a five-day period, Monday to Friday, be our guests but at their own expense and put on a science and engineering seminar for them, which would do two things. It would hopefully titillate them a little bit in terms of science and engineering and it would expose them to the Naval Academy and its laboratories - by the time we had Rickover Hall, of course, with a fantastic laboratory system. It would expose them to the Naval Academy and what we have here scientifically and engineeringwise.

We thought we would have two seminars of 250 people each the first summer, and so we sent out, I think, about 12,000 invitations, hoping we would get 1,000 answers. We got 10,000 answers. We had to winnow these down and the 500 young men we got were fantastically good. They came, the seminar was a great success, and it's continued to this day and is one of the finest recruiting tools we have.

Q: This came out of your academy budget?

Adm. M.: Yes. Well, it wasn't very expensive because they paid their own way and we paid a minimum of food and a few things like that. Of course, the instructors' time came out of this, but it was very inexpensive as far as we were concerned.

Q: Was the roster of instructors augmented by outsiders?

Adm. M.: Oh, no. We didn't need to, we wanted to show them what we had.

Q: I see.

Adm. M.: We had seminars for them, we had scientific experiements, and demonstrations in our laboratories so they could see what we had there.

At the end, they all thought this was fine and we gave

them questionnaires and so forth. At the final point, we had, I think 140 state that they wanted to come to the Naval Academy, and over one hundred did come.

What intrigued me was how about the other 360, 140 said of the 500 said they wanted to come and 360 said no. So I gave them a further questionnaire and said "You indicated you didn't want to come to the Naval Academy. Would you like to come if the circumstances were different? If so, what turned you off? Why do you not want to come to the Naval Academy?" Knowing it was going to be the obligation period, further questions followed one of which was:

"If it is the five-year obligation which turned you off, would you change your mind and want to come if the obligation was four years, three years, two years, one year, and zero years?"

Over half of this group of 360 said yes, they would come, if the obligation were two years.

So I enlisted the help of my friend Admiral Rickover and said:

"Look, I've done this. I have great ammunition here to show that if you want to get the same kind of people as I do and the navy does in here, here they are. This is a pool, but they won't come because the obligation is too long."

Well, he went to congressional friends and I started my campaign and we put so much pressure on Mendel Rivers and the House Armed Services Committee that they got a little mad about it and finally went to the secretary of the navy, and the secretary of the navy called me and said:

"Please stop immediately your campaign to change the obligation to three years."

Q: Which Sec was that?

Adm. M.: Mr. Middendorf.

I explained what I was doing and he said:

"Yes, I understand what you're doing but Mr. Rivers wants the pressure stopped and I have to accede to Mr. Rivers."

So I had to stop and I was told point-blank, "Don't talk about it anymore."

That was a mistake, I think, because what we're doing is we're missing a tremendous group of young men –

Q: It has not been changed since?

Adm. M.: No, it has not. There's no pressure for it.

Q: Is the international affairs seminar of similar nature?

Adm. M.: What that really does is bring in young men already in college. They're not candidates. The young men

men at the science seminar were high-school kids.

Q: Are they still within an age group where they - ?

Adm. M.: No, that's not a recruiting tool at all, except as it is used to talk about telling young high-school people if they come here they can take part in this as midshipmen. What it does is bring college students in and it tries to enhance the foreign-affairs knowledge of the midshipmen who were taking courses involving political affairs, foreign history, and that sort of thing, so it's not really a good recruiting tool.

The other tool I started as - I found that a lot of young men were leaving here in the first few months and did so because they had no idea what the Naval Academy was like, nor did their parents. So I started what's called Orientation Day or Parents' Day, which was done in the spring. After all the class was chosen, we invited them, all the candidates, to come back here, bring their parents, and have a day at the Naval Academy, where we gave them a tour, presentations by the major departments, heads of athletics, military affairs, and so forth. In the evening there was a dinner in the dining hall and a prepared program, including speeches by the superintendent, the commandant, the public works officer, and everybody who could tell them what was going on at the Naval Academy.

Over half of the candidates and one or two parents each showed up the first time, and it was very successful. I hope and think that it contributed to cutting down the attrition among the new entries who now knew something about the Naval Academy before they got here. It was not just an absolutely strange experience to them, and that's good, because we used to lose a lot of very good men because they came here absolutely unprepared for what the Naval Academy was like and they just didn't like it after the first two weeks. When they knew what it would be like after they survived plebe summer, they were prepared to stay and to go through that.

Q: And they knew in advance what plebe summer was?

Adm. M.: Oh, yes, we spared no punches in telling them what everything was like, what it was all about -

Q: What the purpose was?

Adm. M.: Right. They saw what was going on, saw the athletic facilities, saw the laboratories, and some of them were prepared to take a little bit of the bad in order to wait for the better.

I think that was very successful, I know it is. Admiral Lawrence said yesterday that these were two of his chief recruiting tools. So I wanted it put in the record why these came about and what happened first. I think they are good tools. I still think the five-year obligation is too much, too long, and we would get better scholars and certainly better athletes and better all-around men if they were not required to sign up for a terrible period of time in a young man's life. That's nine years, and to require a young man to make up his mind at age eighteen or nineteen what he's going to do for the next nine years is fantastic. This doesn't happen in civilian life.

We were tasked at one time by the Committee on Education to explain why we had such high attrition. The attrition we had here over the four-year period was about 33 or 35 percent per class. I explained that this was not high and, sure enough, we made a study of civilian universities from Harvard on down, from the very highest to the lowest, and we found out that their attrition averaged almost 50 percent at Harvard. What I mean by attrition is that 50 percent of those entering freshman class at Harvard did not graduate with a degree in four years.

Q: For whatever reason.

Adm. M.: For several reason. Either they stayed out two years then came back and finished or they stayed out and never came back or they transferred to another school, but at least they didn't finish at Harvard. This was the same in almost every school in the country, it averaged between 40 and 50 percent, so our 30 to 35 percent really was very modest. It really is an indication of the changing times, the instability of the youth of the country, and what they do and see, but it's another indication that at that age you don't know what they want, and it's not right to ask somebody to make up his mind to obligate for four years at the Naval Academy plus five years obligation. He either makes a good decision, in which case he's happy. If he makes a bad decision, he's unhappy and not a very good contributor for his obligated period, and certainly not for the last two of them. If you want a dissatisfied, incompetent, and inefficient officer for the last two years at some naval station, that's what you've got. My theory was I'd rather let him go and have a chief petty officer take his place or anybody or nobody rather than have a malcontent. But I was never able to prevail. I lost that one.

Q: These examples that you cite indicate such an imaginative approach that you gave to the superintendency. I mean you put a real stamp on it.

Adm. M.: Well, there were some changes made. I repeat

again when I was sent there I had absolutely no charge from Admiral Zumwalt as to what to do, how to run the Naval Academy. He simply said, "Run it as you see fit, and remember that the purpose of the Naval Academy is to train midshipmen mentally, morally, physically, and to prepare them for service in the navy," which is a very general and I think a very good charge. I was asked when I got there what changes I foresaw and I said:

"I don't think any revolutionary changes need to be made, only evolutionary changes."

And what I did for three years was to evolve better systems for doing things and make some changes.

Q: I suppose you could label this "fine tuning"!

Adm. M.: In some ways. It's very difficult to change the course of the Naval Academy quickly. You can't do it. That's why it took three years to make any dent at all in the professional requirements for midshipmen, that is that they know how to serve in the navy when they leave. First, they had instruction and then they had to have mandatory exams without grades, then we had to go to grades through exams. You couldn't just turn in like that. You can do it all right, you can do anything by edict, but it doesn't work very well. You have to put it in so that the people doing it really believe in it if you want to get the best results. So it took about three years to do that.

It took three years to make a significant change in the indoctrination of plebes from the silliness that we used to have when I got there to strictly professional. Now, I understand, it's gone down ever further. Instead of having the first class do it, the first class are doing what they should, learning to be officers, and the second class and third class are indoctrinating the plebes and enjoying it and doing it professionally. No longer are they doing the silly stuff. They are engaged in furthering their own knowledge by having to teach plebes on how many carriers we have, what their characteristics are, and that sort of thing. They like it and the plebes like it. That took some years to start because if you suddenly took a first class and said, "You no longer can do this, you've got to do something else," their answer was, "Well, we went through this ourselves. How come we don't get a chance to try it on somebody else?" The real answer, of course, was, well, be man enough to give it up and do it right, but that doesn't motivate the whole first class. Unfortunately, you've got to change a little bit at a time, so some of these changes did take two or three years deliberately, rather than just change by edict.

Q: I wonder if you'd say something about the physical

plant during your time there, any changes that were made, any additions that came about. Would you include it in some comment on the Nimitz Library?

Adm. M.: When I arrived, the ten-year building program, which was a program laid out by the Navy Department to construct a new series of building at the Naval Academy, was about one-third completed, I guess. In June of the year I arrived at the Naval Academy I thought it was in fine physical shape. One week after I arrived a terrible hurricane occurred and the basements of Chauvenet, Michelson, and parts of the Nimitz Library, which was coming along, were all flooded, and it cost millions of dollars. What happened was the contractor's cofferdam to the utility tunnel broke. It wasn't the Naval Academy's fault, it was the contractor's and he paid most of it, but still it was very expensive and quite a setback for the Naval Academy. At least we survived that and went ahead.

During my period there, the new buildings, which had already been completed, were Chauvenet and Michelson. Nimitz Library was about a third finished and, of course, Rickover was nothing. The Crown Sailing Center had not even been thought about much yet. So in my first year, Nimitz was completed and a start was made during my three years here and Rickover was built, completed, and dedicated, as was about three-quarters of the terrace between them.

Then Sampson Hall was gutted and changed into an electrical laboratory, which is next to Rickover Hall. These were the so-called official buildings that were being changed. Luce Hall was scheduled for gutting and refurbishing but I couldn't get the money for it in the years I was here.

I fought hard for money to put into a new athletic complex. We found that the Naval Academy, strangely enough, had less swimming-pool space per midshipman than did West Point and the Air Force Academy, and yet we're supposed to be a naval service. We were woefully deficient in swimming-pool areas just to teach people how to swim, water survival, and so forth, let alone intercollegiate competition. You couldn't dive, for instance, very high. We couldn't do very well in intercollegiate diving because our pool was too shallow. And we were deficient in wrestling areas, boxing areas, all kinds of inside areas. So in our plan was the new athletic area, which was to be built on top of the stadium. I kept fighting for money for that but it kept being pushed back year by year, then in the final year I got the money for it and it's to be started, I understand, this spring, which will be a tremendous addition to the athletic facilities of the Naval Academy. It's being built on the old Thompson Stadium field.

The other program that Admiral Calvert turned over to me was development of what we thought would be three areas. One would be a complete refurbishing of Dahlgren Hall, which of course in the old days was an armory, into a midshipman recreation center, the building of the sailing center, and then, hopefully, the building of an outdoor swimming-pool complex in the present reflecting pool area. This required the raising of about $3 million. Of course, it wouldn't be funded by Congress, it would be funded by private donations. Admiral Calvert had formed a foundation to take the money involved –

Q: This was separate from the foundation that existed?

Adm. M.: Yes, this was strictly a memorial foundation for these three projects. I spent a good part of my three years raising money, speeches, letters to other foundations, private citizens, and so forth. For instance, I got the money for the Robert Crown Sailing Center from the Crown family.

Q: Yes.

Adm. M.: That was built completely and I helped dedicate it. I started and finished it, and that formed the basis for really a splendid sailing complex there now.

Dahlgren Hall, I got the money for that from individual contributors. The midshipmen themselves went home and got their parents and friends to contribute. Ross Perot helped by loaning us money and giving us a small amount. Many people helped by private donations. This had to be pursued until we got the money for Dahlgren Hall, which we did, and then it became a midshipman recreation center with a convertible dance floor - ice hocky rink, the main part of it, decking over a considerable portion of balcony to make a reception area and a dining area down below this part. This was to be turned over to the midshipmen who could bring their guests in and have a place to eat.

The former visitors' center, which was very inadequate, was formerly in the center of Bancroft Hall and was moved here and, of course, it was a very adequate place for midshipmen where they could all see their guests.

What, I think, stimulated me more than anything when I was here was my first June Week, walking around the yard before I took over from Admiral Calvert, I noticed midshipmen and their families and girl friends sitting on curbs. There was simply not enough space anywhere for midshipmen to greet their guests, certainly not in June Week, and hardly any other time. I think that made me work harder than anything else to get money for Dahlgren Hall and to stimulate the rest of them to work on it and get it done.

It was very satisfying the June Week after Dahlgren

Hall was finished to see, on a rainy day, for instance, all the visitors that the academy could hold practically, midshipmen's families and guests and girl friends in Dahlgren Hall with a place to sit, refreshments, adequate space, it was beautifully furnished - it was just a great achievement. There's a fantastic amount of room there, and nobody was sitting on the curb. So I think that was one of the reasons I really liked that portion of what I was doing, to get this fixed up so that the midshipmen would have a place to take their guests.

Q: You mentioned the approach to various foundations for gifts. Were you successful in that area?

Adm. M.: Oh, yes. I learned a lot about fund-raising. You find that you have to get on the rolls of various foundations really, and to keep it up. Sometimes, they'll tell you the first year that they have no money, they've given it all out, but if you keep after them year after year in a nice way, suddenly the second or third year they'll find money. Their job is to give away money and you just have to make sure you're up on their list of prospective donors so that you get yours in.

Q: Yes, and some of them have pet projects in one area or another area.

Adm. M.: Yes, and many companies have gift-sharing plans, where if an employee will give you $50, the company will match it. We got a lot of that. Gulf Oil would give us a lot of money because of Gulf employees who knew navy types and would give the same amount the employees gave.

We had other methods of raising funds but in the end I was never able to raise the other $2 million, a little less than $2 million, that would be needed for a swimming pool complex. That would be a nice thing for the summertime for the midshipmen because they would have had dressingrooms and picnic areas around the new swimming pool complex. But that's still on the books and as money comes in for various things it's put in the fund for that. Some day, perhaps, it will be built.

Q: Did you have any problem during your regime with the acquisition of books and that sort of thing for the Nimitz Library?

Adm. M.: No. The Nimitz Library, when commissioned, had about 3,000,000 books in it and when I left they had about 3,500,000. We had no problem. As soon as people knew it was there and saw it, they began to give us books and to give us money for books. In general, I think it became a very good library. I'd seen the Firestone Library at Yale, Princeton rather, and the libraries at Yale and

Harvard, in the early years when I was taking my son around to enter him in college. He went to Princeton, and his remark to me always was:

"Daddy, someone has just given $2 million more to Princeton and guess where it's going - rare books for the library. I can't see the books, they won't let you look at them. The only people who can see them are visiting scholars, some of the professors, and occasional graduate students. What's the use? Here the dormitories are falling down, we need money for them, and they're putting more rare books down in the basement of their library."

I think perhaps that impressed me a little bit and I always thought that a book that went into the Nimitz Library should be accessible. A rare book wasn't much good for a visiting scholar if a midshipman couldn't see it. So I think most of our money for accessions went into books the midshipmen could see.

Q: Well, actually, it's a library for the midshipmen primarily, isn't it?

Adm. M.: Yes. It's not like the Firestone Library. It's magnificent, but what's it for? The answer is visiting scholars and graduate students.

Q: Would you say something about the chapel and its

position in the life of the academy?

Adm. M.: Yes, and I am in a unique position to comment on that.

Before I went to the Naval Academy from the Seventh Fleet, I was, of course, deputy assistant secretary of defense for manpower and reserve affairs. There was a suit brought at that time to abolish compulsory chapel and, as you'd expect, the filing of that suit became the province of my office there, together with Admiral Moorer, who was the chairman of the Joint Chiefs at the time, who handled the military end of it.

Mr. Kelley, who was the assistant secretary at the time, passed it to me as a chore to do and I was to make the arguments as to why we should continue compulsory chapel. I said I didn't like it very much, I could dream up some arguments all right, but I didn't believe it, it shouldn't be compulsory. That caused consternation in the ranks. Admiral Moorer couldn't understand it, Mr. Kelley could understand it and followed my reasoning but thought compulsory chapel was a good thing. Mr. Kelley was Catholic and, as you know from the regimen of the Catholic followers their very faith calls for mandatory mass and mandatory observance of holy days and so forth, so it was quite reasonable that that would be the way he would feel. He admitted that and, since I wasn't Catholic,

I could see perhaps more leniency in religious observance.

At any rate, we fought the case and won, to my displeasure. Then, later on, at the Naval Academy I was told that the case was reopened, hearings were coming along, and we were told the Naval Academy could present our position and so forth, which I did, following the Defense direction. I was secretly quite overjoyed when it was overturned and we were told to get ready for voluntary chapel. Everybody thought that was terrible and I thought it was just fine. I followed Father O'Connor's feeling that when chapel opened voluntarily you'd find the same number of worshipers there as before. The only difference would be the attendees who didn't worship wouldn't be there and you'd be better off.

Also, I felt that to make it voluntary would mean that we could do everything we did before, except that perhaps we could make it more flexible, and that's what we did. We started by being low key in how we handled it and decided, of course, we would never go for the business of lining up the volunteers and marching them over just to make a show for the visitors who came to watch people march into chapel. It was to be entirely voluntary. There it was, and the midshipmen could go and they could sit anywhere. At the same time this happened, the first Sunday, I abolished the pew-assignment system. Before, all the central pews had been reserved for not only the

Naval Academy authorities of one kind and another but also retired people and others from the town. As a result, midshipmen sat way back, on the sides, or up in the balcony and so forth, as did their guests. And so I decided the only reserved pews would be for the superintendent, the commandant, and the academic dean. Everybody else would sit wherever they wanted to, which meant a midshipman could bring his guests in or his family and sit wherever he wanted to. That worked just fine.

Also, as I said before, we tried to make it flexible. While the eleven o'clock Protestant service and the then 8:30 Catholic mass were the principal services before, we decided we would change mass to nine o'clock and make the eleven o'clock, as it was, a quite formal service, but that we'd have other services. There'd be several other masses and there'd be a Protestant nine o'clock service somewhere, a so-called communion service. We'd encourage midshipmen to keep on going out in town, if they wanted to, and we'd provide transportation if we had to. We'd have other religious experiences of one kind and another.

What happened was that while attendance at chapel fell off somewhat, considerably, I guess at least down 50 percent, the Protestants fell off a little more than Catholics because they have a little firmer control over their parishioners and tell them they've got to go, whether or not the government says you've got to go, we we found attendance at these other services went up. The various choirs maintained their strength. Whenever a new kind of religious experience was proposed it was received enthusiastically because it wasn't involuntary, it was voluntary, and totally our feeling was that religious observance at the Naval Academy maintained about the same - well, of course, theoretically everybody had gone to something before - but we felt that at least 80 percent of the midshipmen did something every week in terms of going to chapel for communion service or something regarding religious experience, which is what our aim was. The other 20 percent were those who went in the back of the chapel and slept, anyway, through the service, so they weren't hurt.

Q: What did they do on Sunday morning?

Adm. M.: They slept in their rooms! Which cleared out the chapel for those who might like to be there, such as visitors and so forth. So it became a much more honest experience and I liked it. We found that stripers volunteered with very little pressure to continue to usher and, again, the choirs remained filled. It became, again, a much more honest experience and it was for the best. I'm sorry we took that long to get to it. The thing I liked best was seeing a midshipman able to meet his parents in the yard and walk into chapel. If you want to watch midshipmen marching, go to noon meal or go to a parade, you don't have to watch them march to chapel. I thought that was always a rather stilted and unnatural experience, watching midshipmen march into chapel. I never liked it. I had to do it the first year I was there, observe it and do it, but it was much better when it changed.

So I think that was a good contribution to Naval Academy life.

Q: I suppose you regretted the fact that it got into the hands of the Civil Liberties people.

Adm. M.: That was one of my regrets, why did we not have the moral courage to do this ourselves, rather than have it forced on us by the courts. That was terrible. That's what I was saying while I was in the Defense Department. I was told, no, we're not going to do this, you make the argument and we'll fight it. I said, why do you fight it, we'd be better off to do it of our own volition, but I was told to fight it so I had to fight it, not with good grace, I must admit.

Q: Would you say something - I know you have decided feelings on this subject - about the ability of young officers to speak their pieces and to express ideas, constructive or otherwise?

Adm. M.: I felt that if you're going to get somewhere in life, if you have an idea or an opinion, you should not be hesitant to speak it, and, if that's going to be so, then what is an integral part of this is that the person you're speaking to has to receive it gracefully and listen and either tell you why it's a good idea and do something about it, or tell that it's not a good idea, thank you for it, and say no, I'm not going to do it. That's why, when I retired, I made a speech in which I emphasized this. Unfortunately, parts of it were taken out of context and it was thought that what I was saying was I was encouraging young men to be dissenters, that is, to disagree with everything. I didn't say that at all. What I said was that you should always have the moral courage to give your opinions to your seniors, but more than that, as you went along in your career, you should develop a habit of listening to those who dissent from you. And, again, I said either telling them that's a good idea, we'll do it, or telling them no, it's a bad idea and why we won't do it, and then making sure they didn't suffer for offering their opinions. That's what I said, but it was taken out of context and it was said by some people that what I was doing was saying that you should always go around in dissent. Not so. You should only dissent if you have something that you think it's proper to talk about.

Again, the word dissent or dissenter has lots of

meanings and unfortunately the connotation from past decades is that a dissenter is a guy who carries a placard around -

Q: Gets violent about it!

Adm. M.: Yes. A dissenter is simply - dissent means simply to disagree with, and there are two opinions on almost everything. On every military decision, they have a pro and a con, and before you decide to do something you should hear the other side. As a matter of fact, you were wise if you designated somebody to be your dissenter and to tell you everything he can about why he thinks the decision you're about to make is wrong, so you know you've examined both sides of a decision before you take it.

Q: I thought about you yesterday. I spent three hours with Admiral Burke and the current crop of Burke scholars, and the general discussion around the table after the luncheon was over and some of these refreshing points of view that were expressed, because Arleigh gave them all a chance and not only once but several times they spoke up with their ideas of what they were contemplating as officers in the navy and so forth. A very, very constructive thing, which he took and built upon, agreed with them, and then said but there is this other aspect which you should also consider.

Adm. M.: Yes. I find Arleigh Burke a very refreshing person. On the other hand, it's hard for me to reconcile the fact that he brought me in to work for him for slightly less than a year as an official dissenter. In other words, my job was to listen to everything he did and to everything he said and examine his writings, and then give him ideas, tell him where he was wrong, what he should do. This I was doing as a captain when he was chief of naval operations, and he said:

"That's what I want. I want somebody to look at everything I'm doing and give me good ideas and so forth."

I thought that was fine and I enjoyed it no end. I learned tremendously from it and looked up to him as a man big enough to do that sort of thing. I was a little bit surprised, after I made my speech, he never told me that he disagreed with what I said, but in his writings to the Naval Institute discussion column and so forth and other things he said, it was evident to me that he didn't really read my speech, or at least, if he read it, I didn't get through to him because he really made the point that you should not be a dissenter. I kept telling him:

"But, Admiral, I didn't say that. I said you should listen to dissenters. You do. You listened to me."

Somehow I could never get through to him that that's

what I said. I doubt that he ever read the speech because, if he did, he was very good at understanding things and he would have, I think, understood what I said.

Q: Did you have occasion to read the copy of the letter I gave you?

Adm. M.: Yes, I enjoyed it. I think he was just exactly right in what he did. He never enjoyed being a dissenter. I kept talking about, "I'm not talking about the dissenter. I'm talking about when you midshipmen get to be senior enough to have somebody dissent from you, listen to that person because you may be throwing away the best advice in your ship or whatever if you don't listen to this guy. He may be right."

That's what happens so much. I gave three or four examples of it. Sims if he hadn't been listened to we'd have been back in the dark ages in gunnery, and Mahan, of course, with sea power, and Rickover and motive power, if we hadn't listened to these three guys. Somebody had to listen to them or we'd be in terrible shape, and what happened was that military guys, naval officers, did not listen to them. It took a civilian secretary to listen to them, to get their viewpoints and their ideas, and get them out in the open and make them history. That has been one of the bad things about our naval service all the time, that the military fellows have not listened to dissenters. That's what I was saying. I gave these examples, but somehow —

Q: It comes more naturally in civilian life.

Adm. M.: Yes, that's what they do in business, that's exactly it. You can't afford not to listen to a dissenter. If you don't, you lost your profits and your shirt.

In the navy, nothing happens really. You just transfer that guy after you get tired of listening to him, or if you make a mistake, sometimes nobody knows about it. How can you tell?

This is an addendum to the section on the National War College.

After I retired, I was asked back to the National War College to conduct and address a seminar of National War College students and their wives on the subject of morality in government and dissent. This was stimulated by their examination of the retirement speech I made. I did so and I gave a twenty-minute presentation to start the affair, in which I outlined my views on morality in government, dissent, and so forth. What I really said was roughly what I said in my retirement speech, that you should have the moral courage to dissent if you feel something is wrong, and this is certainly highlighted by what's happened in Vietnam. Then I went through the business about one of the things you should learn most is how to listen to other people, encourage those in your command or your group to dissent, because if you don't you're going to make a bad decision because you won't have both sides of the question.

Strangely enough, when I got through and during the discussion period, one officer asked me, "What do you do about this business of dissenting because you know in this day and age in the league we're operating in, if we dissent and our senior doesn't like it one nick in the fitness report is going to kill our career?"

Q: Was this a naval officer?

Adm. M.: It was a naval officer. I said:

"My solution to this would be, if I were in his shoes, to – " and I gave this rationale about the fact that it's very difficult in the services, particularly the navy, to dissent because, if you do, this is what will happen to you. If you dissent from the wrong person, a less than enlightened senior, he can kill your career with one fitness report, even though you're making an honest disagreement with what he's doing and so forth and going within the rules. If he doesn't like it and he's vindictive,

Mack #12 - 821

you're dead. So I said:

"If I had to do my career over again, what I'd do would be to give myself an anchor, that no longer would I be strictly a line officer able to command, I hope, anything, but since there's only one navy, if I did what you say and my career was killed, I can't leave this navy and go to a command in another navy, unless they'd let me in the Soviet Navy or something of that sort, or the British, or somewhere. The merchant marine is not a comparable career, although many naval officers go there. But in a sense if I kill myself careerwise, I have no place to go. I would have to go out and find some kind of a new career.

"So, what I'm advising you to do, and what I would do if I had to start over again, I would have another career, and I would spend all my spare time studying it. I don't care what it is, accounting or law or some kind of a civilian career. I think you can do that in the navy, or in the army and air force, if you spend your spare time and such study time and course time, scholastic time, as the service will give you in preparing yourself. I would certainly have as the heart of this career a postgraduate course in something, and not in too technical a subject. It could be in aviation engineering or mechanical engineering or something, which you can use in the navy but it should have some bearing on what you want to choose as a civilian occupation. I've always studied banking. That's what I'm going to do, but I started late in life and, if I were to do it again, I would study banking or something else very early in life, so that I could always maintain my moral independence. If I had to make a tough choice and disagreed with somebody on a moral issue or a professional issue, I would always think, all right, if that's the way the navy's going to operate and they're going to kill me on one disagreement, let them do it, and I would get out and go do something else."

Q: How was this received by these students?

Adm. M.: Not very well. Their contention was, well, how can you do that. What you're doing is you're stealing time from the country and the government and the navy to prepare yourself to do something else other than be a naval officer.

I might add that, of course, the National War College students are extremely highly selected.

Q: Yes.

Adm. M.: They're superb people, very highly motivated, all of them, and their only feeling, I think, is how do I do my best for my country and my service.

Q: Their reaction to your remarks was on an ethical basis?

Adm. M.: Yes. They said: "Well, how can you justify taking time out, if you're motivated to be a naval officer and the way the navy runs these days and you're going to work eighteen or twenty hours a day for the navy at sea and ashore, where's time left over for that?"

I said, "That's something you'd have to face. I think you can do it. If you do it for two hours that makes your day twenty hours instead of eighteen, but you'd better take it."

Q: You were, in a sense, addressing your argument to a very small percentage of people -

Adm. M.: Exactly.

Q: - because you have to be awfully able to do this.

Adm. M.: That's right.

Q: You have to carry water on both shoulders.

Adm. M.: That's right, but that's why I wanted to address it to them. These are the people I'm concerned about. These are superb officers who have weathered all this sort of thing and are here, and they're just about to step into the JCS and OpNav and OSD, where they face these hard choices, where they have to tell a superior in any service that he's wrong, this is legally wrong or morally wrong and so forth. They're about to make that hard choice and if they don't have a career in sight by now, they'd better start rounding up one, because it's going to happen to them. If they make this hard choice and get the bad fitness report and they have to face it. They're going to get passed over or retire or get out or whatever, or they're going to knuckle under in order to get their promotions and go out to the system, say well, I'll knuckle under here. I know I'm wrong but I have to do this in order to get promoted and go on, and I'll be honest from now on.

Well, that's a choice you make. But my choice, if I had to do it again, would be to prepare myself on my own time, if I had any of my own time, which is hard to find in the navy, and by taking hopefully the right kind of postgraduate courses so that I would have a second career.

Q: You're talking about drawing on your spare time, which would largely inflict on family relationships, so I ask how did the women in this audience react to this?

Adm. M.: The same way the men did. They said, how would you do this. So I said:

"Well, I'll tell you how I would do it. If you don't want to make that sacrifice, then you're going to have to make a hard choice, knuckle under or not. It's going to be very difficult to make that choice, unless you have an additional tool at your disposal such as being able to go outside, if you have to, and make a living."

Many of them had not seen the hard peacetime navy where competition was extremely difficult. It's not hard, if you're a good man, to go out and fight well, but if you try to fight a peacetime war it is moral issues, making decisions, and dissenting on silly little issues that can kill your career. In peacetime it's sometimes a tougher navy than in wartime because what you have is the good paper-shufflers and the bureaucrats and so forth. They tend to come to the top in peacetime, and you have to be able to survive in that league if you want to stay around for the next war. So it's very, very difficult.

Q: You were sounding a note of making personal sacrifice and this is a very difficult thing to get most people to agree to do.

Adm. M.: That's right, but I thought that you could combine personal sacrifice, this is time and effort, together with judicious selection of what you do. In other words, don't take a completely absolutely professional postgraduate course, if you can help it. Take something that has some future in it.

I can name some cases. Admiral Kinney, as you know, took a law degree, but he never took his bar exams and never practiced as a lawyer in the navy. Well, now, I don't know whether that's stealing from the navy or not, but I think he was wise. He would have been a two-bit lawyer for the navy if he'd done that, but his legal training was extremely valuable to him. He could have used that as a profession or anywhere else he wanted to.

Q: I think you've cited before a man whom we both admire and that is Admiral Dennison who, on his own time, got a doctorate in some particular field. He wasn't stealing from the navy.

Adm. M.: No, but he did have a postgraduate course in diesel engineering, which he never used, and, in a sense, he took that on navy time. He could have built on that, had he gone out into the civilian world as an engineering consultant or working for a company involving engineering.

But that can be quite common. By all means, take a postgraduate course in something. The problem is to keep the navy from making you go into the plebeian kinds of billets that are called for to work off your postgraduate obligation. That's where, in a sense, you have to face the business of stealing from the navy. You take the education and then you don't use it to work on these nuts and bolts type jobs or do something else to broaden yourself. But there are so many things you can do. You can study accounting or you can get a law degree on your own time. You can do many things, but you'd better aim toward having some ability to take out into the civilian world, otherwise you're handicapped when you face a tough moral choice.

I told these young people - they weren't young, I guess they were forty-five:

"Here you are, you're a commander or a captain or a colonel. Right at this time you have children who are about to go to college, you have a wife, you have financial and other responsibilities, think what a terrible thing it is if you have to face right now this moral choice, if you disagree with your senior. He's going to nick you and you're not going to make flag rank. How much pressure is on you because you think right away what do I do, do I argue with this guy? I should, but suppose I argue and he doesn't like it and he shoots me down. I've got two kids to get into college. How am I going to get this kind of money on the outside, or what am I going to do if I'm a passed-over captain, and then have to retire? I'm a little short of money to take care of my family at this very critical time financially. How much better for you is it to have in the back of your head, I'll do this and I don't care what happens. If they throw me out of the navy, fine, I'll go do something else.

And if you haven't been careful with what you've done in your career, that "something else" may be running a gas station."

Q: That leads to a related subject that came up yesterday and on which you have some very decided ideas. I was talking to Miles Libbey, a young chap who interests me very much. He's at the Fletcher School on a scholarship and was being quite excited about it, and I said:

"Are you certain now that this thing you're going into won't derail your career?"

"No," he said, "I'm absolutely certain that I'm going to see that it doesn't derail it because I'm a line officer and I want to go to sea, but I also want to write."

What about this, the intellectual development of the naval officer? How far can he go in an area like this without being derailed, so to speak?

Adm. M.: I met him yesterday at breakfast and I didn't have time to talk to him. I wanted to. I know a little bit about his career. He's right on the thin edge.

Going to the Fletcher School of Diplomacy is a great thing -

Q: Sponsored by the navy, of course.

Adm. M.: Yes, of course - and hopefully, if he does his business, which will be to do his sea jobs properly and well, he will become what's called a subspecialist in political affairs. Now, he will be a superb subspecialist because he's going to have the educational grounding of the Fletcher School for it and undoubtedly he's going to the National War College or the Naval War College to back this up, probably the National, and he will become a good subspecialist. But how do you use this on the outside? That's the problem. This is great professional training for him. He'll go along and he'll perhaps wind up on the Joint Staff or Op-60, where high grade commanders go to. That will be great. He's shooting for the top. What you do when you go through this chain of education and billets is you become Op-06 like Admiral Dennision did, or CinC-Lant, or something of that sort in the strategic line. You don't necessarily become CNO but you become something as good or better, CinCLant or CinCPac or CinCPacFlt.

But he has to be kind of careful. What do you do? Do you get out and go over to the State Department and say here, I'm trained in political affairs and that sort of thing, will you give me a job? The answer might be yes and might be no. There's no ready market for a fellow trained in political affairs outside of the government. That's the problem.

Q: Well, in the area of writing books and so forth?

Adm. M.: If he really has outstanding writing talent, yes, he can make a living, but you don't make much money writing books.

Q: No.

Adm. M.: If you're making money, you're writing fiction which is serialized or put in paperback or made a movie from, but a hard book is just a few thousand dollars. That's a tough life to write as an author.

Q: How receptive is the navy, however, to this kind of effort on the part of one of its officers?

Adm. M.: You mean if he becomes an author?

Q: Yes, if he becomes an author.

Adm. M.: As an author strictly nothing, but if he has

something from which to write, that is if he has a successful career and keeps on as he says he's going to do and commands and serves successfully in Op-60 on the Joint Staff and so forth, and write from that, that's fine. But you can't suddenly stop being professional and just become an author. That stops your naval involvement and you don't get anywhere, but if you're going to get out of the navy the kind of money you make writing that sort of thing is not very much. They don't pay very much, the Atlantic Monthly, Foreign Affairs Quarterly and so forth, that's cheap writing.

Q: That leads me to another subject, which is related again. When you were superintendent of the Naval Academy, you were also vice president of the Board of Control of the Naval Institute and at other times you served on the board in a different capacity, and I think you were on the manuscript committee. Do you want to comment on that and on the position of the Naval Institute in the lexicon of the navy itself? The outlet for men to express their ideas and their dissents, too.

Q: I was a member of the Board of Control, I guess, for around twelve years, longer than anybody else. There's a plaque up there that says how many years. I can't read it from here, but for a long time. I started my association with the Naval Institute by writing three articles early in World War II about the campaign in Java.

Q: You were a lieutenant?

Adm. M.: I was a lieutenant. And that started when I was in the John D. Ford and the Asiatic Fleet in those days, and the navy also, had no public affairs system, no photographers, no nothing. So when this destroyer came back to Mare Island after the active part of the war we were in the yard there, a member of the newly formed public affairs system of the navy, I guess, came aboard and wanted to find somebody who knew something about the campaign in Java because - this was a naval officer, I've forgotten who it was - the navy wanted to do something about it, say something about it and they couldn't find anybody. So he sat down and talked to the captain and the exec and then the officers, and finally the captain says:

"Okay, Mack, your detail."

So I said, "All right, I'll write something about it." The guy said, "This is pretty good. Will you expand it and send it to the Naval Institute?"

I said, "If that's what you want, I'll do it. The captain told me to do it, so I'll do it."

So I wrote these articles, submitted them to the Naval Institute and, lo and behold, they published them all.

I'd always been a member of the Naval Institute, of course, and read it all the time, but I'd never thought much about writing, hadn't had time for it, although I'd taken writing courses in high school and, I thought, written well at the Naval Academy. All my writing effort at the Naval Academy was a thesis on the Kuomintang. That was a subject I knew extremely well and I thought I had written a fine thesis on it and, lo and behold, I got it back with an unsatisfactory mark, which was the only unsatisfactory mark I ever got in my entire career at the Naval Academy. I took it to my professor and said:

"I don't understand. This is well researched. I know this subject as well as anybody in the country knows it. I've been in China and I know a lot of these people. To me, it's well written. I've been writing for some time. I don't write poorly. I get As for my themes and so forth."

He said, "Well, I don't like it, it's no good."

I'll not say the name of the professor but at any rate I got a failing mark on my thesis and that really made me unhappy, so I refurbished it and sold it to what was then the predecessor of <u>Foreign Affairs Quarterly</u> as an article, as a midshipman. So at least I knew I could still write. Then when I got to writing for the Naval Institute these three articles, I decided I would continue whenever I could. So I wrote articles occasionally.

And so, when I was back in Washington, there was a

vacancy on the board and I was invited to fill it. That started my association with the Board of Control. I enjoyed my work with them. I was put on the finance committee and then succeeded to its chairmanship. At that time, we had financial problems. We didn't have as much money as we have now and there were other things that had to be resolved.

Q: You certainly did a beautiful job there.

Adm. M.: Well, over the years I changed the investment policy of the institute over a period of more than ten years and finally got it to the point where we're really very solid these days, on a very firm basis, the Bessemer Investment Trust making money for us, and so forth. In those days, we were very, very conservative, bonds and no stocks. We weren't keeping up with inflation and we had lots of problems. No one seemed to want to make any money so we tried to encourage the administration and ourselves to seek more publications in order to make a little bit more money, so we began to make money, as you see now.

So I enjoyed my association over the years with it. I guess I was elected to the board twice after that and then automatically became a member when I was superintendent, so that was easy, although I think I was a member, anyway.

I enjoyed my time. I thought it was very professionally

rewarding. In all those years, of course, there was a succession of presidents who were CNOs. It was a way to get a gauge of the current CNO when he'd come down for meetings.

Q: In perspective, how do you view the institute and its position in the navy, as contrasted with the original concept a hundred or so years ago when it was set up to be - the magazine was to be a vehicle for officers to express themselves, sometimes in great dissent, the Young Turks, and yet with the cooperation with the official navy, because I understand that they had access to ONI documents and so forth to prepare their articles?

Adm. M.: Yes, that's the way it was set up but I don't know how many years it operated that way, because when I came to it as a board member first in 1954, I guess, it was not doing that at all. The Proceedings was simply a succession of historical type articles - and there wasn't a single, in my memory, in the first couple of years, a single article that contributed any knowledge, any information, any ideas, any aggressiveness. It wasn't that kind of a magazine. It was not encouraged to be and the board, I thought, was rather like that themselves. They didn't much care.

Q: It was moribund then?

Adm. M.: Yes. The board membership changed in the first years I was there. I saw this and voted for some of these articles that were coming in, and we began to solicit articles. Commander Bowler became secretary-treasurer early in my regime there, and all he needed was a little encouragement by the board to seek out authors. If you were moribund, as you quite graphically state, to let people know you're alive again you have to get the word out. So we had to seek out new authors and get them to write on subjects we knew would be live and then when that appeared in the Proceedings that encouraged more people to write. And, of course, we had to have some CNOs who were sympathetic again to this viewpoint. We had some CNOs who took a few chances. A couple of them got in trouble with Mr. Sylvester and a few other people from time to time, Admiral Burke being one of them. It wasn't easy but, knowing that you had a CNO who had the guts to do that sort of thing, encouraged you to do something inside the system, and, as a result, over the years we really changed the character of the board, the character of the Proceedings, what it did. I think now it's back roughly to its original state.

Q: That's very interesting, very encouraging, too!

Adm. M.: Yes. The board has the ability now, I think, to look forward to what are going to be issues. The people on the board are much - I don't want to use the word "prestigious," but they are in areas where they are in jobs where the area is prestigious, for instance the CNO's office and what not, and they can bring to the board "this is going to be a vital subject two or three months from now, it's being talked about, you know, and we have to do this or do that." Everybody's very unhappy with the personnel policy or this or that, and then the board would encourage good authors who were knowledgeable in the area to get on this subject and hurry up and give us an article so that when it came time to go to publication we'd have an article which, in some cases, was right on the money as far as timeliness. The problem then surfaced before the article or at the same time, it wasn't a year after the problem.

That was a deliberate policy on the part of the board, to become current again and not historical, as it was for a while. And so we had a deliberate policy. There'd be a few historical articles to please, if you'll pardon the expression, the history buffs, because everybody liked them.

Q: There are quite a few.

Adm. M.: Yes, but everybody liked what happened knowing what happened in the Yangtze in 09 and that sort of thing, as long as you don't overdo it. But some of this had to be current and meeting current problems, some had to be aimed at the younger officers, talking about their problems, not grand strategy, the guy down here, what's he going to do about selection or something a lieutenant thinks about. So we tried to aim at all areas. This was a very deliberate policy and it took a lot of work to try to achieve a format with the Proceedings that would do the things that it does now.

Q: I've noticed a tendency to have some younger officers on the board, too.

Adm. M.: Right, and that was something that I helped start. Of course, the younger officers - we also brought ex officio the successor to the job I'm talking about with Admiral Burke, where I used to be the official dissenter. They're now called White House or CNO fellows, SecDef fellows, and what they are is young fellows who are just sitting there doing what I was doing. But at least one is now a member ex officio of the board. He comes down, and he knows all the problems in the CNO's office, for instance, that are being talked about, so he's a good pipeline to what the CNO wants in terms of things of that sort, and of course there's a regular CNO representative, which is now Admiral Quigley. He's representative to all kinds of organizations and he knows what's going on and he contributes to the board.

In answer to your original question, yes, the institute totally and the Proceedings in particular, are back to their original purpose. They are making waves again, they are financially stable, they are alive and vibrant, they are publishing hundreds of books, where before they were publishing a book every two or three years. This is good and they are now really a premier university press system, as it should be, probably the second best or maybe third best in the country.

I enjoyed my association over a long number of years with the institute and the board and the Proceedings.

Q: I'm certainly glad to get that section.

Adm. M.: I wrote, I guess, a total of ten or twelve articles over that period, and collaborated with Admiral Ageton in revising twice the Naval Officer's Guide.

Q: You're involved in this right now, aren't you?

Adm. M.: Yes, also another book, Naval Traditions, Customs and Usage.

Q: I understand you're also doing another book review?

Adm. M.: Yes. Those sorts of things I like to do just to contribute to the institute and what it stands for.

Q: There's another item on my list. I think this occurred after you retired, however, and that was your defense of a young officer who was judged a homosexual.

Adm. M.: Oh, well, that got more publicity than it deserved. I didn't do anything except state my opinions as I'm required to by law.

What happened is a young midshipman named Berg was a midshipman when I was superintendent and went through the normal course of being a midshipman. He was a member of the Glee Club and the choir, the Masqueraders, and so forth, and apparently he lived a fairly normal life. He was contributing to the Naval Academy. He came before the academic board I guess on two occasions, the last one as a first classman, and the academic board's duty here is to judge whether or not a midshipman is qualified to serve as an officer. He failed his missile course, as I remember it, and we required him to repeat that. His other grades were good. His only bad grade was in this particular course. He made it up, his observations as to professional aptitude, conduct, and so forth were all satisfactory, and the board adjudged him qualified to graduate, to be commissioned, and to go serve. That's all there was to it.

There was no indication that he was homosexual or that he was doing anything improper at the Naval Academy, so when he asked me to testify at his trial, I felt morally obligated to go render my opinion. So I went down and they asked me the same questions. I said, yes, I was superintendent, I knew him, he appeared to be an average midshipman, perfectly normal, doing more than the average because he belonged to all these things like the choir and so forth. That's where I'd seen him because I saw the Masqueraders, I saw the choir every week, and I saw the Glee Club frequently, and so I became acquainted with him. He was in my house as a member of the choir and Glee Club. He had answered all the requirements we put upon midshipmen to become an officer and he'd so been declared by the full board, not just by me. He'd been examined by the entire academic board personally, after the board meeting his record had been gone over and he'd been graduated.

That was all I knew about it. Then they asked me my opinion about whether homosexuals should be allowed to serve in the navy, and I said I supported whatever naval policy was at the moment. When I was superintendent - Then they asked me did I think he was qualified to serve, and I said certainly he was, he was qualified to serve when he graduated. It's up to the navy to decide whether they want a person who has either physical or moral disability, if you want to call it that, to serve in the navy. That's up to the navy to decide, not me, I'm just a member of the navy.

That was the extent of my connection with the case. I did testify, at his request, and I felt I had an obligation to since I was superintendent and as head of the academic board, I had passed on his qualification. So I told them that, as far as I was concerned, yes, he was qualified in every respect except that the navy didn't want him to serve.

Q: I suppose it got caught up in this gay rights drive?

Adm. M.: Yes, and, of course, he was supported by various organizations and so forth, and all of the press, I think, treated him very fairly. There were some people who took it out of context and said what was I doing supporting him. The answer is that I wasn't supporting anybody or anything. I was simply testifying, as it was my duty to do, as superintendent of the Naval Academy.

Q: Well, you retired on the 1st of August 1975. Then you took up something of another career, did you not?

Adm. M.: Yes, I did. As a matter of fact, the first three months after I retired I was asked to come to the Army War College, the Defense Information Institute, the Air Force College, and talk on the subject. I brought up in my speech when I retired. I did at each place, and enjoyed talking to the students.

Q: How was it received in these other places?

Adm. M.: Very well. They listened to everything I had to say, didn't take it out of context, and agreed with it completely. As I said, a little later I talked to the National War College in a seminar.

Q: There it was not really accepted?

Adm. M.: My main thesis concerning morality was accepted. The only thing that wasn't accepted was the idea that you should have a career in mind early on in your life and keep it in mind all through your life.

Q: As sort of a shadow.

Adm. M.: The only thing that wasn't accepted there was how do you do that and not take time away from your obligation to the navy. I said if I were you, I'd find a way to do it because I thought it was important. Everything else - I talked about the need for a new morality and the need to listen to dissenters and so forth, and that was enthusiastically received everywhere. They thought that was great to do that.

But other than that, I decided when I retired that I would spend half my time working for charity or for the navy and the other half working for myself. I was offered and immediately accepted the presidency of Carl Vinson Hall, which is a retirement home for service widows and the parent organization, which is the Navy-Marine-Coast Guard Foundation that raises money for sea service retirement homes, of which Carl Vinson Hall was perhaps the first and maybe the last, but hopefully there'll be another one on the West Coast some day. So I was the president of these two organizations.

Q: You took it over at a difficult time, didn't you?

Adm. M.: Yes, Carl Vinson Hall was in financial trouble. It was undercapitalized when it was formed, contributions were down, expenses were way up, the residents were unhappy about a number of things. I've now been president for almost four years and I think now we're in good shape financially. We've done a lot to repair parts of the hall, the residents seem to be happy, we've got a new manager and some other new personnel, and we're going along just fine.

Q: What's the status of the restaurant there now? That was always a problem.

Adm. M.: Well, we have managed to stop leaks in it, put down new carpeting, get the manager to care about the tastes of older people more, and I got some new equipment from an outfit in Chicago, which made the kitchen able to bake more than one thing at a time. Before, if you had baked potatoes, you couldn't have rolls, so we have enough equipment now to do both.

Q: I know!

Adm. M.: But they're still dissatisfied in the sense that the residents don't seem to understand that you have to have a restaurant in a retirement home, although each resident can and many times does prepare his or her own meals -

Q: They have their own kitchens?

Adm. M.: Yes, but they have to support the restaurant because there's going to be a time when they can't do that or when they get too feeble to do it. There has to be a restaurant there and you have to support the restaurant some way. The only way to do it, as in other retirement homes, is to require everybody to use it. We don't, we just require them to use it a certain minimum time. Well, you can't convince 250 people that that's what they're supposed to do. Two hundred and twenty of them are convinced that that's what they should do and the other thirty don't like it, but they wouldn't like most anything, so that solves your problem there.

Q: I suppose they support the bar, however, don't they?

Adm. M.: There's no bar. But it is a fine home and I've enjoyed being able to contribute to its welfare and doing what I can do. That is my charitable job. It takes a lot of time, a lot of effort, and some money.

I'm also a trustee of the Naval Academy Foundation, a trustee of the Alumni Association, and those are obviously nonpaying but somewhat costly jobs. For instance the foundation takes a heavy contribution every year.

Then, on my side, I am vice chairman of the board of the Northlake Community Hospital in North Lake, Illinois, which is near Chicago. That does pay well and I've been the chairman of that since I retired, or vice chairman, rather, since I retired. That requires about one trip a month to Chicago plus other trips when the hospital has trouble and the executive committee takes over and runs it, as it has done in the last year or so, and so I've spent as much as two or three days there running the hospital, studying their personnel problems, finances, and so forth. But it's a fascinating opportunity and it pays pretty well.

Q: How heavily is it involved with HEW?

Adm. M.: Very much. It's a private hospital for profit. HEW tries to control everything in this country. This little hospital - it's a 115-bed hospital - has the lowest cost per capita in Chicago and yet it makes money. Yet, every time we turn around HEW is trying to regulate us in some way, which defeats our purpose, which makes us charge people more because we had to do that to make money.

I have learned a lot about bureaucracy in government and Chicago politics and that sort of thing.

I'm also director of a bank in Alexandria and a director of the Human Resources Research Orgnization in Alexandria and a director of Premier Industries. I serve as a consultant and a board member to these organizations. This is where I make enough money to make up for the rest of it that I put into charity.

Q: It certainly looks as though your time is fully occupied with all these endeavors! What bank in Alexandria?

Adm. M.: Services National Bank.

    I guess we've come to the end of the tape.

Appendix

Slack In The People Area

VADM WILLIAM P. MACK, the first naval officer to be appointed Deputy Assistant Secretary of Defense for Manpower and Reserve Affairs, thinks the time is soon coming when the Services will be able to "take up the slack in the people area."

Getting skilled personnel out of unnecessary drudgery work and into fields they're interested in is one way to take up such slack and help increase retention, he believes.

Admiral Mack soon will have a chance to find how his beliefs pan out. He and his civilian boss Assistant Secretary Roger T. Kelley will be involved in a study group looking at ways to set up an all-volunteer Armed Force.

Referring to cost estimates for such an all-volunteer force which range from $6-billion to $15-billion above present personnel costs, Admiral Mack says, "It doesn't all have to be pay to retain people."

"I would think hopefully as we move toward lessening of the war and closer to peacetime operations, we can begin to take up the slack in the people area," he says.

He predicted that "in the years to come the Services will seek ways to make military careers more meaningful rather than routine jobs."

He said that "without prejudging" what the study group will come up with, the Services could move toward an all-volunteer force by supplying better housing and transportation, and by moving personnel out of hardship posts more quickly, and out of drudgery work.

"We might even end up with a total Armed Force that trained all morning and went to school all afternoon," he says.

"The Services need smarter, better educated men these days," he said, men who are not content with routine tasks such as "ground pounding and painting ships."

Admiral Mack would like to see Service personnel spending more time doing the jobs they were educated for, commissioned for, trained for, and enlisted for.

He asks: Why have a jet mechanic working in a mess hall? And he quietly stresses again: It's not all money.

Asked how the Services are doing now in retention, Admiral Mack replied, "I don't think we can retain large numbers of these people as long as we have rigorous deployment schedules. We have to look forward to a time when they (personnel) can expect some sort of normal family life with adequate pay and housing. Then we can build up reasonable numbers (of careerists)."

Nevertheless, Mack says, he thinks planning for an all-volunteer force is "a reasonable objective—one that we can get very close to."

This, he said, "is a time in history when we can start toward it."

Before assuming his present duties in January Admiral Mack was Chief of Legislative Affairs for the Navy.

Since 1962 he has served, successively, in the Office of the Special Assistant for Counterinsurgency, JCS; as Navy Chief of Information; and as Commander Amphibious Group Two.

linquish it to another Committee member.

Rivers' action means that the investigatory arms of both Armed Services Committees are headed up by their chairmen.

In recent years, both former Representative Porter Hardy, jr(D-Va) and Representative F. Edward Hébert (D-La) have distinguished themselves in the key House subcommittee post, especially in investigations in connection with procurement and weapons systems.

Hardy was the Subcommittee Chairman in the past few Congresses, but retired from office last year. Hébert, who formerly chaired the panel for a decade, now has moved into other fields of military legislation (although he has been named to serve on the Investigation Subcommittee as a member).

Rivers thus had the choice of naming a new Democrat or taking the job himself.

Other Democrats named by Rivers to the panel (along with Hébert) are Philip J. Philbin(Mass), Samuel S. Stratton(NY), Alton Lennon(NC), William J. Randall(Mo), and Robert H. Mollohan(WVa).

Republican members are William H. Bates(Mass), ranking minority member; Charles S. Gubser(Calif); Charles E. Chamberlain(Mich); Alexander Pirnie (NY); William L. Dickinson(Ala); and John E. Hunt(NJ).

Philbin Heads PX Probe

REPRESENTATIVE PHILIP J. PHILBIN(D-Mass) has been named to head a nine-member House Armed Services Subcommittee that will perform the first Congressional stocktaking of the Services' PX systems in 12 years.

Committee Chairman L. Mendel Rivers(D-SC) directed the Philbin panel—the Exchanges and Commissaries Subcommittee—"to conduct an inquiry into the policies and practices covering the operation of military exchanges and commissaries, and other pertinent or related activities within the Armed Forces."

The Army and Air Force Exchange Service did $2.2-billion in sales last year—just behind Sears Roebuck and J.C. Penney. The Navy and Marine Corps-operated exchanges do another $1.5-billion in business.

Other members of the legislative inventory body are Democrats Otis Fisher(Tex), G. Elliot Hagan(Ga), Speedy O. Long(La), and W. C. Daniel (Va); and Republicans William G. Bray (Ind), Donald D. Clancy (Ohio), Charles W. Whalen, jr (Ohio), and Ed Foreman (NMex).

Mack in Profile

SecNAV and Seamen Agree

By ROBERT J. BOYLAN

Robert Boylan is a retired Foreign Service officer who is now writing as a free-lancer.

A seaman recruit and SecNav could easily come up with the same answer if they asked a computer to give them the name of a Seventh Fleet commander they considered ideal.

The seaman might well want a fleet commander who is ready and willing to listen because he likes people, doesn't pretend he knows *all* the answers, likes sports, even listens to rock once in a while, and has some understanding of the drug problem.

The Secretary of the Navy would call for an officer with extensive command, flag, and Washington experience who knows the Far East, can be both firm and flexible, and who feels equally at home at sea, with Congress, the Pentagon, the press, and world affairs and who, at the same time, has a sensitive feel for the Navy's single most important component — people — at all levels.

In both cases the computer's answer could (happily) be the same: Vice Admiral William P. Mack, whose qualifications and background are impressive! He has commanded two destroyers, one in war and one in peace, a division and also a squadron of destroyers. He has commanded an amphibious ship group, is a graduate of the Naval War College and was naval aide to the Secretary of the Navy.

He also has served as Special Assistant for Counterinsurgency, Joint Chiefs of Staff; Navy Chief of Information, Chief of Legislative Affairs for the Navy and, since 1969, Deputy Assistant Secretary of Defense (Manpower and Reserve Affairs). In this last post he also served as chairman of a Pentagon committee on the problem of drug abuse in the services.

Admiral Mack's new challenge as commander of the Seventh Fleet comes after 34 years of diversified Navy responsibilities by an officer with top marks in nearly every field except self-promotion.

Among colleagues, the single, most frequent comment about Admiral Mack is perhaps the ultimate man-to-man compliment — "he levels with you." A random look at his life (1915-1971) may reveal some key factors as to why his cumulative experience pays off like a five-horse parlay.

In his current assignment, he has had overall supervision of the Armed Services Television Network (one of the world's largest). It's surely a plus for an interest in and an appreciation of entertainment that Mack was once a six-year old scene stealer and movie extra in San Fernando Valley horse operas, sitting next to his uncle, actor Newell Paden, while he was driving one of those 40-mule train wagons.

In real life, in addition to this child labor, he attended glamorous Beverly Hills High School with members of the "Our Gang" comedy troupes and (for balance) Jack Warner, Jr., of the Warner Bros. film family.

Who knows? With his rugged Gary Cooper looks and sturdy frame, which he even now keeps at a trim 190 with summer tennis and winter badminton (his Navy team missed the championship by only one point), he might have made it big in Hollywood.

But films weren't glamorous or appealing enough to distract the new Seventh Fleet Commander from tradition — becoming a second generation Naval officer and marrying the daughter of one of his father's Academy classmates. Two years after graduation from the Naval Academy he joined an old four-stacker, the JOHN D. FORD, on the Asiatic Station and was gunnery officer aboard her in Manila Bay the day of Pearl Harbor.

Intensive study and research have also made him an authority on the problems of drug abuse and he has been called on for television network appearances as an expert on the subject. As Deputy Assistant Defense Secretary, he has been on the peak policy levels in such key areas as military pay, per diem, official travel and transporation allowances, education and individual training, civil rights and equal opportunity, religious, morale, and welfare questions, and even Federal voting assistance.

In terms of "leveling" with a wide assortment of cynical all knowing press types his period as CHINFO (directing the Navy's world-wide information program at the Pentagon) was the single most important time of his career. When he left that post in 1966, after three years, he was guest of honor at a Pentagon farewell reception given by Pentagon reporters — a rare occasion indeed.

Once a Cub Reporter

Maybe having once been a cub reporter for Scripps-Howard in San Francisco gave him a feel for the press. Quietly, one can be sure, and never with the "I used to be a newspaperman myself" response of the incurable PR man. Whatever the source, such a feel should be vitally useful in the Tokyo area with its highly competitive multi-million copy dailies.

Admiral Mack will be the first "black shoe" Commander of the Seventh Fleet in recent years. Understandably, he is looking forward to his new assignment after long Washington service — 15 of the past 17 years. His flagship will be the cruiser OKLAHOMA CITY, with Yokosuka as home base. He, his wife, and their 16-year old daughter, Margaret Ellen, will be living in Yokohama. A son, William Paden Mack, Jr., a lieutenant in the Naval Reserve, is studying medicine at the University of Virginia.

One of the Admiral's interests — landscape gardening (along with some skillful brick-laying and rock arrangements) should appeal greatly to the Japanese, the master gardeners. Both he and his wife have considerable knowledge of Asians and Asia, including firsthand knowledge of China (Shanghai, Peking, and Hankow).

WHAT'S THE FUTURE O[F]

By Vice Admiral W. P. Mack, USN
Deputy Assistant Secretary of Defense
(Manpower and Reserve Affairs)

"We cannot afford in our military business to rest on our oars for long ... we must always be looking ahead, for we must always get ready to fight the next war. History never permits us the luxury of re-fighting the last war."

An NRA Exclusive

This article was prepared exclusively for the Naval Reserve Association and is another in a series of special presentations appearing in this space in the NEWS each month. These articles are designed to increase the professional knowledge of individual Reservists and to provide information for study and discussion by Reserve units.

The accomplishments of the Reserve Forces in the past are well known. During 1968, some 115 units were mobilized for the Pueblo crisis and the war in Vietnam. These contained over 35,000 competent and dedicated Reservists.

On December 15, 1969, the last of these units were demobilized, thus completing another outstanding chapter in the history of our Reserve Forces.

However, we cannot afford in our military business to rest on our oars for long, no matter how pleasant hearing the praise may be. We must always be looking ahead, for we must always get ready to fight the next war. History never permits us the luxury of re-fighting the last war.

Nearly every day in the Pentagon — and in the press — there are indications from which guidelines can be deduced without violating security. For instance, the size of our Armed Forces will almost certainly be reduced in the post-Vietnam era to the neighborhood of two-and-one-half million men. It is evident that the portion of our national budget available for the Armed Forces will be extremely tight, for our national welfare demands that taxes be minimized and that large sums be used for social purposes. The President has announced his intention of moving toward an All-Volunteer Force. This will require increased recruiting efforts, better retention, greater efficiency, and an all-out effort on the part of all of us to do better with less people. It also means that standby authority for Selective Service will continue to be available.

Within these limits we must develop the Reserve Forces of the future.

Obviously with smaller regular forces in the future, Reserve Forces will increase in importance. If they are to do so, they must be built around a relatively small, highly trained, fully equipped, and adequately paid Selected Reserve Force that can be mobilized on extremely short notice to augment Regular Forces in contingency combat operations. This Selected Reserve Force must, of course, be backed up by additional Ready Reserves that can be mobilized on a few months notice to reinforce Regular and Se[lected] Reserve Forces in larger combat [opera]tions, and there must be a po[ol of] unpaid Reserve personnel gen[erally] trained and oriented and availab[le for] mobilization in the event of [major] war. Such a structure is not [too] different from our present stru[cture.] The changes will probably be [an] increased degree of readiness [that] will be required of the Se[lected] Reserve Force and perhaps [some] changes in its size and shape.

In planning for the post-Vi[etnam] period, we are taking a fresh lo[ok at] the total requirements for Activ[e and] Reserve Forces as measured agair[st the] world-wide strategic situation [and] United States interests and obje[ctives.]

Our objective is to achieve a b[alance] between Active and Reserve [Forces] which will provide an adequate d[efense] posture for the least cost. The c[ost of] maintaining Reserve Forces is les[s than] half of that for Regular Forces. [If] it could be accomplished safely, [Regu]lar Forces could be reduced and [more] of our military requirements b[e ful]filled by the Reserve Componen[ts. In] order for such Reserve units [to be] effective toward fulfilling our [total] military requirements, they m[ust be] capable of immediate mobilizatio[n and] prompt deployment. This cap[ability] can be achieved only by main[taining] Reserve units at or near full c[ombat] strength, and by providing the[m ade]quate training and modern equip[ment.]

Our goals for the future then [center] around improvements in four [func]tional areas — personnel, equip[ment,] training, and facilities.

PERSONNEL — One of our p[rime] objectives during the 1970's is t[o pro]vide a military environment for [estab]lishing and maintaining an all-vo[lunteer] military force — both Regular [and] Reserves. Currently and in the [past,] the source of our military man[power] has been largely through, or mo[tivated] by, the Selective Service Syste[m. We] shall continue to rely on the Se[lective] Service System as a motivating [force] for our military manpower r[equire]ments until, eventually, we can [attain] an all-volunteer system.

The establishment of a[n all-] volunteer system will take time, [experi]ence and money. It is estimate[d that] about 70 percent of input t[o the] Selected Reserve Forces is draf[t moti]vated, indicating that most o[f the] Reservists prefer to fulfill their m[ilitary] obligation through the inactive R[eserve] program rather than by inductio[n into] active service. Therefore, the suc[cess]

THE RESERVE FORCES?

of an all-volunteer Reserve dependent on our ability and ation to find substitute means ate voluntary career participa- the Reserves as well as in the forces — in short we must find ns to make Reserve military ufficiently rewarding to *attract* n the manpower required.

Gates' Commission, established President, currently has under e problem of creating an all- r force. While the conclusions ommendations of the Gates' ion are not yet available, it is accepted that new motiva- attracting and retaining volun- npower in the Reserve Forces based on increasing the attrac- of Reserve service.

neral, such steps would include asing Reserve training pay to a hich is reasonably equitable vilian salaries in comparable nent functions, (2) providing and modern equipment for and operations, (3) providing training facilities, (4) seeking fective utilization of training d (5) increasing fringe benefits vel reasonably equitable with the regular forces in such retirement benefits, medical vel allowance, education bene- ernment insurance, promotions, nent bonuses, and PX and ary privileges.

advantages to be obtained in an all-volunteer Reserve force y, including more highly moti- ersonnel, increased utilization ed personnel who have had tive service, reduction in per- turnover rates, increased unit stability, more effective ining, and increased Reserve . The increased costs of creat- ew environment for attracting r Reservists is recognized; how- s believed that the cost reduc- ich will be realized as a result ctions in personnel turnover ic training, as well as more utilization of training time, bstantially offset the cost required.

PMENT — It is absolutely nec- at the obsolete and unservice- uipment now assigned to the Reserves be replaced in an manner by a representative of new combat deployable nt being used by the Active All Reserve Component units eceive at least token amounts cent) of new equipment to accomplish familiarization training. We are developing procedures which will identify and trace Reserve equipment from the formulation of the budget through delivery to the unit.

Once full equipment support is provided and 75 percent is on hand, it is possible to accomplish a higher level of unit readiness training. We will establish a focal point for special emphasis to provide the necessary combat deployable equipment for the Reserve Component units assigned priority status. In short, we desire to improve the equipment status of the Reserve Forces in an orderly and effective manner. In addition, it is desirable to plan for immediate acquisition, early in the mobilization cycle, of the balance of equipment necessary to fill all units to 100 percent.

TRAINING — Every effort must be made to provide sufficient training time and adequate weekend training areas to qualify individuals and units on assigned combat capable equipment. After providing proper equipment and adequate training, we can identify individual and unit training deficiencies and assure initiation of necessary corrective action to improve unit readiness through tests and operational readiness inspections by the Active Forces.

The successful completion of training programs conducted in a realistic manner on equipment being used by the Active Forces, or modern training devices, is the basic requirement to the successful accomplishment of any mission.

In short, we want realistic training on combat serviceable standard equipment to ensure realistic mobilization readiness.

FACILITIES AND MILITARY CONSTRUCTION — Budget constraints and considerations of major force reorganizations curtailed Reserve facility construction during the 1965-1968 period. As a result, a considerable construction backlog has developed. This backlog is a threat to the efficiency and success of the overall Reserve program. This backlog has been the subject of a thorough study seeking to identify clearly and to validate the requirements of the Reserve.

Our objective is to establish a 10-year program which will, beginning in 1972, liquidate the backlog of military construction for the Reserves. In doing this, we seek to improve facilities at field training sites, provide adequate training areas for all major combat units at or near their home stations, and make more use of joint facilities.

The primary consideration in all of these actions is to relate Reserve requirements directly to increased mobilization readiness. In short, we seek to get the maximum amount of readiness for each dollar spent. The net result of these actions should be to produce a Reserve Force able to maintain its key role in the over-all Defense structure in the difficult years ahead.

Use This Form for Notification

IT IS REQUESTED THAT I BE NOTIFIED WHETHER OR NOT MY NAME IS ON THE 1970 SELECTION LIST FOR PROMOTION TO: _____

NAME _____
(LAST) (MIDDLE INITIAL) (FIRST)

FILE NO. _____ DESIGNATOR _____

ADDRESS _____

_____
(ZIP CODE)

I AM A MEMBER OF NRA _____
I AM NOT A MEMBER OF NRA _____

YOU WERE SELECTED _____ YOU WERE NOT SELECTED _____

Please Print or Type

Naval Reserve officers who wish to be notified whether or not they have been selected for promotion should complete the above form and mail it to NRA National Headquarters. But please be sure you are actually in the promotion zone for the year before submitting your request.

COMMANDERS DIGEST

DEPARTMENT OF DEFENSE • WASHINGTON, D.C.

Vol. 8, No. 22   August 29, 1970

Defense Report On Drugs

Vice Adm. Mack Describes New Policy Directions

Revisions in Department of Defense policy on drug abuse have been recommended by a task group headed by Vice Admiral William P. Mack, USN, Deputy Assistant Secretary of Defense (Manpower and Reserve Affairs). A statement of the study was presented Aug. 20 by Admiral Mack to the Subcommittee to Investigate Juvenile Delinquency of the Committee on the Judiciary, U.S. Senate. Following are excerpts from the statement:

The Armed Forces' drug problem stems from the country's drug problem. The exact scope and nature of the country's drug problem has been estimated by many investigative authorities, but statistics are still partial and unreliable. Conservatively, estimates can be made that 10 million Americans have tried marijuana, and that 25 per cent of high school age children are or have been marijuana experimenters. The size of the heroin problem is not known, but an indicator is the 1969 figure of 28,600 addicts in the City of New York (Bureau of Narcotics and Dangerous Drugs) and the estimate that the true figure may have been as high as 75,000. Statistics on use of other dangerous drugs are equally discouraging. In summary, drug abuse has grown radically in this country in the last few years, and particularly in the high school age group from where the majority of Armed Forces recruits and draftees are obtained.

Young people entering the Armed Services bring with them the habits, frustrations, and difficulties they have known in civilian life. To date, there has been no reliable method of examining entrants to determine those who are actual or potential drug abusers. Until one is developed, the Armed Services will continue to receive many young people who have used drugs and many who are psychologically disposed to use them. For many so disposed, tensions and frustrations encountered in the Armed Services may well bring on drug abuse.

Unknown Factor

The extent of drug abuse in the Armed Services is not precisely known, although it is probably not more widespread than in the civilian population. Exact statistics are difficult to produce because of the nature of the offense of drug abuse. Members of the Armed Services are naturally reluctant to answer a drug abuse questionnaire under the eyes of supervisory personnel since an admission may constitute an offense under military law.

Anonymous questionnaires, by their nature, may produce inaccurate responses inherent in such a system and, as in any survey, the results are consequently only approximations.

The abuse of marijuana in Southeast Asia is far greater than in the Armed Services as a whole but the abuse of hard narcotics and dangerous drugs is greater in CONUS and worldwide than in Vietnam. Drugs, particularly marijuana, are cheap and readily available in the Far East. Daily hardship, danger, boredom, and fatigue, aid in producing a climate in which drug abuse may flourish. Today, many young military leaders are technically qualified to perform their military duties but some may lack the maturity and experience necessary in counselling and leading young and inexperienced troops to forego indulgence in drug abuse.

The Department of Defense compiles a summary of investigations of drug abuse cases which shows clearly an alarming increase of cases investigated in the Republic of Vietnam, in CONUS and worldwide. In any event, the incidence of drug abuse can be characterized as very serious. The nature of the problem however is not such that at this point military readiness is considered to be endangered. The real impact is the

(Continued On Page Two)

Secretary Laird Names High Level Group To Act On Blue Ribbon Defense Report

Secretary of Defense Melvin R. Laird announced plans Aug. 26 to appoint a "Blue Ribbon Action Committee" to work on implementation of decisions made by the Secretary and the Deputy Secretary of Defense to achieve improvements in the management of the Department of Defense.

Secretary Laird's Statement

In announcing plans to establish the Blue Ribbon Action Committee, Secretary Laird said:

"It is our objective to make major reductions in overhead staffing throughout the Department. I am convinced that this can be done at the same time we improve our performance. I

(Continued On Page Three)

Defense Drug Report

(Continued From Page One)

...ossibility of permanent damage to the minds and bodies of the thousands of young men who are using narcotics and dangerous drugs worldwide, and who are using strong, dangerous varieties of marijuana and hard narcotics which are available worldwide and particularly in and near the Republic of Vietnam.

Other factors contribute to the nature of the problem. One obvious and over-simplified solution would be to prevent drugs and narcotics from reaching our servicemen. Such a solution is unfortunately not in sight, although extensive coordinated efforts are being made at the highest level of the Executive Branch. Particularly, efforts are being made to divert the Turkish poppy crop and to close the Mexican border to marijuana and other dangerous drug smuggling. For the foreseeable future we must continue to anticipate an atmosphere in which dangerous drugs, including narcotics and marijuana, are relatively easy to obtain.

In summary, the nature of the problem can be described as the necessity to eliminate drug abuse in the Armed Forces in a national atmosphere in which drugs are illegal but readily available and not, unfortunately, universally condemned.

Conclusions

As a result of its investigations and deliberations, the Task Group concluded:

1—There is a serious and growing problem of drug abuse in the United States.

2—This problem extends to the Armed Forces, DoD civilian employees, and to dependents of both.

3—Precise and comprehensive data as to the extent of the problem in the United States and in the Armed Forces does not exist, but sufficient data is available to permit the formulation of possible solutions to the problem.

4—There is no assured, complete solution to the problem.

5—The problems must be attacked within the Armed Services by mustering all possible forces and exerting strong efforts.

6—Every effort must be made to keep past or potential drug addicts, suppliers, or users as defined in the report from entering the Armed Services.

7—A carefully planned, universal educational effort must be expanded beyond past and present programs to cover all members of the Armed Forces including the Reserve Forces, DoD employees, and dependents at all periods of their lives and careers.

8—Where education fails and drug abuse occurs, the abusers must be dealt with quickly, firmly, and fairly, but with enlightened methods that assure that the best interests of the Government and the individuals are served.

9—Where discipline fails, every reasonable effort, subject to available resources, must be made to rehabilitate those who might be of further use to the Armed Services. More serious cases should be considered for sufficient rehabilitation to permit them to re-enter society. A balance between the best interests of the Government and the individual must be reached. Where

Vice Adm. William P. Mack, USN

rehabilitation within the Services' facilities is not possible, liaison with the Veterans Administration and state and local agencies must assure that those discharged as needing further treatment and rehabilitation are guided to those agencies.

10—The discharge system now in effect in the Armed Forces represents a fair and proper method of categorizing service. Changes in it should not be made for the sole reason of allowing drug abusers to receive Veterans benefits. Changes in basic law should be sought to provide a solution to this problem.

11—Research should continue in the Armed Forces and in all agencies of the Federal Government at a rapid pace in all areas of drug abuse and in manpower techniques to permit us to improve the screening, education, discipline, and rehabilitation of personnel and to allow faster, more positive detection and identification of narcotics and dangerous drugs.

Recommendations

The Task Group report made a number of recommendations. These recommendations fall in major categories as follows:

1—Categories of Drugs and Users
2—Screening of Those Entering Military Service
3—Education and Information
4—Discipline and Discharge
5—Rehabilitation

In general, these recommendations buttress and support policies already promulgated and in some cases instituted in various areas of the world on a trial basis. The recommendations in several areas sharpen those policies and where needed, add focus and attention to combat this growing problem. For example, an individual will not necessarily be precluded from serving his country if he has experimented with some of the

(Continued On Next Page)

(Continued From Preceding Page)

dangerous drugs. The report states in Recommendation 11 as follows:

> "It should be the policy of the Department of Defense that acceptance into military service be based on the 'whole man' concept. Each registrant or applicant with a background of drug abuse should be carefully processed to determine the individual's physical and emotional capacity for useful military service. Enlistment and induction standards, including the granting of waivers thereto, should be established by each Service."

In the education area, the Task Force specifically recommends that those disciplines so important to helping us cope with this problem be specifically informed and trained in the area of drug abuse. The categories of professional individuals specifically listed are the Judge Advocates, the Chaplains, and the Medical community. Perhaps one of the most significant recommendations deals with rehabilitating those individuals who are abusing the various proscribed drugs. The Task Force Report specifically recommends an "amnesty program" to encourage voluntary participation by those members who are abusing drugs and sincerely wish to help themselves to eliminate their drug dependence and voluntarily request such assistance before being apprehended or detected. The recommendation of the Task Group suggests such "amnesty programs" be instituted. This, of course, will be up to each of the Services and must be carefully delineated for the situation at the particular camp or station. For example, as the Committee knows, such a program has already been instituted in various parts of the Republic of Vietnam and from all reports is having a salutary and beneficial effect.

Deliberated Long And Hard

The Task Force deliberated long and hard on this recommendation because there must be a balancing of seeking to rehabilitate an individual with the equally important and necessary precept of military life which is discipline.

We must be certain that any "amnesty program" will not deter the maintenance of military posture and discipline throughout the Armed Services. It is for this reason that the recommendation is couched in terms of "an amnesty program . . . should be given a trial." In short, we believe that this is one area of responsibility that appears to have means of aiding some of the less mature members of the Department of Defense who experiment and become trapped through the abuse of some of these dangerous drugs. However, these programs must be tempered by the over-all responsibilities of a military commander to be certain that such programs do not have a back lash or a counter-productive effect on maintaining an effective fighting force which must be ready to fulfill the mission for which it was created.

Secretary Laird Names High Level Group To Act On Blue Ribbon Defense Report

(Continued From Page One)

expect that their action will lead to significant savings in Fiscal Year 1972 and beyond.

"I anticipate that we will make a number of major decisions within the next 30-60 days.

"Dave Packard (Deputy Secretary of Defense) and I have decided to establish an all-Service Blue Ribbon Action Committee to assist us in implementing decisions we make in response to recommendations of the Blue Ribbon Defense Panel. The establishment of this all-Service Action Committee is a part of our program of participatory management.

"It will be the responsibility of the Action Committee, headed by Assistant Secretary of Defense (Administration) Robert F. Froehlke, to work with Dave Packard and me to convert selected basic recommendations of the Blue Ribbon Panel into operation as rapidly as possible. This committee will work out the details of the implementing orders, directives, and instructions so that there will be no interruption to continued combat readiness of our forces.

"Obviously, it would have been possible for us to have unilaterally taken action in response to the Blue Ribbon Defense Panel's recommendations; but, this is not our approach to management of the Department of Defense.

"From the beginning, we have worked to develop a team effort and to decentralize responsibilities to the maximum extent possible, consistent, of course, with our responsibilities for the direction and control of the Department of Defense.

"Serving with Assistant Secretary Froehlke will be a team of experienced general and flag officers from all four Services. There will also be representation from the JCS-Joint Staff and from the Office of the Secretary of Defense.

"It is not our intention that this Action Committee will restudy the work that was done by the Fitzhugh Panel. Instead, it will be the mission of the Action Committee to expedite the implementation of decisions as they are made.

"As to specific decisions, I am not prepared today (Aug. 26) to report any to you, except to express our current thinking that if other proposals made by the Fitzhugh Panel are implemented effectively, it does not, at this time, appear necessary to establish a total of three Deputy Secretaries.

"I can report to you that Dave Packard and I, during recent weeks, have had a number of discussions, individually and collectively, with a broad range of senior civilian and military people throughout the Department of Defense. In these discussions, we have, for example, conferred at some length with the Service Secretaries, the Service Chiefs and the Chairman, Joint Chiefs of Staff, and we will want to have additional talks as we take action to improve the management of the Department of Defense.

"In conclusion, I want to repeat that this is going to be a team effort, for that is the way Dave Packard and I do business."

Index to

Series of Interviews with

Vice Admiral William Paden Mack

U. S. Navy (Retired)

Volume II

ABRAMS, Gen. B. B.: p. 606-7; p. 609; p. 611

AMPHIBIOUS GROUP 2: Mack takes command on May 15, 1966, p. 445-ff; the large scale amphibious exercise (BEACH TIME) on Vieques, p. 447-8; as receiving commander for SPACE recovery shots, p. 449-54; Mack called back to Washington to be Chief of Legislative Affairs for Secretary Nitze, p. 455; discussion of techniques since WW II for Amphibious operations, p. 456-8; the navy's alternatives to Culebra and Vieques, p. 459-60; discussion of command ships, p. 461-2; the ideal AGC, p. 462-3; the use of UDT's out of Norfolk, p. 463;

BAUMBERGER, VADM Walter H.: Taiwan Defense Commander at time of Mack's visit, p. 584-5;

BLANFORD, Brig, General Russ: Chief Counsel to the House Armed Services Committee, p. 470; has a role in killing the FDL proposal, p. 478;

BURKE, Admiral Arleigh: cancels out the proposed change in officer designations, p. 778 ff; p. 782 on dissent and expressions of opinion, p. 816-8;

CARL VINSON HALL: Mack accepts presidency of Carl Vinson Hall upon his retirement - also becomes head of Navy-Marine-Coast Guard Foundation that raises money for the Hall and other retirement homes, p. 844-6;

CHAFFE, The Hon. John H.: Secretary of the Navy - the unusual manner in which he handled the nomination of Zumwalt to become CNO, p. 540-1; his first day in office and first meeting with CNO and Chinfo, p. 571-3; p. 634-5;

CHINFO: Admiral Mack as Chinfo, p. 414 ff; leaking to the press, p. 417; conferences on roll-outs for major aircraft, p. 418-20; press conferences on the SCORPION and THRESHER, p. 420-1; p. 422; remarks about the Press, p. 420-8; the H-bomb accident in Spain, p. 428-30; responsibility for TV movies on the navy, p. 430-2; several difficulties with Mr. Sylvester over Hollywood products, p. 431-3; Combat Art, p. 434; movies for recruiting purposes, p. 435; p. 437; similar problems for other military services under Sylvester, p. 437; the Vietnamese propaganda stories, p. 437-8; problem of clearance for speeches of the Secretary, CNO, etc. p. 439-40; the great assistance rendered by reservists, p. 440-1; trying to coordinate speeches with publishing dead lines, p. 441-2; the navy develops a public affairs plan under Secretary Nitze, p. 443-4; Mack detached (May 1966) to command Amphibious Group 2 in the atlantic, p. 445;

CLAREY, Admiral B. A.: CincPac Flt. p. 629-30; p. 633; p. 636;

CLEMENTS, The Hon. Wm.: Deputy Secretary of Defense - his study of the service Academies, p. 657-8; p. 694 ff; his bias for West Point, p. 696-7; influence of Colonel Dawkins on the Secretary, p. 696-7; Navy's Comdr. Fitzgerald at last has opportunity to aid the navy point of view, p. 698-702;

CNET (Chief of Naval Education and Training): Zumwalt's experiment in putting the Naval Academy under CNET, p. 638-43;

COLBERT, Admiral Richard Gary: p. 643-4;

CONNOLLY, VADM Thomas F.: his testimony on the F-111, p. 474-5;

CROWN, Robert: Chicago business executive - he and his family donate money for a sailing center at the Naval Academy, p. 764-5;

DANANG: see entry under: VIETNAM WAR

DEPARTMENT OF DEFENSE: the prevailing difficulties in the McNamara-Sylvester period for Chinfo. See entries under: CHINFO: McNAMARA: SYLVESTER, PRESS RELATIONS.

DMZ Line - Vietnam: p. 605-6; the line is breached (Apr. 1972) by the North Vietnamese, p. 608; p. 611;

DRUG ABUSE ISSUE: p. 525; Mack became DOD member of White House Drug Abuse Committee (Egil Krogh - chairman), p. 526-7; Vietnam government officials claimed they were helpless to assist with the problem, p. 528; the President's proposal and

and the impossibility of complying, p. 528-30; a summary statement on drug abuse, p. 533-6; the Drug-Abuse report and its acceptance, p. 547-8;

USCGS EAGLE: sailing vessel of the Coast Guard Academy, p. 767-8;

EQUAL OPPORTUNITY: a desire of the Nixon administration, p. 498; the difficulties - example of J. P. Stevens and Co. p. 499; p. 502-3; p. 517-8;

F-111 B: p. 418-20;

FDL (Fast Deployment Logistics Ship): McNamara pushes the idea of this very expensive concept, p. 475-6; the reason given by Nitze in calling Mack to duty as Legislative Affairs Chief, p. 475-6;

FELLOWES, Captain John H.: former POW - his role at the Naval Academy during superintendency of Admiral Mack, p. 713;

FRANKE, The Hon. Wm. B.: Secretary of the Navy, p. 779-81; p. 784;

FROEHLKE, The Hon. Robert: Assistant Secretary of Defense for Installations and Logistics, p. 568-9;

GATES, The Hon. Thomas S.: instigates the proposed changes in officer disignations, p. 779; p. 784;

GOULDING, Philip: replaces Sylvester as Assistant Secretary of Defense for Public Affairs, p. 414; p. 570; he handles Drew Pearson, p. 575;

GROSVENOR, Captain Alexander G. B.: becomes head of sailing program at the Naval Academy and C.O. of the Naval Station, p. 764;

GROVES, General Leslie: his remarks on the A bomb in New York speech, p. 424-5;

GUINN, VADM. D. H.: Chief of Naval Personnel, p. 636-7;

HAIPHONG HARBOR: the mining of the Harbor, p. 616 ff; plan a product of the 7th fleet, p. 617-8; President Nixon's speech on TV determines actual time for mining harbor entrance, p. 618;

H-BOMB OFF SPANISH COAST: the accidental drop of the H-bomb, p. 428-9; the devious manner in which the Navy's rescue operation became known, p. 429;

HEBERT, The Hon. F. Edward: Chairman of House Military Affairs Committe - his opposition to the all-volunteer force, p. 513;

HERSEY, Major Gen. Louis B.: Director of Selective Service, p. 505-6;

HOLLOWAY, Admiral James L. III: relieves Mack as Comdr. 7th fleet - abrupt ceremony on the firing line, p. 622-3; p. 636-7; when he became CNO he changed the command relationship of the Naval Academy, p. 643; p. 648; as new CNO he asks Adm. Mack to retire because no 4-star job is available for another year, p. 649;

HOMEPORTING: Adm. Zumwalt's idea for homeporting certain ships in Japan; Adm. Mack implements his wishes - the problems involved, p. 589-92;

HONG KONG: p. 583-4;

JAPAN: importance of the 7th fleet to the Japanese, p. 582; p. 583;

JAPANESE MARITIME SELF DEFENSE FORCE: close contacts between Commander 7th fleet and senior officials of the Japanese navy, p. 594; Mack comments on the Japanese navy, attitudes, future problems, etc. p. 595-601; p. 631-2;

KELLEY, The Hon. Roger: Asst. Secretary of Defense for Manpower and Reserves - under Secy. Laird, p. 489-90; p. 506; p. 517; his education about the navy's program with Group 4's, p. 522-3; p. 547-8; p. 552; when he first came to DOD he raised question as to why we were involved in Vietnam, p. 553; result was effort to inform the military WHY - in a political sense why were we involved, p. 554-5; his statement on the human goals of the Defense Department, p. 555; p. 566-7;

KOREA: importance of the 7th fleet to the Koreans, p. 582;

KROGH, Egil: Chairman of the White House Committe on drug abuse, p. 526-7; p. 529; p. 535;

LAIRD, The Hon. Melvin: Secretary of Defense, p. 490-1; approves of the new approach to the Reserves system, p. 501; p. 503; p. 523-4; the Zumwalt nomination as CNO, p. 540-1; his Blue Ribbon panel to streamline chain of command from White House to DOD, p. 543-546; Mack on streamlining within the DOD, p. 546-9; p. 565;

LAWRENCE, RADM Wm. P.: Superintendent of the Naval Academy, p. 707; reinstitutes the special course on the Professional Officer, p. 708; p. 714;

LEGISLATIVE AFFAIRS - Chief of: Mack called back from fleet to serve as Chief - description of his duties, p. 464-5; refusal of Appropriations committees to permit any but navy's Comptroller present for budget hearings, p. 465-6; yearly routine in dealing with Congress, p. 467-70; task of getting right witnesses to appear before committees, p. 471-2; Rickover a law unto himself, p. 473; Mack on training men for this job, p. 481-3;

LIBBEY, Comdr. Miles Augustus III: Mack comments on his interest in becoming a sub-specialist in political affairs, p. 828-31;

LINEBACKER: code name for raids against North Vietnam - Haiphong and Hanoi, p. 613 ff; p. 621;

LINE OFFICER DESIGNATION: the story of the attempted change in the system - negated at the last moment by Admiral Burke, p. 779 ff;

LSD: an explanation of how it works on those not psychologically healthy, p. 531-2;

MacARTHUR, General Douglas: Mack points out manner in which the General violated the honor code of West Point in his later career, p. 693-4;

MACK, Vice Admiral Wm. P.: induces Secretary Nitze to let him out of job as Chief of Legislative Affairs, p. 478-9; informed he is to go as Deputy Asst. SecDef for Manpower and Reserve Affairs, Jan. 1969, p. 479; protests and told if he gets out of it the navy would lose interest in him, p.480; his ideas about jobs in Public Affairs, Legislative Affairs and line jobs in the Navy, p. 482-4; his efforts for sub-specialist categories, p. 484-5; Mack and naval aviation, p. 577-8; retired from the navy on Aug. 1, 1975, p. 842; planned to spend one-half time working for charity - one half for himself, p. 844; a trustee of the Naval Academy Foundation and the Alumni Association, p. 846; Vice Chairman Northlake Community Hospital in North Lake, Illinois, p. 846; other connections and duties, p. 847-8;

MANPOWER AND RESERVE AFFAIRS - Dept. of Defense: Mack named as Deputy Asst. Secretary in DOD, p. 479-80; Roger Kelley, the Assistant Secretary was delayed four months and Mack became acting, p. 490; the duties in this office, p. 492-3; armed forces radio and television system, p. 493; the health system for the services, p. 493; overseas school system, p. 493-4; equal opportunity affairs, p. 494; priorities Secy. Laird laid down, p. 494-5; a new pay study, p. 494 ff - also p. 503-5; the President's desire for an all-volunteer force, p. 495; in second year of Nixon Administration - cutting budget of the DOD, p. 518-19; growing problem with Group-4 enlistees, p. 521-2; problem of jobs for Veterans, p. 524-5; the drug abuse problem, p. 525-6; Mack's comments on the streamlining of action in Defense under Laird, p. 546-49; dealing with the ROTC program, p. 550 ff; effects of Vietnam on development of DOD manpower policies, p. 549 ff; a visitation of students and Mack's conversation with them about Vietnam, p. 552-3;

MARIJUANA: The report from the National Institutes of Health, p. 532-3;

McCAIN, Admiral John Sydney, Jr.: (Jack) CincPac - his delay in getting signal for the mining of Haiphong Harbor, p. 619; p. 621;

McKEE, VADM Kinnaird R.: p. 707;

McNAMARA, Robert Strange: Secretary of Defense - his tight rein over Sylvester - and resultant problems on public relations, p. 414-6; p. 428; p. 432; p. 444;

MOORER, Admiral Thomas H.: p. 574-5;

MOOT, The Hon. Robert: Assistant Secretary of Defense for Comptrollership, p. 568;

NATIONAL WAR COLLEGE: Mack's remarks after retirement to the students - on wisdom of being prepared for a second career, p. 819 ff; p. 843-4;

NASA: Amphibious Group 2 responsible for recovery of SPACE shots - the use of a monkey, p. 449-50; GEMINI X, p. 450; use of expensive and effective equipment, p. 450; NASA instructions to the navy, p. 451-4;

U. S. NAVAL ACADEMY: Mack named as Superintendent, p. 621-2; p. 626-7; arrives at academy, p. 633 ff; p. 637; Zumwalt puts the Academy under the Chief of Naval Education and Training, p. 637-43; Mack tries to make plan work in spite of unanimous opposition of Board of Visitors, p. 640 ff; Mack's prior knowledge of the Naval Academy, p. 651-2; areas ripe for reform, p. 654-5; also p. 658; military vs civilian instructors, p. 655-7; race relations and the Naval Academy, the Zumwalt policy, p. 673-4; also p. 678-9; the special course on "The Professional Officer - A Human Person," p. 675-7; also p. 716 ff; the effort to provide professional attainment for every Academy graduate, p. 681-4; Mack's major steps as Superintendent - p. 684; strengthen science and math curriculum, p. 684; getting all students qualified professionally, p. 684; ridding academy of practicie of "silly stuff," p. 684-5; first class given responsibility for plebe summer, p. 686-7; naval academy honor system, p. 690-2; p. 701; p. 704-5; women at the naval academy, p. 715-22; improvement of the curriculum, p. 722 ff; Mack's personal experience in the Navy from the old 4-stackers to present technicalities has bearing on his concept of curriculum, p. 726-7; preparation of the future PAO on board ship and in the navy, p. 729-31; contrasting background of the Naval Academy graduate and the West Pointer, p. 732-5; a broad background - other than technical - is acquired outside the Academy, p. 736; the Burke Scholars, p. 736-8; summer cruises, p. 738-746; athletes - the help of the Foundation, p. 747 ff; the selection of George Welsh to be football coach, p. 748-51; general attitude of average brigade member towards varsity teams, p. 751-2; funding of athletics, p. 753-4; Naval Academy Foundation, p. 756 ff; the sailing program, p. 759-68; the lynchpin is the football team, p. 769; teamwork and athletics, p. 769 ff; the Army-Navy game, p. 772-3; aviation summer, p. 774; submarine summer training - marine training, p. 774; plebe summer - purpose, p. 775-6; the five year obligation to remain in the navy after graduation, p. 790-2; the <u>science seminar</u> at the Academy for high school grads, p. 793-4; the international affairs seminar, p. 796-7; Mack's comments on the gradualness of change at the Academy, p. 800-2; the Chapel, p. 810 ff; the change over from compulsory attendance at chapel to voluntary, p. 810-814; comments on right to dissent - to express opinions, p. 814-9; Mack's testimony in the Berg Case - to the effect that this young man had met the qualifications of the Academy - was certified by the Academic Board to graduate and be commissioned, p. 840-1; Mack's summary of building program, p. 803-807;

U. S. NAVAL ACADEMY - BUILDING PROGRAM: Admiral Mack's summary of the status of things when he came as Superintendent - subsequent developments, p. 803-7;

NAVAL ACADEMY FOUNDATION: p. 756-7; the trustees, p. 758;

U. S. NAVAL ACADEMY - SAILING ASSOCIATION: p. 762; Mack's motivation for the establishment of the Association, p. 762-3; Captain Grosvenor becomes C.O. of the naval station and head of the sailing program, p. 764;

U. S. NAVAL INSTITUTE: Mack a member of the Board of Control for twelve years, p. 831 ff;

USS NEW JERSEY: her usefulness in Vietnam bombardments, p. 613 ff

NITZE, The Hon. Paul: Secretary of the Navy - his insistence on a public affairs plan for the navy, p. 443; wanted Mack to take a cruiser division when he left Chinfo, p. 445; calls Mack from fleet to serve as Chief of Legislative Affairs, p. 455 ff; Adm. Connolly reports to him about this testimony on the F-111, p. 475; McNamara orders Nitze to sell the FDL proposal to the Congress, p. 475-6;

NIXON, The Hon. Richard M.: the President's insistence on the equal opportunity provisions of the law, p. 497-500; his anger over drug addiction and the military - his order in the matter - and Mack's response, p. 528-9; accomplishments during his administration in military matters, p. 549-50; Nixon and the DMZ in Vietnam, p. 613;

NIXON DOCTRINE: for the protection of the SEATO nations, p. 581-2; p. 586; p. 600;

O'CONNOR, The Rev. John (Captain - Navy chaplain): co-creator of the course on the "Professional Officer and the Human Person", p. 675; p. 706; p. 714;

USS OKLAHOMA CITY: flagship of the 7th fleet - visit of the Japanese chairman of their JCS, p. 600-2; p. 606-8; Mack gets word in Yokosuka that DMZ has been breached - speeds to Tonkin Gulf, p. 608; p. 614;

OKUBO, Takeo: first director general of the Japanese Maritime Safety Agency, p. 594;

PACKARD, The Hon. David: Deputy Secretary of Defense, p. 489; p. 566;

PEARSON, Drew: p. 575-6;

POLARIS: p. 784 ff;

POWs: the influence exerted in the navy today - impact of their experiences, p. 709-12;

PREMINGER, Otto: his movie - "In Harm's Way", disapproved by Sylvester, p. 433;

PRESS RELATIONS: p. 420-1; accountability, p. 422-4; the illustration of Gen. Groves speech about the A bomb, p. 424-6; the policy of papers they represent governs the attitude of reporters, p. 427-8;

PROFESSIONAL REQUIREMENTS: see entries under: U. S. NAVAL ACADEMY

PROJECT 100,000: the policy of President Lyndon Johnson for the military services to utilize one hundred thousand recruits with low mental attainments, p. 521-2;

PROMOTIONS IN U. S. NAVY: p. 486-8; difficulties enhanced by rapid promotion system, p. 488-9;

RABORN, VADM Wm. F., Jr: p. 784; words of praise for his achievement with the POLARIS project, p. 784-790;

RACE RELATIONS: see entries under: U. S. NAVAL ACADEMY

RECRUITING: money put into new barracks to improve living conditions - p. 511;

RESERVES: p. 500; calling up reserves - the new system of providing first class equipment, p. 556-9; reserves in WW II, p. 560-2; the ready reserve, p. 563-4;

RICKOVER, Admiral Hyman: his cautious attitude towards news on the SCORPION and THRESHER, p. 420-1; a law unto himself with Congressional Committees, p. 473; p. 652; p. 654; his ideal for the Naval Academy regimen, p. 658-9; his method of selecting Naval Academy men for his program, p. 659-64; p. 667; Secy Warner decrees the new engineering laboratory at the Naval Academy shall be named RICKOVER HALL, p. 668; the ceremony, p. 669-70; additional comments on Rickover, p. 671-3; p. 702-4; p. 707; p. 724; p. 755; p. 786; p. 787-8; Rickover urges Adm. Mack to get the "best young brains" into the Academy, p. 793 ff; the science seminar, p. 795-6;

RIVERS, The Hon. Mendel: Chairman of the House Armed Services Committee, p. 470; his opposition kills the FDL proposal of McNamara, p. 478; p. 792; p. 795-6; p. 797;

SCHLESINGER, The Hon. James: Secretary of Defense, p. 647-49;

USS SCORPION: press conference covering, p. 420-1;

SEATO: The SEATO nations and the 7th fleet, p. 481-2; p. 586; p. 600;

SEVENTH FLEET: Chinfo builds a press staff in Vietnam through the 7th fleet, p. 416-7; Zumwalt names Mack to command the 7th fleet - the first non-aviator, p. 543; p. 576-7; extent of Mack's briefing before taking over, p. 578-9; the matter of Japanese customs, his navy sword and change of command ceremonies, p. 580; importance of 7th fleet to SEATO nations, p. 581-4;

visit to Taiwan, p. 584-6; Mack uses occasion to reassure government of Taiwan, p. 586-7; problem of fleet base at Yokosuka, p. 588-9; obligations for intelligence collection in Sea of Japan, p. 592-3; year 1972 sees a build-up in operations in area of Vietnam, p. 602-3; a "day to remember" - p. 603-5; difficulties placed on Mack to remain in Vietnamese waters in anticipation of developments, p. 606-7; the big build-up in Tonkin Gulf after DMZ has been breached, p. 609-11; Linebacker, p. 613 ff; story of the mining of Haiphong Harbor, p. 616 ff; Holloway relieves Mack on board the OKLAHOMA CITY as she interrupts firing against the enemy, p. 622; nature of naval war against the North Vietnamese, p. 623 ff; Mack asks to stay on as 7th fleet commander until official change of command could be arranged for Holloway and Japanese officials could attend, p. 629-30; request denied, p. 630-32;

STENNIS, The Hon. John C.: Senator from Mississippi - Chairman of Senate Armed Services Committee, p. 470; Mack sells him on concept of the FDL, p. 477; his opposition to the all-volunteer force, p. 512-3; p. 644-5; p. 650;

J. P. STEVENS CO: The textile company forced to comply with Equal Opportunity provisions of the law, p. 499;

STRATTON, The Hon. Sam - member of congress: conducted an "end run" around the House Armed Services Committee to get women in the Naval Academy, p. 718-20;

SUB-SPECIALISTS IN NAVY: a new concept of duty in the U. S. Navy, p. 484-5;

SYLVESTER, Arthur: Assistant Secretary of Defense for Public Affairs, p. 414; his attitude on public information about Vietnam, p. 415-6; p. 420; p. 428; p. 430-1; his strong opposition to several movies involving the navy, p. 431-3; p. 442; his resistence to the development of a DOD public affairs plan, p. 444;

TAIWAN: Mack's visit came just after announcement of President Nixon's forthcoming trip to Red China, p. 584-5;

USS THRESHER: press conference covering, p. 420-1;

TURNER, Admiral Stansfield: p. 634-5; p. 650;

VIETNAM: propaganda, p. 437-8; p. 446; the resentment that built up in the United States, p. 549-50; the ROTC program, p. 550 ff; repercussions felt in the DOD, p. 552-3; The Vietnam War and the 7th fleet, p. 602 ff; restraints placed by Washington on U. S. forces vis-a-vis the DMZ, p. 605-6; p. 610-13;

VOLUNTEER FORCE - FOR ARMED SERVICES: the President's Council headed by Mr. Gates, p. 495; the plan to train and use Vietnamese and so reduce the draft, p. 496-7; p. 505-6; discussion of All Volunteer Force vs the draft, p. 506 ff; opposition of Senator Stennis and Cong. Hebert, p. 512-3; prognosis for the future, p. 514-5; discussion of the navy's problem, p. 516-7;

WARNER, The Hon. John: Secretary of the Navy - p. 644; p. 648-50;

WEST POINT (The United States Military Academy): p. 687-90; the West Point honor system, p. 692-3; Gen. MacArthur's violation of the system in later career, p. 693-4; Secretary Clements desire that Naval Academy change over systems and practices to be more like West Point, p. 696-7; after the cheating scandal West Point comes around to Navy's honor system, p. 699-700; background of the West Pointer contrasted with the academy ensign, p. 732-3;

WELSH, George: selected as football coach at the Naval Academy - his method of building a team, p. 748-51;

WESTMORELAND, General Wm.: his control of press affairs in Vietnam, p. 416-7; p. 438; his initial opposition to the all-volunteer force, p. 512;

YOKOSUKA: Zumwalt's idea for homeporting certain U. S. ships - Japanese desire to use the port as a fleet base for their naval units - also to expend facilities for merchant ship building, p. 588-92; p. 631-3;

ZUMWALT, Admiral Elmo: his nomination to be CNO - as handled by Secretary Chafee, p. 540-2; his request that Mack as Cinc 7th fleet resolve the matter of the U. S. base at Yokosuka - also to homeport a carrier and DD's in Japan, p. 588-9; names Mack as Superintendent of the Naval Academy, p. 621-2; denies request of Mack to remain in 7th fleet until an official ceremony could be arranged with Japanese

present for change of command, p. 629-30;
p. 634-6; p. 644; p. 646-7; p. 650; p. 673;
p. 801;

www.ingramcontent.com/pod-product-compliance
Lightning Source LLC
Chambersburg PA
CBHW080625170426
43209CB00007B/1514